International Intervention in a Secular Age

International intervention is not just about 'saving' human lives: it is also an attempt to secure humanity's place in the universe.

This book explores the Western secular beliefs that underpin contemporary practices of intervention—most importantly, beliefs about life, death and the dominance of humanity. These beliefs shape a wide range of practices: the idea that human beings should intervene when human lives are at stake; analyses of violence and harm; practices of intervention and peace-building; and logics of killing and letting die. Ironically, however, the Western secular desire to ensure the meaningfulness of human life at all costs contributes to processes of dehumanization, undercutting the basic goals of intervention. To explore this paradox, *International Intervention in a Secular Age* engages with examples from around the world, and draws on interdisciplinary sources: anthropologies of secularity and IR, posthumanist political philosophy, ontology and the sociology of death.

This book offers new insight into perennial problems, such as the reluctance of intervenors to incur fatalities, and international inaction in the face of escalating violence. It also exposes new dilemmas, such as the dehumanizing effects analyzing violence and of 'transformative' peace-building processes and will be of great interest to students and scholars of Political Philosophy, Social Anthropology and Ethics.

Audra Mitchell is a lecturer in the Politics Department at the University of York, UK.

Ex Libris

Independent Social Research Foundation

Interventions
Edited by: Jenny Edkins
Aberystwyth University
and Nick Vaughan-Williams
University of Warwick

'As Michel Foucault has famously stated, "knowledge is not made for under-standing; it is made for cutting." In this spirit the Edkins–Vaughan-Williams Interventions series solicits cutting edge, critical works that challenge main-stream understandings in international relations. It is the best place to con-tribute post disciplinary works that think rather than merely recognize and affirm the world recycled in IR's traditional geopolitical imaginary.'
Michael J. Shapiro, University of Hawai'i at Mãnoa, USA

The series aims to advance understanding of the key areas in which scholars working within broad critical post-structural and post-colonial traditions have chosen to make their interventions, and to present innovative analyses of important topics.

Titles in the series engage with critical thinkers in philosophy, sociology, politics and other disciplines and provide situated historical, empirical and textual studies in international politics.

Critical Theorists and International Relations
Edited by Jenny Edkins and Nick Vaughan-Williams

Ethics as Foreign Policy
Britain, the EU and the other
Dan Bulley

Universality, Ethics and International Relations
A grammatical reading
Véronique Pin-Fat

The Time of the City
Politics, philosophy, and genre
Michael J. Shapiro

Governing Sustainable Development
Partnership, protest and power at the world summit
Carl Death

Insuring Security
Biopolitics, security and risk
Luis Lobo-Guerrero

Foucault and International Relations
New critical engagements
Edited by Nicholas J. Kiersey and Doug Stokes

International Relations and Non-Western Thought
Imperialism, colonialism and investigations of global modernity
Edited by Robbie Shilliam

International Intervention in a Secular Age

Re-enchanting humanity?

Audra Mitchell

LONDON AND NEW YORK

First published 2014
by Routledge
2 Park Square, Milton Park, Abingdon, Oxon OX14 4RN

and by Routledge
711 Third Avenue, New York, NY 10017

Routledge is an imprint of the Taylor & Francis Group, an informa business

British Library Cataloguing in Publication Data
A catalogue record for this book is available from the British Library

Library of Congress Cataloging in Publication Data
Mitchell, Audra.
International intervention in a secular age : re-enchanting humanity? / Audra Mitchell.
  pages cm -- (Interventions)
Summary: "This book explores the Western secular beliefs that underpin contemporary practices of intervention – most importantly, beliefs about life, death and the primacy of humanity"-- Provided by publisher.
  Includes bibliographical references and index.
1. Intervention (International Law)--Moral and ethical aspects. I. Title.
  JZ6368.M576 2014
  172'.4--dc23
    2014000974

ISBN: 978-0-415-70506-6 (hbk)
ISBN: 978-1-315-89005-0 (ebk)

Typeset in Times New Roman
by Taylor and Francis Books

MIX
Paper from
responsible sources
FSC
www.fsc.org   FSC® C013604   Printed and bound by CPI Group (UK) Ltd, Croydon, CR0 4YY

Contents

Acknowledgements

A number of colleagues, friends and students made valuable contributions to this book. In particular, I would like to thank Roland Bleiker and Severine Autessere, who read initial drafts of the proposal and/or chapters and offered valuable insights. I would also like to thank the organizers and participants of the workshops and conferences at which early versions of this book were presented, in particular: the 'Category of Violence' workshop at the University of Aberdeen in June, 2012 (thanks to Trevor Stack); the British International Studies Association conference panel on 'Interpretivism in International Relations' in June 2012 (thanks to Oliver Daddow); the LSE Programme on Religion and Non-belief seminar in January 2013 (thanks to Matthew Engelke); and the panel on 'Anthropology and Peace-building' at the 2013 International Studies Association Convention in San Francisco (thanks to Catherine Goetze). In particular, the discussions at the Ontological Security workshop at Koc University, Istanbul in January 2013 helped me to sharpen many of the ideas explored in this book—thanks to Bahar Rumelili and all of the participants. Thanks also Oliver Richmond for our conversations on the significance of ontology in IR. Many colleagues at the University of York have patiently listened to my ideas through the various phases of this project, offering their insights and moral support—special thanks to Adam White, Carole Spary and Mihaela Mihai. Sydney Calkin was a great help in tracking down some of examples discussed in chapter five. I would also like to thank the students on my module 'Violence in International Politics' in 2012 and 2013, whose sharp questions (and willingness to stare into the void) helped me to hone several of the ideas presented here. Thanks to Jenny Edkins, Nick Vaughan-Williams and the editorial team at Routledge for their enthusiasm for this project.

Finally, thank you to Liam Kelly—the centre of my universe—for his love, support, and unwavering belief.

1 Introduction

The world is in our hands, or so the cliché goes. It reflects an assumption common in Western societies: that human beings are ultimately responsible for the fate of humanity, and everything else. The logic behind it is simple: if we fail to protect ourselves, or the world around us, who or what else will? In fact, this assumption corresponds to a distinctive set of beliefs about the universe and humanity's role in it. Specifically, it expresses the belief that humans are the only source of agency and protection. In the course of human history, this belief is, in fact, quite unusual. According to many past and current belief systems (including the Judeo-Christian tradition on which most Western societies draw), humans occupy an intermediate role, with deities or divine forces at the helm. The idea that human beings are alone in the universe, and must take responsibility for what happens in the world, is a signature feature of Western secular cosmology.

The image on the cover of this book symbolizes many of the assumptions of Western secular beliefs. In this image, the world is not only 'in human hands', but actually embodied in human form—just as, in Western secular cosmology, all meaning and value are measured in human terms. The universe is understood from a human's-eye perspective—that is, in terms of space, time and scales comprehensible to human minds and subject to the manipulation of human hands. Non-human forces can make things happen—for instance, bio-chemical processes can produce life, and gravity can determine the movement of matter. But humans are understood to be the only creative forces, the only beings that can *intervene* in events or trajectories in order to alter the conditions in which they exist. From this perspective, human agency is the sole source of creativity and rationality, and humanity offers a single source of light and colour in an otherwise blank universe.

The gesture made by the hands in the image is also symbolic. The palms are opened as if making an offering or an act of supplication. Therefore, they resemble some of the practices familiar in Judeo-Christian and other transcendent systems of belief. This represents the idea that Western secularity is a belief system, with its own worldly forms of faith, piety, ritual. However, these practices are not oriented towards pleasing or placating a deity, or living according to transcendent laws. Rather, they glorify human life and work to secure its dominance over the universe. The hands pictured on the cover also offer a powerful image of the desire for redemption, or perhaps for the expiation of wrongdoing. As this book will argue, the Western secular desire to respond to evil and to redeem humans is expressed through the various large and small-scale processes through which intervention is carried out.

However, the image also hints at vulnerability and weakness. Although they are covered in images of hard rock, volatile seas and jagged ice, these hands are nonetheless made of soft flesh. They call to mind other clichés: the idea that we are 'only' human, and that certain things are 'out of our hands'. In so doing, they highlight the massive, perhaps even quixotic, scale of the task that humans are faced with when they take on custodianship of the whole universe. Doing so means assuming tasks and responsibilities previously assigned to gods, without the advantages of omnipotence, omniscience, immortality, ubiquity, or any other superhuman powers.

These are the conditions in which contemporary international intervention takes place. Intervention, as this book argues, is not only an attempt to 'save' the lives of people threatened by large-scale violence. It is also an assertion of the primacy of human life against the threat of death. By attempting to halt, reverse or redirect trajectories of violence, intervenors work to secure the boundaries of humanity and to affirm its dominant place in the universe. In other words, beyond the legal, political and ideological dimensions of intervention lie fundamental beliefs about the nature of the universe and humanity's role within it. As this book argues, these beliefs make human intervention into large-scale violence seem both possible and necessary. They simultaneously inspire the desire to intervene, and constrain the actions of intervenors. Moreover, they help to promote human life and its flourishing, but also undermine it.

This book explores a profound source of the beliefs that shape contemporary international intervention: Western secularity. Although it is often treated in negative terms, as an absence of religion or belief, Western secularity is, in fact, a distinctive belief system based on its own cosmology—that is, its understanding of the universe and the role of the various beings in it. Within this cosmology, human beings sit at the top of the hierarchy of being; transcendent or divine figures are either absent or subjugated to human agency, and all other beings are treated as objects for human use. As a result, human beings are framed as the ultimate arbiters of meaning, solely responsible for ensuring the value of human life and the order of the universe. They attempt to do so by projecting meaning onto other beings, and by restoring it when it is lost.

Within this belief system, human life is the highest ideal and death is considered abhorrent. In particular, violent death is despised because it instrumentalizes human beings, and treats them as if they were nothing but 'mere' objects. As this book will argue, the category of 'humanity' is, in Western secular frameworks, forged and sustained by separating 'enchanted' humanity from all other beings. The latter are treated as 'disenchanted' objects, to be disposed of as humans see fit. However, by ruthlessly instrumentalizing human lives and deaths, violence dissolves the boundary between 'enchanted' and 'disenchanted' beings, and undermines the exceptional status of human life. From this perspective, violence threatens to disenchant humanity.

Even within this belief system, however, humans are not taken to be totally helpless in the face of violence. They can respond to the threat of violence by interposing themselves, halting or redirecting its trajectories, and enfolding 'disenchanted' beings into their own frameworks of meaning. Indeed, this book argues that international intervention is concerned precisely with these tasks. It is a large-scale effort to re-enchant humanity, to reverse the effects of violence, and to affirm the exceptional value of human life. This impulse drives a vast range of strategies used by intervenors—from the interpretation of acts of violence to the measurement of deaths, to the social transformation of societies affected by violence to the killing of violent actors.

Yet, as this book will argue, the attempt to re-enchant humanity through intervention has ironic consequences. The strategies mentioned above reproduce the distinction between 'enchanted' and 'disenchanted' life. They, too, subject human lives and deaths to instrumental processes, which confirm their status as disenchanted objects. In other words, the desire to re-enchant humanity in this way contributes to its disenchantment, and heightens its vulnerability to violence. Understanding the sources of this paradox is crucial if we are to address some of the perennial problems of intervention: its inconsistency, the reluctance of intervening actors to risk their own lives to save others, and the logics of killing and letting die that shape intervention.

What does it mean to intervene?

In international relations (IR), the term 'intervention' is highly loaded and used in a very specific sense. It almost always refers to situations in which state actors use military force to bring about changes within the boundaries of another state. Yet, as a concept, intervention is much broader. In everyday life, we speak of 'intervening' in a quarrel, to stop a friend from making a bad decision or pursuing a dangerous behaviour, to contribute to an argument, and so on. At its most basic level, intervention is a way of imagining action, predicated on a simple belief: that humans can change the course of events by interposing themselves in it. In this book, I use the term intervention in precisely this sense—to describe the wide array of actions through which humans try to change trajectories of events by 'acting into' them. I explore intervention as a particular way of conceptualizing and exercising human agency—and one that is rooted in distinctive ideas of humanity's role in the universe (see Chapter 1). From this perspective, an uninvited military mission across state borders can certainly be an act of intervention, but so can the speech-acts of public figures attempting to influence warring actors, the efforts of 'grassroots' peace-builders to restore social order in the wake of violence, and even the calculations of researchers attempting to predict and control the outbreak of conflict.

This understanding of intervention will no doubt raise the hackles of IR theorists who insist on defining the concept in a narrow way. Indeed, they have very good reasons for doing so. In contexts where decisions must be made about the use of military force, it is necessary to be precise about the exact kinds of action that are permissible in order to uphold international law. It is also crucial for international actors to have a means of differentiating between acts of aggression or military expansionism and efforts to protect a threatened group of people (see below). For these reasons, in IR discourses, 'intervention' almost invariably refers to the use of force by states (often, but not always, approved by international organizations), and the set of constraints placed upon this by international law and conventions (see, for instance, Walzer 1977, 2004; Welsh 2003; Wheeler 2000; Chesterman 2001). The defining feature of intervention, from this perspective, is that it undermines the principle of state sovereignty: the idea that each state should have ultimate control over affairs within its own territories and the use of violence within them. Intervention raises a significant dilemma in this context: in some cases, it seems necessary to violate the sovereignty of states in order to uphold international security and law—for instance, in cases where states commit grave acts of violence against their 'own' citizens. On the other hand, if states were permitted to intervene in any case when they disagreed with the policies of a particular state, it is feared that the entire international system, based on stable relations between sovereign states, would collapse into disorder (see Chesterman 2001). In this context, intervention is defined negatively, as an exception to the normal order of things, which occurs when prohibitions against it can be overridden. For this reason, most discussions of intervention in IR are concerned with constraining the circumstances in which it can be permitted, and identifying when violations of these rules have occurred.

Even within the specific context of military intervention, these debates are restricted almost entirely to the direct use of force. For instance, the norm of *responsibility to protect* (ICISS 2001) devotes substantial attention to setting out limits for the use of coercive force. However, it does not set similar limitations for the other activities which (it insists) should attend military action: for instance, peace-building activities, or the provision of financial and technical assistance. These activities take place across state borders, and alter affairs within a sovereign state's remit, but they are not generally treated as problematic in discussions of sovereignty. What is most important to theorists of intervention is not simply the alteration of conditions across state borders, but rather the use of violence and the perceived intentions behind it.

In this context, the effects of action and the norms to which it is explicitly oriented take centre stage. The deep-seated beliefs of intervenors are not examined in any detail. The principles of just war theory, which lie at the foundations of contemporary norms of intervention, insist that those who use military force have 'just cause' and the 'right intentions' (see Walzer 1977; Wheeler 2000). That is, military force can be used only in cases where there is a severe threat to a civilian population and when the actors using force are doing so for the express purpose of protecting this population. These criteria refer to the *conscious intentions of decision-makers*, and their stated values (e.g. the belief in humanitarianism or legal concepts such as war crimes and genocide). However, they do not capture the unconscious beliefs or assumptions of these decision-makers, nor sources of the beliefs (conscious or not) of the many people who carry out the various aspects of intervention. These approaches can tell us a great deal about how international order is conceptualized, but much less about intervention as a form of human agency. So, throughout this book, I will use the definitions discussed above to refer to some aspects of *military* intervention. However, I will use a much wider and more complex conception of intervention to capture the various (military and non-military) acts through which it is carried out.

Most importantly, I approach intervention in *ontological* terms. That is, I understand it as an attempt by human actors to alter the basic conditions of their existence, and the spatio-temporal trajectories that produce and alter these conditions. By interposing themselves in trajectories (such as the instrumental processes of violence—see Chapter 3) intervenors may attempt not only to maintain the stability of existing conditions, but also to bring about new ones (see Chapters 7 and 8). This conception of agency is based on the idea that human beings *can* act in ways that change ontological conditions—and, in fact, that they are the only beings capable of doing so (see Chapter 1). From this perspective, intervention is distinguished not by the use of specific kinds of action, but rather by the ways in which humans understand their capacity to act and what they are doing by acting. Moreover, it is not limited to cases in which state sovereignty is formally challenged, but expanded to include any case in which human actors attempt to interpose themselves into trajectories of change that upset the existing order or threaten 'humanity'.

Indeed, the idea of 'humanity' is integral to the notion of intervention that will be used throughout this book. I refer frequently to the 'category of humanity' (see Chapters 4 and 5). This is an ontological category—the central ontological category within Western secularity—which sets particular parameters for what kinds of beings can be considered human. Membership in this category offers 'fully human' beings (see Chapter 4) protection and priority vis-à-vis all other beings. As the following chapters will argue, this category is defined by the belief that human life is the highest form of being, and that human actors are solely responsible for ensuring that it is protected and enabled to flourish. It is created and sustained through human actions that uphold the ideal of human life and protect it from threats. While it is not coextensive with the international social imaginary, the latter is understood as a crucial line of defence for the former. In other words, the value of the international social imaginary lies primarily in its perceived capacity to express, embody and protect the category of humanity. Throughout the book, I will explore a number of the actions through which this category is created and sustained—from aerial bombing to conflict transformation, from the instrumental use of non-humans to the performance of death rituals.

By the same token, however, the category of humanity is deeply vulnerable to human action. Without an external (that is, divine) guarantor to ensure its durability, any actions on earth that undermine the ideal of human life or violate the boundaries of this category constantly threaten to dissolve it. If this were to occur, human beings would lose their privileged place in the universe, along with the protection that this offers. It is in these situations of threat that intervenors interpose themselves. They attempt to shore up the category of humanity by interrupting, halting or redirecting trajectories that threaten it. From this perspective, intervention is not an exceptional act that threatens systems of order, but rather an integral, positive action that upholds it.

Since intervenors 'act into' spatio-temporal trajectories, time plays a very important role in intervention. Specifically, intervention is a *diachronic* process: is embedded in processes that unfold over time, and it can only be understood in the context of these processes. The mainstream definitions of intervention discussed above examine only the *synchronic* aspects of intervention—for instance, the moment in which sovereignty or international law is breached, the threshold at which a number of killings is recognized as an act of ethnic cleansing (see Chapter 6) or the instant in which UN Security Council approval is issued for a military action.[1] However, from a diachronic perspective, intervention does not begin or end with a formal action or declaration, but rather unfurls in multiple, overlapping processes. One such process might span from the moment in which an act of violence is initially apprehended by an international organization through the lengthy processes in which a decision is taken on whether and how to respond. Another begins when a decision is taken to intervene, through the deployment of staff (whether military or civilian) to the site of intervention, through the various practical and logistical processes in which the aims of the mission are carried out. The processes through which external actors are withdrawn (sometimes suddenly, sometimes gradually) from a site of intervention, and in which communities living at this site return to 'everyday life' or attempt to create new structures and institutions are also part of this broader temporal spectrum.

Understood in this way, intervention also involves numerous actors working at different levels (from interpersonal to international). In some cases, as in the 'integrated missions' carried out by the UN, there is a deliberate attempt to coordinate the efforts of various military, civilian, local and international actors pursing similar goals. However, in many cases, various actors approach the same goals with different, and perhaps even conflicting, motivations. For instance, in NATO's intervention in Libya in 2011, the 'rebels' fighting the ground war, the NATO bombers supporting them from the sky, and the various organizations who provided humanitarian aid used different forms of agency, and with varying motivations, to carry out what is considered to be the same intervention. The legal language of IR discourses identifies particular individuals or corporate bodies as being 'responsible' for actions which they have approved and/or executed (whether or not it is possible to ascribe 'responsibility' to a corporate actor like the UN—see Erskine 2004).

However, the interpretation outlined here belies the unitary or corporate agency which is usually ascribed to states or international organizations in contexts of intervention. From this perspective, intervention is carried out through forms of agency that are dispersed across multiple actors, each with their own motivations, goals and repertoires of action.

Indeed, in any given case, thousands, and perhaps even millions of people can be called 'intervenors', so long as they understand their acts in the manner I have outlined above. In fact, this is arguably the case even in the narrower concepts of intervention discussed above. Aside from pronouncements about who is responsible for the decision to intervene and its consequences, who actually carries out the act of intervening, or realizes its aims? Is it the soldiers 'on the ground'—or, in more contemporary terms, those who 'push the button' to launch weapons from afar? Is it their commanders, the heads of states to whom they are responsible, or perhaps even the populations who invest these leaders with authority (see Ignatieff 2001)? Is it the member states of the international bodies (e.g. the UN Security Council or NATO) who approve and oversee the actions, or perhaps the individuals who sit on particular decision-making bodies within these organizations? And what about people who live at the sites of military interventions and contribute to the activities of intervenors, say, by providing information or assisting in peace-building activities? Approached in this way, answering the question 'who intervenes' seems much more complex than identifying the person(s) who can be held legally responsible for an action.

From the perspective adopted throughout this book, all of these actors (and many more) can be said to intervene. I shall use the term 'intervenors' to define any actor(s), individual and corporate, at all levels of analysis, who understand their actions as efforts to interpose themselves in trajectories that threaten the category of humanity. Rather than attempting to define all potential categories of intervenors (an impossible task), I shall focus instead on concrete practices of intervention and the people or organizations that carry them out. It is important to note that this approach does not discount the idea that certain actors carry more responsibility (and, indeed, capacity) for intervening in specific ways. This does not mean that all intervenors should take equal responsibility for responding to mass violence; moreover, certain actors may be legally defined as being more responsible than others. It simply broadens the range of actors and actions that can be analyzed as contributors to intervention.

This approach recognizes that intervenors are not always states, or even acting on behalf of states. In fact, in the context of contemporary intervention, states are rarely the sole or even primary subjects of intervention. International and regional organizations such as NATO, the European Union and, of course, the UN regularly frame themselves as the major actors in interventions (whether or not these include a military element). Intervenors may also take the form of non-governmental organizations (NGOs) that assist or contest the actions of state and international or regional organizations; the 'local' actors who cooperate with or resist the presence of intervenors; the network of scholars, consultants and experts who shape policies and influence practices of intervention; and the publics whose normative commitments or moral censure can alter the decision to intervene or the nature of an intervention. In addition, as Chapters 5 and 7 demonstrate, the subjects of intervention are increasingly framed not as individual states or even multilateral organizations, but rather as representatives of the 'international community' (see below), or even of 'humanity' itself. When any organization or individual claims to act 'in the name of humanity' or 'on behalf of the international community', she or it invokes a concept of subjectivity that is very different from that of the state or the individual. This notion of subjectivity is ontological in the sense I have discussed above: it claims to represent an entire category of being (humanity) or sphere of existence (the international), not just specific instantiations of it. As this book will demonstrate, all of these forms of subjectivity are invoked by different actors across the temporal trajectories of intervention.

Moreover, it is misleading to think of states as the *objects* of intervention. In the rubric of 'human security' (see Chapter 5), the recipients of intervention are no longer defined in political, territorial terms, but rather in the language of demographic and ethical categories—for instance, 'the victims, the men being killed, the women being raped, the children dying of starvation' (Evans 2008). Similarly, the targets of contemporary intervention are only sometimes states, or factions dominating a government (as in the case of Saddam Hussein in Iraq, or the Taliban in Afghanistan at the point of the US invasion). Often they are non-state groups, such as tribal groups or the warring factions within states (for instance, Al-Shabab in Somalia, or the Taliban in post-2001 Afghanistan). In this context, while it is still most common to talk about intervention *in* Libya or Timor Leste, the state itself is not always the object of intervention.

In a related sense, the approach to intervention used throughout this book differentiates the forms of agency through which intervention is realized from the normative status often ascribed to it. Defining intervention in a normative way is highly problematic, for a number of reasons. It can be undertaken for genuinely altruistic reasons driven by care for other human beings. However, the motivations of intervenors are complex—particularly if we take into account the myriad people that may act as intervenors in a given case. Acts of intervention may be undertaken to end the suffering of others, to ensure the safety of one's 'own' people, to impose a particular way of life as a universal truth—or all of the above. Moreover, as Wheeler (2000) points out, even where actors explicitly state their intentions, these are not necessarily borne out in the events that follow. He points out that military actions undertaken for non-humanitarian purposes may actually enhance the well-being of a threatened group of people. Similarly, acts of intervention undertaken for seemingly 'ethical' reasons may simply mask the realist strategies or domestic political constraints of intervening actors (see Chandler 2004). Acts of intervention are overdetermined: they are influenced by ethical, practical and strategic considerations, emotions, precognitive reactions or reflexive responses and, as this book will argue, deeply held but subconscious beliefs. Precisely because the motivations for intervention are overdetermined, intervention, as a concept of agency, is ethically *indeterminate*—that is, we cannot prejudge the entire category of intervention as either 'good' or 'bad'. This shift in thinking has implications that might disturb normative proponents of humanitarian intervention. Simply put, it suggests that the NGO workers delivering aid to refugee camps and the controllers of unmanned 'drones' carrying out signature strikes in Pakistan are part of the same category of action. In the ontological sense described above, this is true. However, it certainly does not suggest that there is a moral equivalency between these two actions. In fact, it is precisely to avoid the making of such moral equivalencies that the normative connotations of the term 'intervention' need to be removed. Only by doing so is it possible to approach intervention as a category of human agency, and to understand the full, ambiguous consequences of exercising it.

So, the concept of 'intervention' used throughout this book departs significantly from standard definitions and discourses within IR. To sum up briefly, I have argued that standard definitions focus exclusively on the negative characteristics of intervention, as a threat to the sovereign state and the system of international order based on it. These accounts focus on the assignation of responsibility for military action and its consequences to discrete actors at particular, synchronic moment. In contrast, I have argued that intervention is a unique, positive category of human agency—which, as I shall argue shortly, is an expression of distinctive cosmological beliefs. Fundamentally, intervention is an *ontological* project—it is an attempt to interpose oneself into spatio-temporal trajectories that threaten the category of humanity. This book focuses almost exclusively on acts of intervention in trajectories of large-scale violence. However, this limitation is simply a function of parameters of the book; similar interventions take place regularly in response to natural disasters, famines, or projects of development. Intervention can be understood as an act of protection, a means of bolstering the category of 'humanity' against its most profound threats. However, it is also an act of *resistance*, an expression of the desire to assert the priority of human life against death (see Chapters 4 and 8). It is a diachronic process which unfolds at various levels of analysis, through the diverse actions of many different kinds of actors. Moreover, it is not a normative category, but a form of agency that can have many normative outcomes and implications. By framing intervention in this manner, this book seeks to understand how and why human beings have come to imagine themselves as capable of exerting a form of agency once (and in many contexts, still) reserved for divine beings and forces. It explores the sources of this image of agency, the moral commitments that animate it, the ontological and ethical principles that constrain it, and the expectations that it generates. To understand all of this, I shall now argue, we need a deeper appreciation of

Western secular cosmology, and this calls for a different approach to the subject.

Approaching the 'international'—an anthropological lens

Intervention is, above all, a conception of human agency. It is *enacted* in a range of practices and rituals, each of which express beliefs about the conditions in which human life is embedded. As I have argued above, most accounts of intervention have focused on its legal definition or the high politics of international decision-making. Instead, this book seeks to understand how intervention is realized through a series of everyday acts and social structures. For this reason, it adopts the social–anthropological approach taken by scholars such as Charles Taylor (2004, 2007), Talal Asad (2003, 2007) or Bruno Latour (1993). This approach does not involve 'on-the-ground' or ethnographic methods, but it pays attention to the way in which beliefs shape social formations (or transformations) and the way humans interact within them. By studying human action and practices, it makes us alert to the way that beliefs and materiality intertwine, to the intermingling of the biological and the transcendent, and to the coexistence of life and death. In short, it seeks to capture the cosmology posited by a belief system. Cosmology, in this context, refers to the images of the universe which shape the beliefs of a particular group of people. It offers a model of symbolic order, which designates the place of all beings in the universe, and their 'proper' relations to one another. It also reflects beliefs about the spatial and temporal conditions of this universe, and metaphysical beliefs (such as the existence, or not, of a transcendent realm, or of life after death). This book seeks to understand how Western secular cosmology shapes the practices of intervention—and vice versa.

Anthropology explores the ways that humans forge their lives in conjunction with specific geographical, material and 'natural' settings—for instance, a particular community, region or culture. The context for intervention, however, is the massive, unbounded, poorly defined realm of 'the international'. To date, there has been little anthropological work on the international. However, several innovative studies document the anthropology of specific international organizations—for instance, the abstract structures or decision-making processes of international organizations, the organizational cultures of international NGOs, or collective perceptions of phenomena that involve a super-domestic or transnational dimension (see, for instance, Brigg and Bleiker 2010; Autessere 2010; Pouligny 2006; Darby 2006; Debrix and Weber 2003; Pink 1998; Fox 1998). This book builds upon this emerging approach and poses a wider set of questions. For instance, what does it mean to believe in the 'international'? What specific forms of agency are made possible by this belief? And what assumptions about life, death and cosmology shape it?

Adopting this approach requires that we look at the international in a very different way. It requires that we view it not as an abstract level of analysis, or a residual space produced by the relations between states, or even an emergent property produced by their interactions (see Wendt 1999), but rather as a set of real places, populated by actual people and things. In short, it requires that we treat the 'international' not only as an abstract category, but also as a concrete form of life.

A useful way of grasping this approach is to treat the 'international' as what Taylor (2004) calls a 'social imaginary'. For Taylor, social imaginaries entail:

> The ways people imagine their social existence, how they fit together with others, how things go on between them and their fellows ... the expectations that are normally met, and the deeper normative notions and images that underlie these expectations ... a sense of how things usually go ... interwoven with an idea of how they ought to go, of what missteps would invalidate the practice.
>
> (Taylor 2004: 23–4)

Social imaginaries are constituted and preserved through:

> The discriminations we have to make ... knowing whom to speak to and when and how, carry an implicit map of social space, of what kinds of people we can associate with in what ways and in what circumstances.
>
> (Taylor 2004: 26)

In other words, social imaginaries are not specific places, but rather images of the relationships among people, things and structures that produce particular rules and forms of behaviour. As I shall argue in the next chapter, they sustain certain forms of agency and enable others. According to Taylor, social imaginaries produce a number of distinctive social formations: contemporary images of the public sphere, in which people imagine themselves to be participating in national or even global discourses; market economies, in which people act individually, but help determine global trends; social movements, which link people across time and space; and the modern citizenship-oriented state, upon which individuals make direct demands. The common thread between these imaginaries is that they connect individuals 'translocally and internationally into a single collective agency' (Taylor 1998: 40). Taylor contends that these imaginaries have emerged from the transformations that brought about Western secularity, which 'disembedded' individuals from rigid, collective social structures and forced them to reconfigure their relations (see Chapters 2 and 3).

The international realm, I shall suggest, is another example of a social imaginary. It, too, links millions of people indirectly through intangible but nonetheless very real social formations.[2] It is created and sustained through human agency, and held together by mutual expectations and beliefs. It is instantiated in, but not reducible to, specific places or objects. Moreover, like markets or social movements, it has the quality of being everywhere at once and transforms itself frequently, yet does not seem to lose its integrity.

Although it has no fixed form, it has positive features, and is viewed by millions of people as a 'real' thing. The international is the purest form of diaspora—one with no single 'homeland', fluid, mobile and multilingual, with constantly shifting internal cultures and tensions. It is populated not just by rules, norms and processes, but by actual people: employees of international organizations, aid workers, volunteers, soldiers, researchers, 'third-party' consultants and mediators, citizens who witness its work, and the 'local' cultures which it confronts and constructs.[3] It is also made of material things: buildings, vehicles, robots, parcels of food, websites, weapons, computers and the networks that link them, medicines and so on. Each instantiation of the international is composed of combinations of these people and things, and so its manifestations are varied. They range from the sleek headquarters of international organizations in New York, Geneva or Brussels, to the makeshift structures of refugee camps; from the 'field' offices of NGOs, to the neighbourhoods or cafés frequented by 'internationals' at sites of intervention; to the public parks, government buildings, 'reconstructed' houses and places of worship built through the funding of international donors; to the living rooms, classrooms and streets through which people critique the work of 'internationals'. Moreover, moving within these social imaginaries produces specific kinds of subjectivity. It is possible for people to identify themselves as 'internationals' or recognize others as such; to possess 'international' mindsets and careers; to occupy 'international' spaces or acculturate themselves within 'international' social structures and norms. These features are not reducible to specific job titles or training.[4] Rather, they reflect particular expectations about the ethical motivations, skills, values, experiences, mindsets, social standing and lifestyles of 'international' people and institutions.

In order to approach intervention from an anthropological perspective, it is necessary to focus on these features of the international. Of course it would be impossible to capture all of them, but this is not necessary. By focusing on various instantiations of the international—that is, specific, practices, settings, artefacts and discourses—we can begin to grasp how particular beliefs shape human agency, and vice versa. In order to do so, this book takes the idea of intervention as its focal point and focuses on the many contexts in which it is realized.

Why this book is not about 'religion' (some caveats)

At the conferences and workshops where early drafts of this book were presented, one of the most common questions I was asked was: 'What is your religious background?' The assumption was that, because I took a critical orientation towards Western secularity and attempted to relativize it in relation to other beliefs, I was writing about it from the 'outside'. Moreover, the fact that I used language like 'belief', 'faith' and 'cosmology' to describe Western secularity contrasted with my interlocutors' understanding of secularity as the absence of these features (see Chapter 1). In actual fact, this book is intended as an immanent critique of Western secularity, the belief system which has shaped my understanding of the universe. It is an attempt to bring this system of belief out from the background in order to critique its dominance and the paradoxes it produces. Reducing Western secularity to the absence of 'religion' both denies its positive features and shields if from critique, and I aim to counter both problems. This does not mean that we should reject Western secularity wholesale (see Chapter 8); it should be treated with the same respect as any other system of belief, but not arbitrarily privileged or treated as 'neutral'. This requires an approach to secularity that highlights its positive features and engages with its contradictions.

However, this is a difficult task in the context of IR, in which it is almost impossible to mention the word 'secularity' without being immediately drawn into a discussion of 'religion'. Indeed, as Chapter 2 explains, secularity usually only enters IR through debates about the perceived 'resurgence of religion', or 'religious violence'. In these discussions, secularity is usually treated merely as the absence or opposite of 'religion', and not as a belief system in its own right. In contrast, this book espouses an approach in which, as Jose Casanova puts it, the 'experience of being "secular" is not tied anymore to one of the units of a dyadic pair, "religious/secular", but is constituted as a self-enclosed reality' (2010: 67). In other words, Westerns secularity is treated as one belief system among many that shape international politics. However, due to its profound influence on Western societies, it has attained a dominant (if largely implicit) role in international structures and discourses—one that needs to be explicitly critiqued.

Moreover, for the purposes of this book, I bracket discussions of the perceived clash between 'religious' and 'secular' actors. As this book will argue, the most potent threat to Western secularity is not actually 'religion', but rather death and the denigration of human life. So, I join others (MacFarlane *et al*. 2004; ICISS 2001) in deliberately *not* using the seemingly mandatory discussion of '9/11'and counter-terrorism as my starting point. On the contrary, I argue that Western secular ideas of international social formations and modes of agency have evolved as a powerful counter-current *throughout* the history of IR.

In Chapter 2, I will explain in detail how the idea of Western secularity is used throughout the book. However, it is useful to begin with a few caveats. First, to argue that intervention is profoundly influenced by Western secularity is not to assert that it is either (1) non-religious (2) overtly secular*izing* that is, hostile to religion or transcendence or (3) bereft of people who hold religious beliefs and express them through international work. On the contrary, the practice of intervention is rooted in 'religious beliefs' (see Chapter 1), overtly religious organizations continue to play a major role in various practices of intervention (see Chong and Troy 2011) and active religious belief motivates the work of many 'internationals' (see Lynch 2011; Barnett and Stein 2012). Western secular structures are neither wholly atheist or religious. They bind together numerous forms of belief and disbelief within a shared cosmology and central ideal: the primacy of human life.

Moreover, this book moves away from *ad hominem* arguments which suggest that an act can be defined as 'religious' or 'secular' based on the personal beliefs of the individuals involved in them. For instance, during the early 2000s, several military interventions were launched by two world leaders whose religious beliefs were well known: George W. Bush and Tony Blair. Certainly, it is likely that the ethics instilled by their faiths had an effect upon their actions and their personal motivations for undertaking them. However, their primary justifications for engaging in Afghanistan and Iraq were not theological or transcendent in nature; they did not *explicitly* call for the glorification of God or the fulfilment of his will. Instead, they appealed for public support by emphasizing the need to save lives, ensure international security and promote forms of governance that would enhance human flourishing. All of these goals are, as I shall argue in Chapter 3, hallmarks of Western secular beliefs about life and death.

Furthermore, as Chapter 2 will argue in more detail, Western secularity is characterized by the intermingling of various forms of belief and unbelief. So, in the example discussed above, the world leaders in question may have been motivated to intervene by 'religious' and 'non-religious' forms of belief simultaneously. In addition, those who do not believe in a transcendent realm may nonetheless draw on transcendent beliefs, subjugating them to the Western secular ideal of human flourishing. For instance, the Western vogue for yoga is not typically driven by a genuine desire to achieve spiritual transcendence, but rather to enhance one's health and experience of life. These examples suggest that *ad hominem* judgements about the beliefs that drive human action can be misleading, especially when they characterize a person as wholly 'religious' or 'secular' in all respects. Instead, it is important to focus on the acts themselves and what beliefs they embody.

It is also important to note that I restrict my analysis to *Western* secularity which, I shall argue, forms the basis of the contemporary idea of intervention and many of the practices surrounding it. Western secularity refers, broadly speaking, to the conditions of belief that have emerged from the transformation of Judeo-Christian beliefs[5] and shaped societies (previously) dominated by these beliefs. There is a tendency to conflate Western secularity with Westernness and the processes associated with it—for instance, modernization, industrialization and scientific process. However, I argue that secularity is not reducible to Westernness (and vice versa). On the one hand, secularity cannot be conflated with 'Western' ideologies, in particular liberalism, democracy or market-based forms of economic organization. As William Connolly (1999) and Akeel Bilgrami (2004) point out, there is ample evidence of theological liberalism (e.g. that of progressive Catholics) and non-liberal secularism (e.g. in Baathist Iraq or communist Europe). Moreover, simply focusing on one of these aspects cannot capture the complexity of contemporary Western secular social formations. A critique of 'Westernness' might explain why international actors often promote market-based economies and liberal democracy as strategies of peace-building. However, it cannot explain the underlying attitudes towards life, death and killing that frame these goals as appropriate responses to violence (see Chapters 4, 7 and 8). So, throughout this book, I focus on critiquing the Western variant of *secularity*, instead of reducing secularity to a feature of Westernness.

In this vein, it is also important to resist the temptation of viewing secularity as a uniquely 'Western' phenomenon. Hybrids of Western secularity belief systems other than Judeo-Christianity have emerged around the world (Bhargava 1998; Jakobsen and Pellegrini 2008; Hurd 2008). Moreover, the extension of Western secularity through processes of globalization and intervention has been resisted through the assertion of various forms of transcendent belief (Nandy 1998; Keane 2000; Juergensmeyer 2011). These forms of resistance help to reshape Western secularity and render it heterogeneous (see Chapter 2). For these reasons, we should not see Western secularity as a stable system, but rather as a rapidly evolving assemblage of beliefs that is very much in the process of 'becoming' (see Connolly 2011). In other words, the processes through which Western secularity expands ensure that it can never become entirely dominant. As Casanova claims:

> If … globalization entails a certain decentering, provincializing, and historicizing of Europe and of European secular modernity … then it is unlikely that 'our' secular age will simply become the common global secular age of all humanity.
>
> (2010: 279)

With all of this in mind, my decision to focus on Western secularity is not intended to ignore non-Western experiences of secularity, non-secular experiences of Westernness, or non-Western, non-secular beliefs. It is certainly not intended to reproduce a Western-centric account of secularity, but rather to expose, critique and relativize Western secular beliefs that are too often treated as 'neutral'. To this end, I follow Taylor in taking Western secularity as my central subject, but:

> In a way that is so fine-grained that one would both lose any remaining temptation to see it as the universal road on which humanity as a whole is embarked and gain some interesting points of contrast with other civilizational histories.
>
> (2011a: 37)

By giving flesh to Western secularity as a particular 'civilizational history' among many, this book seeks to identify its distinctive influence on how we understand the sphere of the 'international' and the powerful idea of intervention. Equipped with this understanding of Western secularity and the anthropological lens discussed above, we can now begin to unpack this idea.

Outline of the book

In this chapter, I have set out the basic premise of the book, and the major concepts that will be explored within it. In particular, I introduced the idea that Western secular beliefs play a profound role in shaping international intervention. Chapter 2 begins to explore the sources of these beliefs by turning its attention to the founding mythology of IR. According to this myth, the 'Westphalian moment' that gave rise to the modern state was also a watershed, after which 'religion'[6] was gradually excised from the state. This myth promotes a negative or secular*ist* account of Western secularity, which draws sharp dichotomies between 'religion' and 'secular' spaces or ways of life. It has produced an image of the international sphere as a space from which 'religion' has been purged or pushed out, or which emerged with no 'religious' influences. In contemporary IR, this idealized image of the international sphere is perceived to be under imminent and serious threat from a 'resurgence of religion', in the form of terrorism and political violence. Within these discourses, 'religion' and the 'secular' international sphere have been securitized (see Buzan *et al.* 1999) in a reflexive way: each one is framed as a threat to the other. In response, many 'post-secularists' have called for an approach to IR that can accommodate 'religious' actors and forms of agency, or even 'bring religion back in' to IR (see Thomas 2005). However, Chapter 1 argues that the rush towards post-secularism may efface a powerful counter-narrative within IR's story: the 'transformation thesis' and its distinctive account of Western secularity. According to this version of events, Western secularity emerged not from the displacement or dilution of 'religious' belief, but rather from the transformation of Judeo-Christian beliefs into earthly, human-centred terms. These transformations have produced a distinctive cosmology which is neither devoid or 'religion' nor determined by it. Rather, it fosters various forms of belief and unbelief, all subjugated to a single ideal: the promotion of human life and its flourishing. Building on the work of major thinkers in this tradition, such as Charles Taylor and Talal Asad, I demonstrate that the 'transformation thesis' sheds light on the sources of some of the key concepts of contemporary IR—including humanitarianism and the contemporary concept of intervention.

Chapter 3 explores two of the most important contributions of Western secularity to IR: its concepts of life and death. Drawing on Taylor's concepts of 'human flourishing' and 'authenticity' (Taylor 2004, 2007, 2011a), I argue that the image of 'humanity' central to contemporary intervention is based on the idealization of everyday human life ('high life'). In this context, almost all forms of death are 'bad', since they mark the total and irreversible negation of high life. However, violent death raises a particular threat. It undermines the sanctity, integrity and self-ownership that are central to the ideal of high life, and can destroy human flourishing on a large scale. Within Western secular beliefs, there are two major ways of conceptualizing violent forms of bad death: dying or being 'killed for/as nothing', or as 'bare life' (Agamben 1995); and dying or being killed 'for something', or as an act of sacrifice. As the following chapters illustrate, these images of high life and bad death shape the way in which episodes of violence are framed by intervenors, and the nature of their responses to it. In Chapter 3, I explore how they influence one of the perennial paradoxes of humanitarian intervention: the desire to 'save' others, and the simultaneous reluctance to risk the lives of intervenors.

Building further on these ideas, Chapter 4 introduces a paradoxical belief at the heart of Western secularity: the idea of disenchantment. Standard accounts of 'disenchantment' refer to the belief that the instrumental–rational actions of humans have stripped the non-human elements of the world of their intrinsic meaning. These beings are treated as mere objects, empty vessels onto which humans project meaning, and 'raw materials' for human use. In a universe without a divine arbiter, preserving this distinction between 'enchanted' and 'disenchanted' beings makes it possible to guarantee the unique status of human beings, and to prioritize their needs above all else. However this, as Chapter 4 argues, is a risky strategy—especially when the ability to define these boundaries is placed in human hands. Specifically, the logic of dehumanization underpins the process of dehumanization. In Chapter 4, I argue that dehumanization is not an objective phenomenon that inheres in specific actions, but rather an *inter*subjective process. In order to carry out dehumanization, one or more actors must believe that a particular being has been moved across the human–inhuman boundary, and therefore can be disposed of instrumentally. This belief only makes sense in a context in which being human is defined by this boundary, and non-human beings are treated as mere objects. Chapter 4 explores three forms of dehumanization made possible by the belief in disenchantment. In 'direct' dehumanization, actors deliberately equate other humans with non-human beings. Their ability to do so relies on 'effective' dehumanization, in which one or more parties—including, in some cases, intervenors—'recognize' the being in question as dehumanized. 'Categorical' dehumanization occurs when human actions cause the boundaries of the category of humanity to shift, leaving certain beings outside of it and exposing them to instrumentalization. By exploring how Western secular cosmology makes dehumanization possible, this chapter introduces a dilemma with which contemporary intervenors must grapple. Namely, the cost of elevating earthly human life to a supreme ideal is that nothing is sacred—not even human life.

However, as Chapter 5 argues, humans are not entirely helpless in the face of disenchantment; Western secularity is defined by the belief in disenchantment, but also in the impulse to resist or combat it. This chapter explores the powerful dialectic of disenchantment–re-enchantment, in which intervention plays an integral role. This dialectic produces ambiguous results: it simultaneously re-enchants and disenchants humanity. More specifically, the form of meaning-making that defines Western secularity—instrumental rationality—is simultaneously the driving force behind disenchantment. So, each attempt to encompass 'disenchanted' beings within Western secular structures of meaning reproduces their disenchantment. To illustrate this dialectic, I explore how it is reflected in the strategy of 'human security', which simultaneously elevates individual humans as its ultimate end and reduces them to objects of instrumental 'bio-political' control. Then, I examine how the dialectic of disenchantment–re-enchantment helps to determine the basic categories through which violence, bad death and dehumanization are apprehended by intervenors. I examine how this dialectic shapes the strategies through which 'bad deaths' caused by mass violence are counted, measured, analysed, predicted and represented in the materials used by intervenors. These processes help to create the basic ontological categories against which the scale and urgency of an event is measured, and responses to it are considered. As this chapter suggests, they attempt to re-enchant humanity—or to activate forms of agency that might achieve this aim—in ways that confirm the disenchantment of certain groups of people.

This problem is reflected on a much larger scale in the logics of killing and letting die that shape military intervention. Chapter 5 explores the conditions in which Western secular cosmology (which abhors death) can accommodate certain forms of killing and death in the context of intervention. It examines four circumstances in which death is, if not always celebrated, tolerated within this framework. First, as discussed in the previous chapters, intervenors shape their responses to mass violence on the basis of ontological categories. These categories, in turn, are based on thresholds that allow intervenors to make distinctions between elements such as the scale or severity of an act of violence. As the previous chapter outlines, these categories are produced through the literal counting of deaths and harms. In Chapter 5, I draw on Alain Badiou's (2007) ontological framework to explain how these processes of counting bring particular categories of violence into being for intervenors. The thresholds for these categories must be crossed before particular forms of agency—and especially military action—can be taken. Ironically, this means that a certain number of 'bad deaths' are required before the particular kinds of agency associated with military intervention can be activated. Second, this chapter looks more closely at the logic behind the abstention from military action in some cases, and its use in others. Specifically, it suggests that intervenors sometimes find it necessary to abstain from intervening in cases where failure might undercut belief in the agency of intervening organizations, and their capacity to protect and embody the category of humanity. In such cases, the imperative to protect 'humanity as a whole' sometimes overrides the good of protecting *specific* groups of people. The converse is also true: where the survival of specific groups of people is framed as a threat to 'humanity itself', intervenors find it easier to justify military action. Third, this chapter examines the specific circumstances in which killing can be framed not as the antithesis of high life, but rather as an expression of it. It argues that military intervenors sometimes adopt a concept very like Walter Benjamin's notion of 'divine violence', in which violence is construed as a direct expression of human life and needs. This image is invoked in two cases: when individuals constructed as enemies of 'humanity' (for instance, Osama Bin Laden and Muammar Gaddafi) are killed in its name; or when the killing of civilians is linked to the goal of enhancing human flourishing. If the killing of these people can be linked to the production of human flourishing, it is treated not as an excess but rather as an 'economy' of death. So, despite appearances, the logics of killing and letting die that shape military intervention do not contradict Western secular ideas of life and death but actually embody them. In other words, Western secularity has its own 'culture of death' (see Asad 2007) and its own secular angels of death in the form of intervenors.

Indeed, contemporary forms of intervention are deeply concerned with bringing closure to death and the ontological ruptures it creates. Chapter 7 explores the 'immortality strategies' (see Bauman 1992) and death rituals that intervenors use to complete this task, which is integral to the project of re-enchantment. It begins by exploring the strategies used by intervenors to 'make something good come out of violence'. Returning to Badiou's ontological framework (see above), it argues that intervenors 'reclaim' lives lost to death by altering trajectories of violence. Specifically, they sever these trajectories from their original ends, and suture them to new outcomes: for instance, the creation of conditions of 'peace', or the formation of a new state. In so doing, they offer a Western secular form of immortality to those who die, by embedding their deaths in the structures and social formations of the 'new' society. Chapter 7 analyses a range of strategies—conflict transformation, peace-building, even the militaristic doctrine of nation-building—that deploy this strategy. Second, this chapter explores the rituals that intervenors use to put the dead in their place, insulate the living from their presence, and seal off the ontological holes that violence has rent in the category of humanity. In some cases, intervenors use quite literal and direct forms of re-enchantment. That is, they appropriate elements of transcendent belief systems (for instance, tribal customs or ceremonies) in order to expedite their projects and increase resonance of these projects among 'local' actors. However, Western secularity also offers its own death rituals, which can be found in the public processes of self-transformation, rituals of 're-humanization' and strategies of healing that characterize the strategy of 'conflict transformation'. This chapter argues that these rituals and immortality strategies offer a sense of hope and infuse intervention with a redemptive quality. Yet they, too, are ensconced in the dialectic of disenchantment–re-enchantment. They instrumentalize the deaths of others towards Western secular ideals, and may fragment or even desacralize elements of transcendent belief systems.

It seems, then, that the dialectic at the heart of Western secularity undermines itself: every attempt to protect or re-enchant humanity drives forward its disenchantment. Does this mean that Western secularity is irretrievable as a basis for human action, and for intervention specifically? Drawing together the elements explored in the previous chapters, Chapter 8 argues to the contrary. It claims that rejecting Western secularity wholesale is neither practical nor desirable—but nor is privileging it in an uncritical way. Rather, it is necessary to rethink the role played by violence, death and disenchantment within Western secularity. Chapter 8 offers two possible pathways for doing so. First, I assess Taylor's (2007) claim that Western secularity needs to find a place for transcendence, even when it takes the form of violence. He argues that, instead of rejecting violence and death wholesale, humans should seek to meet a 'maximal demand': that is, they should strike a balance between the ideal of everyday life and the need for transcendence. In the context of intervention, this might involve embracing more robustly the forms of killing and dying discussed in Chapter 6. It might also require the cultivation of an ethics of sacrifice among intervenors, which would counter the paradox discussed in Chapter 1. Furthermore, it might entail restoring some of the meaning-making capacities of violence, perhaps by magnifying its sublime aspects. However, I ultimately argue that this approach reproduces the Western secular dichotomy between violence, death and meaning, and that it concedes too much of the ground that Western secularity has claimed for the importance of earthly existence. An alternative can be found in Jane Bennett's (2001) rejection of the standard Western secular story of disenchantment. Rather than staking protective action on the fear of mutual or even total dehumanization, it would advocate action rooted in attachment and commitment to the world. Instead of attempting instrumentally to re-enchant humanity, it would rest on a sense of enchantment *with* humanity (and other forms of being) even in the face of violence. Adopting this approach would dissolve the boundary between human and non-human, enchanted and disenchanted being, rendering the problem of dehumanization moot. However, aside from the practical problems which this approach raises, it also involves a massive gamble. Specifically, intervenors currently rely on the fear of mutual dehumanization to motivate and legitimate their actions, and it is not clear that the affective sensation of enchantment could do the same. Moreover, there is a risk that removing belief in dehumanization could produce toleration for, or at least diminish outrage at, terrible crimes and injustices perpetrated against humans. Bennett's work suggests that the cultivation of enchantment could overcome both problems, but further exploration of the connection between enchantment and human action is needed in order to ascertain this.

So, although both of these pathways raise problems and risks of their own, they suggest that Western secularity is not a lost cause. By engaging explicitly with its core beliefs—and with other systems of belief—it may be possible to find ways out of the current trap in which intervenors find themselves. In order to begin this discussion, we need to turn our attention to the role of Western secularity in IR, and to the forms of agency it enables and constrains. *International Intervention in a Secular Age* begins this task.

Notes

1 Wheeler (2000) examines the diachronic process through which norms of military intervention have changed (see Chapter 2), but he does not explore the diachronic processes through which individual acts of intervention unfold.
2 This is also, of course, the central feature of cosmopolitan theories of IR—see Kaldor (2006) and Held (2010). However, cosmopolitan theories are concerned primarily with how individuals constitute social structures and the demands they

can make upon them, not with the social practices and beliefs which constitute them. For this reason, the two approaches should not be conflated.

3 The term 'local(s)' seems to have emerged within contemporary international relations scholarship and practice (in particular that concerned with intervention) as the standard term of demarcation for people who are contrasted with intervening actors. In other words, these people are deemed 'local' only in relation to the presence of 'internationals'; otherwise they would simply be 'Somalians' or 'Sarajevans' or 'citizens'. In other words, the very positing of a positive category of the 'local' presupposes a set of distinctive 'international' cultures and structures which need to be distinguished from the 'local'. There has, to date, been almost no attempt to theorize or explain the idea of a 'local', except in relation to either geographic location or in contrast to 'internationals'.

4 Although immersion in a particular institutional environment can help to inculcate an 'international' mindset, as Michael Barnett's (2010) work shows. Also, as Catherine Goetze (2013) argues, certain cultural backgrounds (shaped by education, social status and cultural influences such as literature) are predominant within international organizations.

5 However, it is far beyond the scope of this book to explore the theological roots of Western secularity, a subject which has been amply treated in the theoretical works upon which this book draws (see Chapter 2). Rather, I take the social imaginaries of Western secularity as my starting point and explore how they shape contemporary intervention.

6 I put the word 'religion' in quotation marks because, in IR discourses, a vast array of religious beliefs are often conflated, as are the ways of being 'religious' (e.g. through pious observation, social and political activities, as a matter of one's heritage, and so on). It is necessary to use this shorthand in order accurately to reflect the discourses in question, but I reject the idea that we can speak of 'religion', 'religiousness' or 'religious actors' in general terms. The quotation marks are not intended to denigrate religious beliefs of any kind.

2 Beyond belief

Telling a new story about secularity in IR

International intervention is shaped by beliefs about death, the meaning of life, and the place of humanity in the universe. As I shall argue in this chapter, many of these beliefs derive from a distinct system of belief: Western secularity. Yet IR discourses are dominated by a negative conception of secularity, which defines it merely as the absence of, or even an antidote to, 'religion'. This conception is buried deep in the guiding stories of mainstream IR, in particular the founding myth of the Westphalian moment. For many IR scholars, this moment marked a cosmological watershed, at which point the violent, messy politics of 'religion' cleaved from a new, pure, orderly space—the 'international' sphere. As the modern state and its laws developed, or so the story goes, 'religion' was gradually excised from the 'international' realm until it remained only as a stubborn vestige. Until the present day, that is, when the seemingly dormant forces of 'religion' burst into the international realm, in the form of 'new wars', 'religious' terrorism and millenarian foreign policy. Indeed, concern over the destabilizing effects of 'religion' on the international sphere has been elevated to the status of an urgent security issue. 'Religion' has been framed as a force that threatens, and is threatened by the presence of, an international sphere defined by the absence of 'religion'. Conversely, this sphere is increasingly understood to be embattled by, and overtly hostile to, a plethora of 'religious' actors and spheres of action.

This story is reproduced in a recent turn towards 'post-secularism' in IR theory. Post-secularists suggest that it is inaccurate, if not outright dangerous, to treat the international sphere as if it were, ever was, or ever could be entirely devoid of 'religion'. Instead, they suggest, we should acknowledge the constitutive power of 'religious' beliefs, actors and actions in the international sphere. This theoretical turn draws on a set of theories developed largely in domestic politics, which emphasize plurality, multiplicity, difference and disruptive action. However, in the international sphere, the imperatives of security override even the most pluralistic impulse. As a result, most post-secularist arguments are instrumentalized to the goal of reducing 'religious' violence or threat. Even though they contest certain aspects of the foundational myths of IR, the moral of their stories are strikingly similar.

I want to tell another story and, with it, offer a different way of approaching the role of belief in international politics. Specifically, I shall argue that instead of (only) debating the meaning and role of 'religion' in international politics, we (also) need to pay much more attention to what secularity is, means and enables. There is an alternative way of framing secularity—not as the absence of, or opposition to religious belief, but as a powerful, diverse *belief system*, which transforms, rearranges, combines and translates beliefs from various other frameworks of meaning. Crucially, it translates the basic tenets and beliefs of transcendent frameworks into worldly or human terms. Not only is this form of secularity a powerful force within our societies, as scholars such as Charles Taylor and Talal Asad claim, but it is also at the heart of the international sphere. Indeed, the notion of secularity produced by this 'trans-formation thesis' has helped to create ideas and forms of agency such as humanitarianism and even intervention itself. It provides a powerful counter-current to the negative or *secularizing* accounts of secularity embedded in IR's foundational myths. Moreover, it explains in a way that these myths cannot the beliefs that inspire and inhibit contemporary intervention.

A foundational myth: secularity in IR

Mainstream narratives of IR owe much to a single founding myth. Specifically, the Westphalian moment is treated as a turning point, in which 'religion' was relegated to the domestic realm in order to make way for the emergence of a new international realm. Most ways of telling this myth are remarkably secular*ist*: that is, they adopt a negative account of secularity, framing the international sphere as a space marked by the absence of 'religion'. Although this story remains quite consistent across IR theory, there are different ways of telling it. Each gives rise to a distinct understanding of secularity, and I shall explore the two dominant ones here.

One account suggests that the signing of the treaties of Westphalia in 1648 marked the end not only of two major wars involving factions associated with particular religious sects, but of *all* religious wars. The modern, sovereign states that emerged from this process became regarded as bulwarks not only against violence, but against 'religious' violence in particular (see Laustsen and Waever 2000; Philpott 2002; Thomas 2005). Conversely, as Luca Mavelli (2012) argues, the exclusion of 'religion' from the workings of the state became firmly linked to the provision of security and stability. As this narrative took hold and shaped the formation of modern states, 'religion' was consigned to the 'outside' of IR—and, increasingly, of politics itself. It came to be viewed as a matter of personal choice, a set of beliefs held by *some* statespeople and citizens, or a feature of 'local' culture. This account of the 'secular' international sphere reached its apex during the Cold War, which was framed in terms of the frictions and confrontations between worldly political ideologies, in which theology played almost no explicit role (see Barbato and Kratochwil 2009).

This story invokes the idea of laicism, which is best known as the basis for domestic, state-sponsored policies such as *laïcité* in France and *laiklik* in Turkey (see, for instance, Balibar 2004; Bilgin 2008). Laicists argue that the peaceful coexistence of both 'religion' and 'secularity' depends on their careful separation. In practice, this usually means that overt 'religious' practice and belief must be excluded from the public sphere and prevented from influencing its formal institutions and their functions. One way of understanding laicism is as an ironic inversion of the idea of the 'taboo' or 'ban' in Judeo-Christian (and many other) belief systems. Within these traditions, taboos or bans are used to separate bodily, mortal and profane objects from sacred spaces or practices in order to protect the higher realm from being corrupted by the demands and denigrations of this world (see Kristeva 1982). This belief is directly reversed by laicists, who view the transcendent, ritual or sacred as corrupting forces in society, and seek to protect the worldly, human realm from their influence. According to Rajeev Bhargava (1998), this work of separation is precisely what the secular state is 'for': filtering out aspects of religious belief or practice that exert dispropor-tionate influence on politics and society, and embedding them firmly in the private realm. It is important to note that laicists are not necessarily 'anti-religion'—on the contrary, Jurgen Habermas (2006) points out that the roots of laicism lie in the desire to protect religion and its expression. Specifically, the intention behind the formation of the Westphalian state was to create a public sphere in which people of many religious beliefs could coexist without the threat of persecution (see Taylor 1998). For Habermas, this means framing the public as a space in which citizens can step outside of their religious beliefs (and those of others), viewing them with objectivity and mutual respect. Beliefs derived from religious frameworks may play a role in public life, but only if they are 'translated' into forms that do not undermine the equality of citizens or, indeed, their rights to religious practice and expression.

Laicist views of IR define the international sphere as a global public, whose institutions should be free of overt 'religious' influence. This means that states and international structures are given the rather imposing task of separating the divine and the earthly. How they do so has important implications for world politics. Perhaps most (in)famously in Samuel Huntington's 'clash of civilizations' thesis, this idea has led policy-makers to imagine a geo-strategic sphere in which sharp boundaries are drawn between a secularized West and a 'religion'-dominated rest, characterized by poverty, violence and disorder (see Debrix 2007). According to Elizabeth Shakman Hurd (2008), this kind of thinking has dominated contemporary political leaders and international organizations, producing an image of 'religion' (and of Islam, in particular) as an unwelcome, exogenous intrusion that threatens international stability and security. Imagining geopolitics through this laicist lens places pressure upon international actors to protect the hard-won spheres of secularity from the (perceived) encroachment of 'religion'. In its translation from the domestic to the international sphere, the idea of laicism has taken on a distinctly realist hue at the expense of pluralism. That is, it generates fear of the effects of 'religion', without evincing the impulse to protect and cherish 'religious' beliefs as found in its domestic variations.

The second version of this story is both more descriptive and more normatively charged than the laicist account. Secular*ists* argue that (a) religion is declining in the world, or (b) that this decline should be celebrated—or both.[1] This story, too, starts with the Westphalian moment. According to Simon Chesterman (2001), this marked the point at which human beings began to see their laws and the actions of their leaders not as direct manifestations of divine will, but rather as the results of human effort. This, of course, meant that states could no longer rely as readily on the divine to substantiate their authority. As Habermas (2006) suggests, at this moment modern states faced the challenge of 'fleshing out' the authority and legitimacy formerly provided by the divine. In response, they present themselves as replacements—that is, as an ultimate source of power and authority in worldly affairs. And, as people began to rely more heavily on states and other worldly institutions to protect them, care for them and address their needs, popular reliance on the divine decreased in turn.

This story reflects the 'secularization' thesis: the notion that 'religion' has been gradually eroded, not only through the rise of the state, but also through phenomena such as modernization, liberalism, economic and scientific development, the diversification of social bonds, and a rise in the quality of life (Habermas 2006). Secularists present this trend as an irreversible, linear progression towards a more 'advanced' or 'modern' way of life. However, empirical evidence suggests that this image is inaccurate. For instance, the political scientists Pippa Norris and Roger Ingelhart set out to study what was presumed to be 'a systematic corrosion of religious practices, values and beliefs' around the world (2004: 5). They collected data on 'religious' activities and values (such as church attendance and prayer, moral orientations, and beliefs related to life after death, heaven and hell) across a range of countries (Norris and Ingelhart 2004: 40–1). Their findings were not as straightforward as some secularists might have expected. 'Religious' practices had declined in certain countries, but actually increased in others (particularly across the global south). Drawing on this evidence, they argued that, while secularization was clearly a real process, it was neither natural nor inevitable. Specifically, 'religious' activity declined only in those places where human institutions did a relatively competent job of meeting human needs for economic well-being, security, or social cohesion—that is, where 'the feeling that survival is secure enough that it can be taken for granted' (Norris and Ingelhart 2004: 4). In contrast, they claim, there is a relatively inelastic 'demand' for religion (as well as a competitive 'market' of providers) where quality of life or life chances are relatively low. Similarly, it is often argued that the 'demand' for religion is strong where secular(izing) social systems have failed to live up to popular expectations (Keddie 2003) or where 'secular' systems of belief, such as those associated with communism or 'salvational' liberalism have collapsed (Barbato and Kratochwil 2009: 3).

Although they are not necessarily normative in their implications, these arguments set the stage for deeply secularist approaches to 'religion' within IR. Specifically, by pointing out that secularization is not inevitable, and that its 'progress' can be reversed, they raise warning flags for those who are invested in it. Moreover, empirical evidence of the type presented by Norris and Ingelhart gives the impression that 'religion' is, in fact, resurging. When combined with the concerns of laicists, they warn that the 'pure', secularized spaces of the international realm are under imminent threat from 'religion'. This anxiety courses through some of the most heated discourses and controversial policies in contemporary IR.

Secularity and securitization

Writing in response to the events of September 11, 2001, Daniel Philpott argued that the scholars, policy-makers and political leaders who shape IR had fallen asleep at the wheel 'like a watchman who nods off as the creature he surveils himself falls asleep' (2002: 67). That creature, 'religion' had lain quiescently under the structures of the secularist state and international sphere. But on September 11, he argues, the very foundations of this system were 'shaken by the fitful rumblings of a Rip Van Winkle awakening from long centuries of slumber, a figure whose identity is public religion' (Philpott 2002: 67). This fable, common in IR debates, contains two important assumptions. The first is that 'religion' disappeared, or was neutered by development of the contemporary state and international structures. The second is that 'religion' is back, and with a vengeance.

The first of these assumptions reflects the post-secularist thesis: the idea that the world is no longer on a one-way path to secularization, but in fact is being *de*-secularized by a 'resurgence of religion'. The second one reflects the deep anxieties that drive the process of 'securitization' (see below). In combination, they set the parameters in which 'religion' and 'secularity' have entered contemporary discussions in IR.

Among IR scholars and in public debates, the claim that the events of 9/11 offer indisputable evidence of the 'resurgence' of 'religion' has become a truism. Acts of violence undertaken by 'religiously-motivated' people, or associated with 'religious' purposes have been reframed as the primary security issue facing the contemporary world—often at the cost of attention to other pressing issues, including episodes of mass violence (MacFarlane *et al.* 2004). In order to respond to the challenges this raises, a number of scholars have advocated a 'post-secularist' orientation. This approach is designed to break the discipline's 'secularizing silence' (Sheikh 2012: 391) by recognizing the central role that religious actors and actions play (and perhaps always have played) in the international sphere.

Although diverse in their arguments and motivations, post-secularists tend to explain the idea of the 'resurgence of religion' in the following manner: secularity has become a hegemonic world-view in IR, one which has devalued (or marginalized, or simply ignored) 'religious' belief and practice. This has, in turn, sparked widespread frustration, anger and, ultimately, retribution in the form of 'religious' violence. Thus, in order to prevent or halt this violence, it is necessary to *accommodate* 'religion', to 'bring it back' into IR theory and practice.

Post-secularist arguments have emerged in several strands, each of which provides an alternative to the negative concepts of secularity discussed above. The first strand is empirical,[2] and does not necessarily carry normative or ethical implications (although, as we shall soon see, it does carry instrumental ones). It suggests that the world *is* not, may never have been, and likely will never be fully secularized. Its main message is that analysts and political leaders should take this into account when formulating policies, in order better to understand the motivations and likely behaviour of other actors. This is the kind of argument implied by Norris and Ingelhart's study, as well as Philpott's fable and the work of Mark Juergensmeyer (see below), who warns that a secularist approach to foreign and domestic policies may provoke fear and anger among actors with strong religious beliefs.

A second major strand of post-secularism takes its cues from domestic models of politics which value pluralism and diversity. One version of this approach suggests that the demands of justice require the toleration of 'religion' in the public sphere (see Dallmayr 1999), whether or not secularists like it. However, toleration, as Wendy Brown (2008) argues, is not an always an affirmation of plurality or the value of other ways of life; on the contrary, it is often a way of masking fear or revulsion, and regulating the objects thereof. It also might call for a Habermasian model of the secular public sphere, which recognizes the value and contributions of 'religious' frameworks, but calls for a secular public sphere capable of accommodating, mediating and equalizing them (see above). However, within this strand, there is also a more robustly pluralist account. It includes the radical and challenging work of William Connolly (1999) who argues that the 'visceral' and transformative experience of various forms of transcendence (whether religious or otherwise) underwrites the diversity, energy and inspiration necessary for a robust democracy. It can also be found in post-colonial thought or protests against the homogenizing force of secularization. This approach can be found in the work of Ashis Nandy (1998) who presents processes secularization as acts of violence inflicted on 'developing' countries by the West, and argues that other traditions and ways of life should be afforded a value equal to Western secular ones. These concepts suggest that the accommodation of 'religion' in public is a good in itself, and that creating a just public (or international) sphere necessitates this. However, although these concepts form the basis of fascinating academic debates, they have not, for the most part, translated well into mainstream IR theories and practices. Instead, they have been instrumentalized in the service of 'security' due to the powerful strategy of securitization.

'Securitization' (Buzan *et al.* 1999), in brief, refers to a process through which specific threats are elevated to the status of existential threats to specific 'referent objects' (the victim of perceived harms). These threats, and the referent objects they menace, are artificially lifted 'above' public debates and invested with extreme urgency. By labelling any event or problem as a 'security' issue, entrepreneurial actors are able to leapfrog them to the top of the priority lists of leaders and policy-makers and to expedite responses. Securitization is driven by the production of constant anxiety, punctuated by the occasional stab of intense fear. It relies on the presence of an audience that accepts the belief that a referent object at existential risk produced by the threat in question. Securitization, according to its framers, precludes measured debate and democratic contestation, instead fostering a kind of policy-making at gunpoint.

As Carsten Bagge Laustsen and Ole Waever (2000) suggest, 'religion' has been heavily securitized in contemporary international politics. On the one hand, 'religion' is treated as a profound threat to the stability of the international system and human life. On the other hand, attempts to preclude or constrain religious actors are often experienced by these actors as threats. According to Mark Juergensmeyer, many groups of 'religious' people around the world 'perceive themselves to be fragile, vulnerable, and under siege from a hostile secular world' (2011: 185). As a result, he claims, the public expression of religion has become a kind of protest against this looming threat. That is, as Laustsen and Waever claim, 'religion' is framed as a threat *to*, and an object of threat *from* secularization and the institutions by which it is propelled. Likewise, these secularized phenomena are equally interpreted as threats to, and the objects of threats from, 'religion'.

In this case, securitization is a reflexive process—that is, the phenomena in question are simultaneously threats and referent objects. So, in the same process, the image of a 'secular' international sphere has been securitized. Within secularist discourses alike, 'religion' is framed as the ultimate threat to the creation and preservation of 'secular' spaces. However, depending on the kind of secularism one espouses, the object of this threat may look very different. From one perspective, the threat raised by a 'resurgence' of religion is that processes of secularization may be rolled back, inviting a 'reversion' to 'religious' ways of life. For laicists, the perceived intrusion of 'religion' into the international sphere threatens to corrode the *cordon sanitaire* that separates the domains of 'religion' and 'secularity', breaking the reverse taboo discussed above. Both of these discourses frame the international as a 'public sphere [that] needs to be secured from religion' (Mavelli 2012: 178). In other words, 'religion' becomes an international security threat when it is associated with violence that undermines international security or, say, the human rights regime. The specific content of the theologies in question is irrelevant unless it can be directly linked to actions which threaten these phenomena. As Talal Asad (2007) claims, the power of 'religious terrorism' lies not in the mere act of suddenly killing, but in the expression of a belief system that can challenge the Western secular ideal of life (see Chapter 3). So, the referent object in this project of securitization is very specific. It is not the international sphere perse, or even human life, but rather a secular*ist* model of the international sphere.

The reflexive securitization of 'religion' and of a secular*ized*/laicized international sphere has diverted the post-secularist impulse away from pluralism and towards a much more instrumental aim: the prevention or cessation of 'religious' violence. Even within pluralistic post-secularist discourses, there are few calls to recognize, accommodate or even celebrate 'religious' actors or practices in their own right, or for the sake of plurality itself. For the most part, the call to 'bring religion back in' is driven by the belief that this move is necessary in order to ensure security. Crucially, awareness of 'religious' actors and their beliefs is promoted as a means of predicting, identifying and intervening to stop acts of 'religious' violence. For instance, Scott Thomas (2005), a leading proponent of 'bringing religion back into IR', urges policy-makers to pay closer attention to 'religion'. He claims that ignoring the role of 'religion' as a catalyst for social mobilization left policy-makers flabbergasted in the wake of the Iranian revolution, the Solidarity movement in Poland and, indeed, 9/11. Policy-makers, he states, should pay attention to 'religion', not *necessarily* because they ought to, or because it is a good in itself, but rather because it is essential in order to uphold security. This is also the crux of Philpott's fable of the sleeping watchman—fail to keep an eye on 'religion' and it will become a source of immense insecurity. So, although these post-secularist accounts call for more attention to 'religion', they do so in a way that contributes to the process of securitization. This has two knock-on effects. First, by accepting the 'secular' international sphere as a referent object of security, it reproduces the secularist image discussed above instead of contesting or diversifying it. Second, it instrumentalizes the ethics of plurality—inclusion, acknowledgment, accommodation, respect for difference—as security strategies or prophylactics against threat. As a result, the pluralistic modes of post-secularism discussed above are translated into the international sphere in a way that subverts their underlying values and reproduces negative images of secularity. So, ironically, the rush to 'bring religion back in' to IR may do so in a way that magnifies the processes of secularization.

Why not bring secularity (back) in to IR?

A second problem with the post-secularist approach is that it focuses almost exclusively on how 'religion' should be interpreted and responded to in the international sphere. For the most part, the standard secular*ist* accounts of secularity go unchallenged. When they are criticized, the strategy is often to demonstrate that they were never really that 'secular' at all. For instance, Mavelli (2012) argues that stories of secularity recounted above are based on a misinterpretation of history. For one thing, he states, the Westphalian moment was characterized not by the emergence of states 'purified' of 'religious' belief and practice, but rather of 'sacralized' states that drew many of their central symbols and practices from (Christian) religion. He also casts doubt on the assumption that these states were always sources of security *from* 'religious' violence. On the contrary, he suggests that the early nation-states manipulated sectarian differences in order to generate insecurity and thus consolidate citizens' reliance upon them. In addition, he claims that the modern state's preoccupation with security arose not from secular sources but rather from 'religious' ones. Mavelli's strategy is to show that 'religion' is always already an integral part of the genealogy of IR, not an external (or externalized) force. Its basic message is that secularization or the creation of laicist boundaries has not been successful; 'religion' permeates what we think of as 'secular' structures. This thesis challenges the negative concept of secularity as an absence of 'religion', and acknowledges some of its positive content. However, followed to its logical conclusions, this strategy swings too far in the other direction. It invites us to view secularity as a form of religion in disguise, and fails to acknowledge the distinctive features of secularities in themselves.

In order to understand the powerful force of Western secularity on international politics, it is necessary neither to dismiss it as the opposite of 'religion', nor to reduce it to an outgrowth of existing transcendent belief systems. Instead, it is crucial to extend to secularity the same kind of attention that has been applied to 'religion' by post-secularists. This does not *only* mean critiquing the effects of secularity on 'religion', as a number of authors have done effectively. It also requires asking more basic questions about what secularity is, and what it enables people to do. Such questions are already frequently asked about 'religion' in the context of IR. Secularists and post-secularists alike tend to agree that 'religion' enables specific repertoires of action. Three of these are explored by Sheikh (2012). First, she claims, adherents of a particular religion have access to a 'belief community' which shapes their decisions and values. Second, they may leverage their beliefs or this community as a form of soft power to influence decision-making. Third, by invoking 'religion', securitizing actors use the very word as a speech act that lends credence to their framing of threats and referent objects. Sheikh's answer to the titular question of her essay—'how does religion matter [in IR]?'—is that it makes certain kinds of action possible.

How, then, does Western secularity 'matter' in IR? What features of social and political life, what forms of agency, what notions of life, death and meaning are produced and enabled by this belief system? While negative, secularist accounts can tell us little about the substantive features of Western secularity, there is an alternative, positive conception of secularity that does just this. It has played a foundational role in the development of international politics and, as I shall now argue, furnished some of its key concepts. This narrative has been submerged within mainstream, secular*ist* genealogies of IR, and it threatens to be further sidelined by the post-secularist debates outlined above. As Stephen Chan claims, 'in its rush to secularity, IR has forgotten the need to tell stories that are sacral' (2000: 588). I worry that the rush to post-secularism, entwined with the project of securitization, may efface important stories about *secularity* and its role in IR. These, too, are 'sacral' stories—stories about belief, aspiration, ontology and the role of human beings in the cosmos. In order to understand the fundamental basis of international politics, it is necessary to bring these stories (back) into IR.

The 'trans-formation thesis'

The alternative story I want to focus on has no beginning—and no end—precisely because it is non-linear. From its perspective, secularity is neither the opposite of 'religion' nor a form of theism masquerading as its own absence. Instead, it is a set of beliefs, social features and ways of life that have emerged from the trans-formation of 'religious' world-views. I use the hyphenated term 'trans-formation' to refer to a process in which something entirely new emerges from the alteration of existing phenomena, without destroying them in the process. Trans-formations are messy: they do not neatly transfigure objects from one form into another. Rather, they create fragments and remainders, they move forward, in reverse and in multiple directions and dimensions. They combine features, practices and beliefs from different periods of time and they give rise to genuinely novel phenomena—all without totally entirely replacing, or displacing, that which they trans-form. To appreciate this, we need to see secularity (and, indeed, religion) as an assemblage of beliefs, bodies, objects and acts whose interactions produce the very energy that transforms them. Like other vast assemblages—the global economy, for instance—their form is by the complex movements, evolutions and processes of 'becoming' that unfold within them (see Connolly 2011). And, just like global economic trends, the features of belief systems may ebb and flow, expand and contract in various directions. But, although they may not be linear or teleological, these movements have visible trajectories. The current dominant form of Western secularity has emerged from the refocusing of Judeo-Christian beliefs in a very specific direction: earthward.

When we view the emergence of Western secularity as a trans-formation of these beliefs, the picture that appears is very different than that offered by secularist or laicist accounts. Instead of a sphere purged of transcendence or the waning of belief, we see new conditions of belief and distinctive forms of agency that respond to these conditions. To introduce the trans-formation thesis[3] as an alternative way of understanding Western secularity, I shall now examine these two facets and their influence on two important features of contemporary IR: humanitarianism and intervention.

Conditions of belief

The trans-formation of Western secularity has been characterized by very distinctive conditions of belief—that is, cosmological assumptions that shape belief and how it is enacted. These conditions of belief are both the product of internal evolution within Judeo-Christian theology and the catalysts for its continued trans-formation. Perhaps the most important of these conditions is exclusive immanence—that is, a firm grounding in *this* world, in the spaces and time in which human lives are lived. Immanence can be understood in many ways—as a closed system in which human life is insulated, 'flattened' and cut off from 'higher' forces and sources of meaning (see Taylor 2007); or as a rich, dynamic system of interacting forces that produce their own moments of inspiration and awe (see Connolly 2011). In any case, in an immanent cosmology, the source of life and meaning is internal, rather than external, earthly rather than divine.

Western secularity involves an inversion of traditional Judeo-Christian beliefs, such that human life is framed as the ultimate ideal and eclipses beliefs in, or aspirations towards the divine. Charles Taylor argues that, for many people, this trans-formation is experienced as a loss—of specific repositories of belief, or even of belief itself. However, in a Western secular framework, people still feel the intense need for meaning or 'fullness'; they still call on forces larger than themselves to guide and protect them; and they still attribute hope, fear and expectation to these forces. The main difference is that these forces are now understood in 'exclusively human' terms (Taylor 2007). This involves the belief that 'morality should be based solely in regard to the well-being of mankind in the present life' (Connolly 1999: 21). In a sense, this is not a radical departure from the transcendent belief system in which it is rooted. As Taylor points out:

> What people ask for when they invoke or placate divinities and powers is prosperity, health, long life, and fertility; what they ask to be preserved from is disease, dearth, sterility, and premature death ... divinity's benign purposes are defined in terms of ordinary human flourishing.
>
> (2011b: 44)

In other words, people have historically called on deities to protect them or enhance their mortal, biological lives. The difference in a Western secular framework, he claims, is that the weighting of the divine and earthly elements of belief have shifted radically, so that the will of the divine, or the idea of an afterlife, are no longer primary considerations. Instead, 'human flourishing', or the collective well-being of humans (see Chapter 3), is the ultimate end. From this perspective, Western secularity does not involve a sudden break with Judeo-Christian belief, but rather the magnification of an important aspect of it.

Indeed, a Western secular universe is not necessarily devoid of belief. As Connolly avers, 'there is no place called "unbelief". Every existential stance is infused with belief' (2011: 85), but it may take very different forms. Western secularity is better understood as a world-view in which not believing in the *divine,* or believing in it to a lesser extent, or believing in various conceptions of the divine, along with some immanent values, are all *possibilities*. As Jose Casanova (2010) suggests, Western secularity offers a range of different degrees of (un)belief: 'mere secularity', or the belief that being religious is one of many possible and valuable life choices; 'self-sufficient and exclusive secularity', in which religion is viewed as totally unnecessary to human life; and 'secularist secularity', or the experience of being 'liberated' from religious doctrine and belief.

However, Western secularity has also, perhaps ironically, multiplied and recombined elements of various transcendent belief systems. Taylor contends that the rise of the immanent frame involved a loosening of formerly rigid belief systems. This led to what he calls a 'nova effect': the proliferation and dissemination of myriad forms, experiences and practices of belief. According to Casanova, the processes of globalization have magnified this trend, producing a 'supernova' effect in which:

> All religions of the world are available for individual appropriation anytime and anywhere, thus multiplying the options of conversion, cross pressures and the individual search for transcendence.
>
> (2010: 279)

In other words, the rise of Western secularity has made it possible for human beings to adopt beliefs from various transcendent traditions—religious, spiritual, mystical and otherwise. It has multiplied belief as well as unbelief. According to Taylor, few people ensconced within this framework believe in an overarching notion of '*the* Good', but the desire to attain *a* sense of goodness or 'fullness' is actually amplified and, due to the (super)nova effect, the opportunities to attain it are multiplied. At its best, then, Western secularity can produce an 'ethos of engagement between multiple constituencies honouring a variety of moral sources and metaphysical orientations' (Connolly 1999: 39). This is different from the 'resurgence of religion' argument, which pits 'belief' against 'non-belief', and which treats human action as if it embodies either one or the other. Instead, the transformation thesis suggests that other currents of Western secularity have actively fostered (as well as fragmenting or rupturing) transcendent belief systems. The multiplicity of beliefs and orientations produced is a feature of this cosmology, rather than an intrusion into it. Moreover, it suggests that human action is shaped by a range of different kinds and degrees of belief, and is expressive of them.

In a related sense, faith, too, plays a role in Western secularity. It has been reframed and applied to earthly forces or phenomena. For instance, Craig Calhoun and his co-authors suggest that people living in Western secular social systems continue to put faith in the forces that affect their well-being, such as financial markets. However:

> This is not, in any strict sense, religious faith. For most, it is not faith in divine intervention but, rather, faith in the honesty and competence of

human actors, the accuracy of information, the wisdom of one's own investment decisions, and the efficacy of the legal and technological systems underpinning market exchange. In short, it is a secular faith.

(Calhoun *et al.* 2011: 10)

This suggests that faith remains a crucial, even constitutive, element of secular social structures. Indeed, 'religious' and 'non-religious' (or distinctly secular) modes of belief need not conflict; they may even reinforce one another. People may have religious motivations for undertaking secular practices, or secular motivations for espousing religious ideals (Taylor 1998; Asad 2003). For instance, an individual might champion the doctrine of basic human rights because of a religious belief that human beings are children of God, because of a secular belief in universal human dignity—or both. So, contrary to secularist accounts, people living within Western secular social systems have a great deal to believe in. The trade-off is that none of these beliefs is comprehensive; rather, they are experienced as something akin to 'lifestyle choices', which enhance one's earthly life and sense of meaning but cannot guarantee much beyond that.

To explore how these conditions of belief have shaped IR, I shall briefly explain how they have shaped the contemporary ethos of humanitarianism. They explain its immanent focus, its emphasis on earthly, human flourishing, its provenance in various forms of transcendent belief and the kinds of secular faith and piety that it inspires. However, most accounts of the emergence of humanitarianism reproduce the negative stories about secularity discussed above. This is particularly true in accounts of human rights, which are framed as artefacts of 'religious' belief that were secularized as they became embedded within the structure of the Westphalian state. Michael Freeman makes this kind of argument. He claims that:

The concept of human rights emerged in the West, to an important extent, as a *religious* response to a set of problems that was both religious and political at a time when religion and politics were inseparable. Gradually, the concept became secularized.

(Freeman 2004: 386)

By 'secularized', Freeman is referring to the stripping-away process discussed earlier in this chapter, in which 'religious' principles are denuded of their transcendent content. According to Freeman, the emergence in Europe of non-transcendent philosophies such as positivism and utilitarianism eclipsed the belief that the law was a medium of divine will. From this perspective, the moment that rights became human was the point at which they were divorced from belief and tied to human rationality. Alternatively, anti-foundational approaches (see Malachuk 2010) suggest that human rights did not emerge from the secularization of 'religious' principles, but rather that they were created by humans for humans, without any divine influence.

An alternative account can be found in genealogies of humanitarian thought and action which focus on the *practices* associated with humanitarianism, not just the development of human rights. Paying attention to practices enables us to see how the shift towards a totally immanent frame produced new understandings of 'good action'—not by excising transcendent beliefs, but rather by translating them. For instance, Calhoun *et al.* (2011, following Taylor 2007) demonstrate how the idea of humanitarian work sprang from changes taking place within Christian theology in the late medieval and early modern eras. Specifically, Christian ethics began to emphasize care for the earthly dimensions of human life. The humanity of Jesus Christ, and his attention to the worldly needs and ills of human beings, was increasingly emphasized, and believers were encouraged to imitate this. As a result:

> By the nineteenth century, to be a good humanitarian was to be somebody who helps humanity in general and advances progress in society. This was ultimately a secular project, although it might have distinctly religious motivations.
>
> (Calhoun *et al.* 2011: 14)

According to these authors, the same ethos animates contemporary humanitarian action in situations of natural disaster, war or refugee displacement. Care for the earthly lives of the people caught up in these disasters is, they point out, an important goal of many overtly religious people and organizations. However, they claim, 'it is organized very much in terms of ministering to the needs of people in the secular world' (Calhoun *et al.* 2011: 14).

From this perspective, the trans-formation of Judeo-Christian theology towards immanence is central to the humanitarian ethos. Humanitarianism is not, by this account, a 'religious' idea that has been stripped of its theological content. Rather, it has emerged from the magnification of particular aspects of 'religious' belief. In other words, it is not a matter of unbelief, but a means of expressing different degrees and kinds of belief through human action. Another articulation of this can be found in the work of Michael Barnett and Janice Gross Stein, who point to two intertwined trends in contemporary humanitarianism. On the one hand, they argue, humanitarianism is increasingly dominated by instrumental–rational logics such as outcome orientation, the pragmatics of fundraising, the role of states and commercial enterprises, and the 'encroachment of earthly matters such as governance, processes of bureaucratization and professionalization' (Barnett and Stein 2012: 8). This, they contend, has de-sanctified humanitarianism and even rendered it inhospitable towards the 'religious' actors whose various traditions gave rise to it (see also Lynch 2011). This sounds like a rather straightforward secularization story. On the other hand, however, they suggest that a powerful current of *sanctification* is also occurring within this field—but not of a 'religious' kind. It involves processes analogous to the 'religious' sanctification of objects and practices, but its objects are distinctly immanent and human centred. In explaining this process, they refer to the:

> Establishment and protection of a space that is viewed as pure and sepa-rate from the profane ... in the insistence on a space free of politics, and in the calling of a humanitarian ethic that acts first and asks questions later, insists that motives must be innocent and altruistic, and guards against a world in which interests and instruments trump values and ethics.
>
> (Barnett and Stein 2012: 8)

In other words, humanitarianism has sanctified certain *human* spaces and repertoires of action. Accordingly, many people working in the field of humanitarianism are driven by the kind of Western secular faith discussed above. Barnett observes that:

> Members of human rights and relief agencies frequently refer to forms of the international community and humanity that appear to have a religious-like standing. For many the transcendental pivots around God; for others, though, around a secularized humanity.
>
> (2010: 205)

From the perspective of these authors, humanitarian action is an expression of belief, and its practices are a form of piety—perhaps to 'religious' doctrine, but also to distinctly secular values.

Interestingly, the objects of Western secular faith is also increasingly espoused by overtly religious actors. Consider, for instance, Pope John Paul II's address to the UN General Assembly in 1995. In this speech, he claims that:

> There are indeed universal human rights, rooted in the nature of the person, rights which reflect the objective and inviolable demands of a universal moral law ... these rights tell us something important about the actual life of every individual and of every social group. They also remind us that we do not live in an irrational or meaningless world. On the contrary, there is a moral logic which is built into human life and which makes possible dialogue between individuals and peoples.
>
> (Vatican 1995)

He also espouses the 'universal longing for freedom' of the world's peoples, and pays tribute to the 'non-violent revolutions of 1989'.

Similarly, consider Pope Benedict XVI's speech to the UN Assembly on 18 April 2008. In expressing support for the norm of responsibility to protect, he states that:

recognition of the unity of the human family, and attention to the innate dignity of every man and woman, today find renewed emphasis in the principle of the responsibility to protect ... Every State has the primary duty to protect its own population from grave and sustained violations of human rights, as well as from the consequences of humanitarian crises, whether natural or man-made. If States are unable to guarantee such protection, the international community must intervene.

In these quotes, two successive heads of the Catholic Church—one of the most visible religious offices in the world—articulate the Church's support for political norms in language almost exclusively concerned with human life on earth. Both quotes invoke moral laws and logic, human rights, non-violence, the daily life of individuals and social groups, the importance of the 'international community' and its capacity for *non-divine* intervention. Although one can presume that both speakers had 'religious' motivations, the speeches themselves are not overtly evangelical or even theological. Instead, the language adopted in both speeches emphasizes human-made objects of Western secular faith which are compatible with, but distinct from, Catholic doctrine. This reverses the idea, discussed above, that seemingly secular organizations and practices are simply facades for 'religious' beliefs. Instead, in these speeches, an overtly religious organization acts as a mouthpiece for distinctly Western secular ideals. This, in turn, exemplifies the conditions of belief that mark Western secularity, in which people can adopt 'secular' beliefs for 'religious' reasons, and vice versa.

So, in discourses of humanitarianism, we can detect the influence not only of belief and unbelief, but also of various degrees and combinations of belief. There is also ample evidence of new forms of faith and piety, expressed in the actions associated with humanitarian work. Certainly, secularist and laicist trends have shaped humanitarianism—for instance, by creating pressure on international humanitarian actors to adopt overtly non-religious aims and identities (see Barnett and Stein 2012; Lynch 2011). However, there is also significant evidence that the trans-formation of transcendent belief has produced new outlets and expressions of belief, and, in some cases, new beliefs. This is one of the most important contributions of Western secularity to IR.

New forms of agency

The forms of belief discussed above are based on very specific understandings of the conditions in which human life takes place. These include the dimensions of time and space, but also the possibilities and constraints that these place on human action. Most importantly, perhaps, the trans-formation of Western secularity has produced the belief that human beings are on their own in the universe. The perennial problems that they struggle with—the need to survive, the need to find meaning in life, the need to resist harm or evil on a massive scale—remain unchanged. But without a deity to meet these needs, it seems incumbent on humans to adopt this role. Human institutions must offer meaning, protection and, if necessary, wrath; they must respond to harm and ensure flourishing; they must offer inspiration and a place to put one's faith. As a result, Western secularity has demanded new concepts of human agency, which frame humans as capable of—and responsible for—responding to the central problems of human existence.

One of these problems is that of evil. Within Western secular cosmology, 'evil' has been rearticulated as a property of the human world rather than a metaphysical one. That is, it is understood as something that derives from human nature rather than gods or demons. Talal Asad (2003) argues that, in Western secular social systems, 'evil' is framed not as an expression of trans-cendent, superhuman forces, but rather as the superlative form of whatever is considered to be bad and shocking in human behaviour. Evil is imagined as something that emanates from humans, and something which is immanent to them, rather than a battle between abstract cosmic forces. This reformulation of evil has two important implications: first, it suggests that humans are the *source* of evil; and, second, by placing evil within the scope of human action, it implies that they must be responsible for addressing it. Taylor summarizes this belief as such:

> If things go wrong, it's always someone's fault. One can identify the evildoer and act against him. What's more, because the responsible agent is always an evildoer—not the unconscious and unwilling cause of some misfortune, but a malevolent, even criminal agent—action against him means not just neutralizing his action, but also punishing him.
>
> (2004: 130–1)

These responsibilities—of judging someone as evil, taking action against him, and punishing him—are placed firmly in human hands. But how can humans, who lack the scope, power and omniscience of deities, hope to carry out these tasks?

According to Taylor, the trans-formation of Western secularity has made this appear possible by offering new conceptions of human agency. These correspond with distinctive understandings of human social structures, which are, in turn, based on Western secular notions of time and the exclusively immanent world-view discussed above. As Taylor argues, the trans-formation of Western secularity brought about the collapse of rigid, hierarchical social structures. Individuals, he argues, have been cut loose from the structures that held them together and mediated their connections with others. These indivi-duals have re-aggregated, but in a very different way: instead of being medi-ated through layers and hierarchies that strictly regulate their relations, they can connect directly to social wholes. So, for instance, an individual might envision herself as being connected in an immediate way to the state, and able to make direct demands upon it, rather than having to 'go through' a church, family, or other social structure (see Taylor 2007). Through the re-aggregation of individuals into 'direct-access' social structures (see Chapter 1), individuals in Western secular social imaginaries believe that 'each of us is equidistant from the centre … immediate to the whole' (Taylor 2004: 158). Individuals see themselves as being connected directly to wholes—markets, the internet, trends, social movements and a plethora of other modern social imaginaries. Crucially, they also imagine these social wholes as being directly connected to them.

Time place an important role in these social imaginaries. As Bhargava (1998, drawing on Taylor 1989) argues, the trans-formation of Western secularity was characterized by a movement from the 'high time' of Judeo-Christian beliefs to 'secular time'. 'High time' refers to the realm of great moments (for instance, biblical events, miracles, acts of creation or the eternal time of the divine). This register of time and the events that punctuate it are not accessible to the average person, but only, to a certain extent, to privileged persons such as kings or priests. Human beings cannot act in high time, or on its scale; this form of agency is reserved for deities. Secular time, on the other hand, refers precisely to the register of time in which human lives are lived—the time of states, families and individual lifespans. Indeed, as Taylor points out, the Roman root word of 'secularity', *saeculum* originally referred to idea of a 'century', or the unit of time against which the functions of the state were measured. However, secular time also refers to the accelerated time of globalization and rapid political and material change (see Connolly 2011; Jakobsen and Pellegrini 2008). According to Bhargava, the fact that many people now understand themselves to be situated in secular time has had a profound effect on the way they understand and enact their agency. As a result of this shift, he claims, large-scale action can now take place in 'real time'—that is, simultaneously. So, he claims:

> A key idea has now taken hold of people's imagination: that together, by our action here and now, we can create and sustain large solidarities … Hence the link between the idea of simultaneity—events occurring in different places at the same time completely unrelated to higher time—and the understanding of a large, interconnected social whole to which everyone has direct access.
>
> (Bhargava 1998: 12)

In other words, the combination of 'direct access' social imaginaries and the adoption of secular time makes large-scale action seem possible. Through this lens, it becomes possible to imagine large social wholes such as the 'international community' intervening directly in the lives of individuals. As I shall now argue, the combination of these two features—the reformulation of evil as a human problem and the reconceptualization of human agency—has helped to produce the ethos of interventionism in contemporary IR.

During the period in which this book was written, the international sections of most Western news services were filled with reports about the implosion of

Syria. Every fresh revelation of evidence about systematic killing on the part of the Assad regime was accompanied by 'will they or won't they?' speculations regarding the likelihood of intervention by the US, the UK or a coalition of states. Despite significant evidence of war crimes on the part of the Syrian state, including the use of chemical weapons against its citizens, Western leaders took pains to explain the need for caution in contemplating military intervention of any kind (see, for instance, Roberts 2013). What is interesting about this situation is not the reluctance of these states to intervene militarily, but rather that they felt it was necessary to justify *both* their possible reasons for intervening and their reasons not to. This exemplifies a major shift in the way intervention is understood by state leaders, international organizations and the global public.

For most of the twentieth century, the sovereignty of states was treated as sacred—literally, at first, and later in the secular manner that I have discussed above. External intervention was considered to be a dangerous and unacceptable challenge to an international system based on territorial sovereignty. However, since the mid-1990s, sovereignty has increasingly been framed as a potentially revocable privilege, rather than an absolute law. Normative demand has risen for intervention of various kinds—whether by the UN, individual states or security organizations like NATO—when human lives are at stake on a large scale. This trend is clearly reflected in *The Responsibility to Protect*, which frames the privileges of sovereignty as contingent on states' ability to protect their citizens, and justifies military intervention in *some* cases when it is violated. But whether or not states and international actors fully espouse the principles of responsibility to protect, the burden of justification is now placed on decisions *not* to intervene as well as decisions to intervene. That is, decisions about intervention now take place in a 'climate of heightened expectations for action' (Welsh 2003: 2). What can account for the emergence of these expectations, which cut so sharply against the grain of international power structures and conventions?

The answer given by most historians of military intervention is a secularist one—that is, an explanation which makes no reference to the role of transcendent ideals or their Western secular trans-formations. I call this narrative the 'double negative' hypothesis: it suggests that the demand for intervention arises when the principle of non-intervention is overridden (Chesterman 2001; Morgenthau 1967; Walzer 1977). Nicholas Wheeler (2000) traces this process through the series of interventions that took place in the 1990s. He argues that, in a gradual and ad hoc way, specific interventions eroded the legal barriers to military intervention and produced significant changes in the interpretation of the UN's Chapter VII (which deals with threats to 'international peace and security'). This, he suggests, created an environment in which interventionist norms could emerge. I do not wish to argue that this account is inaccurate, but simply that it is incomplete. Wheeler explains how the removal of certain constraints created an environment in which normative change could take place. However, it does not tell us what drove that normative change, or provided its compelling content. In order to challenge such entrenched norms as sovereignty and non-intervention, this concept must have deep resonance for human beings across a range of cultures and traditions, and tap into a profound source of collective belief about the capabilities and duties of humans. This is where Western secular beliefs come in. In the next few chapters, I shall explore how Western secular beliefs about life, death and the category of 'humanity' help to drive desires to intervene, and to refrain from intervention. For the moment, I want to argue that these beliefs affect intervention in a more fundamental way: they make it seem possible.

Above, I argued that Western secularity furnishes a new image of human agency: the capacity to 'intervene'. Belief in the existence of 'direct-access' social structures discussed above makes it possible to conceive of a form of agency in which humans can interpose themselves directly in the fates of others, and on a massive scale. This notion of intervention is premised not on transcendent power, but rather on the desire to protect human lives on earth. Michael Walzer (2004) traces this story to the roots of just war theory. He suggests that this ethos arose from an Augustinian idea—that pious Christians could fight not only for holy purposes, but also to defend their 'worldly cities', as long as doing so did not violate their theological beliefs. In other words, just war ethics emerged from a transmutation of agency, or at least of conceptions thereof. Soldiers who previously saw themselves as fighting in the name of God, or as vehicles of divine will, began to envision their fight as an effort to protect human life. This narrative reflects the trans-formation thesis discussed above: a distinctly secular form of agency has transformed 'religious' beliefs, without entirely negating or displacing them. Belief in the divine is not destroyed, but it is mediated by a new belief that humans, too, have a role in securing their own destinies—and those of others.

Over the following centuries, this belief has been magnified to the extent that many Western secular people believe that they are the only source of agency in the universe. As a result of this shift in cosmology, human life has, to borrow a concept from IR, lost its external guarantor. When secular 'evils' such as large-scale violence threaten the ideal of human flourishing, either human institutions must respond—or nobody will. So, as Neta Crawford puts it:

> At issue is the future of millions of people who, if not rescued by the international community, or some benevolent power, may be left to suffer or die at the hands of brutal dictators and genocidal aggressors.
>
> (2002: 400)

Crawford's assertion is telling because it suggests the possibility that 'some benevolent power' may intervene, but does not take it for granted. Such an idea would have been unthinkable in Western civilization until very recently; it would be assumed that a divine agent would step in if and when necessary to decide the fates of human beings. Most importantly, however, it suggests that human beings have no one but themselves to blame if they fail to protect human life and its meaning. This helps to explain the demand for 'action' discussed above, and the urgency attached to it. It also helps to explain why states and international organizations are expected to offer reasons for deciding to intervene *and* for opting to abstain from exercising this form of agency. Simply put, if they are expected to act as arbiters for the fate of groups of people (or perhaps even 'humanity' itself) they had better demonstrate that they have taken it seriously.

Indeed, the ability to act in the name of humanity (and in the place of the divine) has become tightly bound up with ideas of goodness in Western secular thinking. As Taylor puts it, where human efforts to protect or enhance human life fail:

> It is not only our security that is threatened; it is also our sense of our own integrity and goodness. To see this questioned is profoundly unsettling, ultimately threatening our ability to act.
>
> (2004: 182)

In other words, the failure to exercise the form of agency usurped from the divine might strike a blow to human agency in (secular) faith in it. This idea is reflected in the following passage from *Responsibility to Protect*:

> Nothing has done more harm to our shared ideal that we are all equal in worth and dignity ... than the inability of the community of states to prevent genocide, massacre and ethnic cleansing ... We must be prepared to act. We won't be able to live with ourselves if we do not.
>
> (ICISS 2001: 75)

This passage suggests that, in a context in which humans and their institutions are solely responsible for their own fate, the failure to 'act' in the name of humanity constitutes a major abdication not only of duty but of moral status. This negligence, it hints, might make us impossible to be human, and to 'live with ourselves' as such. This helps to explain why decisions on intervention now take place in a climate in which it is widely believed that those 'who decide not to exert their humanitarian faculty when they have the possibility, indeed the duty, to do so must finally be either deterred or punished' (Debrix 1999: 184–5). From a Western secular perspective, is not only the humanity of victims of violence that is at stake, but also the capability of humans to secure their own lives and destinies without divine help.

The demand for intervention also reflects a particular kind of ethical reasoning associated with an immanent, Western secular cosmology—what Taylor (1991) calls 'strong evaluation'. This mode of reasoning, he contends, is a response to the loss of rigid, hierarchical, universal belief systems rooted in 'religious' doctrine. Within traditional Judeo-Christian societies, he argues, people envisioned themselves as embedded within cosmic hierarchies in which the 'right' and the 'good' were determined by timeless, divine laws that guided all action. However, the social and political trans-formations of modernity loosened these hierarchies and fragmented the various beliefs they once bound together. Suddenly, the people in question were confronted with a plethora of possible, competing goods and, in the absence of rigid, hierarchical rules, the need to decide between them. Taylor claims that they began to think of competing values in terms of goods and 'hyper-goods'. Whereas a number of values could potentially qualify as goods, 'hyper-goods' are those values or actions which most enhance, promote or guarantee human flourishing, and are considered essential to it. According to Taylor, a Western secular person confronted with a threat to a 'hyper-good' feels compelled to give a very good reason for refusing to act. For instance, she cannot say that she failed to help the suffering because she was 'otherwise occupied' or 'not interested' (Taylor 2011b: 294–5). Rather, she must demonstrate that a larger moral consideration—a greater and conflicting 'hyper-good'—prevented her from doing so. This distinctly Western secular form of reasoning also helps to explain one of the central tensions in contemporary decisions on intervention: the trade-off between sovereignty and the protection of human lives. From a Western secular perspective, one possible hyper-good (the preservation of sovereignty) is confronted directly with another (intervention to protect human lives). Both potential 'hyper-goods' seem to offer crucial protection to human flourishing: the first through preserving the stability of the existing international order, and the second by attempting to halt processes of systematic violence. In the absence of a divine arbiter, or of a hard-and-fast hierarchy to determine the relative value of each one, these potential 'hyper-goods' are placed into conflict. So, the cosmological beliefs of Western secularity set the context in which the protection of human lives can be framed as an ultimate good—but also in which this good can be contested.

According to these arguments, the contemporary impulse to intervene cannot be understood solely in terms of the 'double-negative' account. This explanation helps us to understand the context in which new normative demands for, and against, intervention have emerged. But to appreciate the driving force behind this demand and belief in its possibility, it is necessary to understand the belief system that has produced it. I have argued that Western secularity has produced a new conception of agency and responsibility: the capacity for *human* intervention. This form of agency has emerged in a highly charged situation, in which the failure to exercise it has profound consequences for humanity as a whole. By highlighting these possibilities and threats, Western secular beliefs have exerted a strong and pervasive influence on contemporary international politics.

Conclusions

Discussions of secularity in IR have been dominated by the same old story. Specifically, secularity is treated as an empty, sterile phenomenon, as the absence of belief and a source of hostility towards it. Post-secularists caution IR scholars and practitioners against the 'blind spots' created by this kind of secularity, and seek to moderate it by recognizing the role of 'religion' in international affairs. However, I have argued that it is also necessary to reconsider the nature of secularity (in its many forms). Certainly, secularism and laicism have real and important effects on how human societies are structured and how politics is performed on the world stage. But there is also a more nuanced account, which focuses on the trans-formation of transcendent beliefs, and which highlights the new, profound but often taken-for-granted possibilities that Western secularity offers. In this chapter, I have told this alternative story about Western secularity in order to highlight the central role of its *positive*, substantial features in contemporary IR. From the perspective of the 'trans-formation thesis', Western secularity offers various forms of unbelief, but it also multiples the possibilities of belief and makes possible new conceptions of human agency. This account suggests that:

> Secular societies are not just mankind minus the religion. They are very specific kinds of societies, imaginable only as the outcomes of long histories ... constituted by a distinct set of ethical goods, temporal frameworks, and practical contexts.
>
> (Warner *et al.* 2010: 25)

These features, I have argued, have helped to produce the ethos of humanitarianism, the demand for intervention and the fundamental ethical imperatives that both drive and frustrate it. For this reason, I shall focus primarily on this strand of Western secularity throughout this book, highlighting the important influence it exerts on the way that intervention is imagined and enacted. To do so, I shall now delve deeper into Western secular belief to show how some of its most profound tenets—beliefs about life and death—shape intervention.

Notes

1 It is important to note that empirical secularists are not *necessarily* normative secularists. That is, it is possible to posit that there is a decline in 'religious' belief around the world without framing this as an ethical claim—see Philpott (2002).
2 Again, there is an important distinction between empirical post-secularism, which simply claims that there is evidence of a 'resurgence of religion' and normative post-secularism. The latter suggests that actors and scholars in international relations *should* alter their beliefs and approaches in order better to understand and respond to contemporary challenges in IR.
3 Thank you to Matthew Engelke for suggesting this terminology.

3 A matter of life and death

For many people living in Western societies, it seems second nature to assume that avoiding death at all costs is the ultimate goal. However, this is not the case in all cosmological frameworks, and is a recent belief even in societies that are now dominated by Western secularity. Indeed, the idea that life is the highest ideal, and death its antithesis, is an innovation of Western secularity. This idea, I shall argue, lies at the heart of the impulse to intervene in situations of mass violence. According to the anthropologist Talal Asad, the impulse to end violence and alleviate suffering 'is not simply a matter of eliminating particular cruelties, but of imposing an entire secular discourse of "being human"' (2003: 124). Indeed, as I shall argue, the use of various forms of intervention to respond to death and affirm life produce a specific image of humanity.

This chapter explores the distinctive concepts of life and death that Western secularity has contributed to the practice of intervention, and to IR more generally. Drawing on Taylor's linked concepts of 'human flourishing' and the 'authentic' self (2004, 2007), I argue that this conception of humanity treats human life as the highest form of being, and the individual self as sacred (in a secular sense). Human life is not quite divine, but nor is it reduced to mere biology. Rather, it is a form of 'high life'[1] that is thought to rise above all other forms of earthly being, without entirely transcending them. Western secularity also provides its own distinct images of death, which is framed as the diametric opposite of high life. In a totally immanent cosmology, which lacks the concept of an afterlife or a transcendent realm, death is quite literally, a dead end. Violent death, in particular, threatens the sanctity and propriety associated with the individual self. It also undermines the ideal of robust, prosperous everyday life central to human flourishing. But, even in this context, some kinds of death are deemed to be 'worse' than others, depending on the extent to which they negate the ideal of high life. Two kinds of death in particular undermine this ideal: dying or being 'killed for/as nothing', or as 'bare life' (Agamben 1995); and sacrifice, or being killed 'for something'.

These Western secular images of 'high' life and 'bad' death form the foundation of many of the activities through which international actors respond to mass violence. They shape the basic categories used to measure violence and threat, decisions about appropriate strategies of response, and calculations about the relative value of human lives. They help to explain the urge to intervene in episodes of extreme violence, *and* inhibitions regarding the 'sacrifice' of life that intervention sometimes demands. Moreover, these concepts shed light on the sources of implicit prohibitions against certain kinds of killing, or the killing of certain people. In so doing, they help us to understand precisely what kind of human life is protected—and produced—by contemporary intervention.

High life

What does it mean to make human life the highest ideal? This is not simply the outcome of removing a layer of the cosmic hierarchy—the divine—and allowing the next level to take its place. It involves a more radical rethinking of immanence, of the profane and mundane. These words are not, in a Western secular framework, synonyms for meaninglessness or inferiority. On the contrary, the very phenomena which were formerly contrasted against the divine—the everyday, the mortal, the living, the worldly—are framed as the sources of value and meaning. This belief comes with its own distinct ethical prescriptions, not least that the flourishing of human life should be the ultimate focus of human endeavour. According to Taylor, Western secular social systems promote 'a single-minded focus on the human good' (2007: 548) and the use of scientific reason to maximize the life, and quality of life, of humans. This is a profound contrast from the transcendent ethics from which this belief system emerged. Instead of exhorting people to orient all of their efforts towards transcendent norms, such as piety, adherence to divine law or the pursuit of an afterlife, they direct human action towards 'ordinary goals', such as the preservation of one's own life and the well-being of one's family. According to Taylor, the idea that 'the life of production and reproduction, of work and the family, is the main locus of the good life flies in the face of what were originally the dominant distinctions of our civilization' (1989: 23). Indeed, as Taylor (2007) points out, the acts of sacrifice and self-denial demanded by transcendent belief systems are often, within Western secular systems, recast as 'mutilations' or 'humiliations' in relation to the ideal of high life. What is important to keep in mind is that this change does not constitute a loss of a 'higher' purpose; the divine has not simply been swapped with the banal. Rather, what was formerly considered to be banal has been invested with a 'higher' meaning and purpose.

In this cosmological framework, the most potent expression of the ideal of high life is human flourishing. As the name suggests, this phenomenon goes beyond the mere survival of human beings, or the quantity of human lives. It emphasizes what we normally think of as 'quality of life'—that is, life that involves some form of meaning and self-realization. Moreover, the maintenance and multiplication of this kind of life is viewed as an ethical end, not simply a biological imperative. For instance, economic activity is understood not only as a means of meeting the daily survival needs of humans but also, and because of this, as an affirmation of the primacy of human life. Moreover, the possession of rights, or of a legal status (as a citizen, say, or even a consumer) is expected to offer the kind of security and value previously provided by membership in a church or religious community (Taylor 1985). So, just as human life has been reframed as the embodiment of higher meaning, the processes and institutions that sustain it are sanctified in the manner described in the previous chapter.

For this reason, it is important to resist understanding the concept of human flourishing exclusively in terms of survival, biology, or, indeed, biopolitics (Foucault 2003; Agamben 1995; Arendt 1976). The notion of biopolitics refers to the exertion of sovereign power in and through living bodies—more specifically, through the regulation of their means of life and manner of death. Contemporary states use biopolitics when they attempt, for instance, to control the size of a population or to regulate the use of violence, but also in everyday spheres such as regulation of work, the maintenance of public hygiene, and the provision of healthcare. Biopolitics is a distinctly secular*ist* theory, or what Taylor calls a 'subtraction story' (see the previous chapter). It suggests that human life is *reduced* by the structures of government and the circulations of power to 'mere' biology. In making this claim, biopolitical analysis retrenches the division between the divine and mundane derived from Judeo-Christian cosmology. Specifically, it preserves the idea that the 'biological', worldly or mortal is somehow a 'lower' or debased form of life—a status to which humans are *reduced* through processes that disenchant them (see Chapter 4). The ideal of high life differs from this image in a subtle but important way. It suggests that humans 'are in an order of "nature", in which we are part of this greater whole, arise from it, and don't escape or transcend it, even though we rise above everything else in it' (Taylor 2007: 547). In other words, *human* life alone is believed to be higher than all other forms of life and, indeed, being. In fact, Taylor claims, many Western secular people experience '[a] sense of wonder that something like ourselves arose out of lower nature' (2007: 547). By referring to 'lower nature', Taylor suggests that there is a dichotomy being drawn, not between 'nature' and the divine, but within 'nature'. Instead of acting as a boundary that divides *life* from higher forms of being, it sections off *human* life (including its biological aspects) as an inherently 'higher' form of being in contrast to everything else.

The source of this dichotomy is, Taylor (2007) claims, the fact that human beings consider themselves to be the sole legislators of meaning in an otherwise empty universe. In other words, while other beings may have meaning attributed to them, humans are the only beings *for which* something may have meaning. Instead of an eternal hierarchy in which every being is locked firmly into its divinely ordained cosmic place (see Taylor 2007), the universe is understood as a field populated by beings that have, at different times, more or less meaning *for* humans. In this framework, non-human beings are understood as mere receptacles for the meanings created and projected by humans; they have no inherent meaning or value in themselves. Moreover, humans consider themselves the only beings capable of making meaning, and of making decisions about what possesses or lacks it. The creative control over the universe previously attributed to the divine is translated into the more worldly process of producing, distributing and projecting meaning. The ability to make meaning and take it away gives humans the power to determine—and to alter—the structure of the cosmos.

According to Taylor, within Western secular belief, it is this very ability to make and decide on meaning that renders human life *inherently* meaningful. Taylor uses the rather clunky term 'metabiological' to describe this image of human life. He states that:

> We enter the realm of the metabiological when we come to needs like that for meaning. Here we can no longer spell out what is involved in biological terms, those with animal analogues, nor state what kinds of things will answer this need, like a sense of purpose, of the importance or value of a certain kind of life, or the like.
>
> (Taylor 2011a: 189)

In other words, the *need* or *desire* for a meaningful life (which Taylor assumes to be unique to humans) is used as a marker of its exceptional status. However, the ideal of high life does not prescribe precisely how a human life should be made meaningful, simply that the quest for meaning should drive it. It does not offer a single, overarching image of the 'good life'; indeed, as the previous chapter argued, Western secular beliefs draw on multiple sources and registers of meaning. Indeed, it is this impulse to find and make meaning *in itself* that renders a life 'metabiological'. It requires that humans seek, as Zygmunt Bauman puts it, a life 'forgetful of death, life lived as meaningful and worth living, life alive with purposes instead of being crushed and incapacitated by purposelessness' (1992: 7).

The sanctity of the self

If collective human flourishing is the highest ideal in Western secular cosmology, what role do individual humans play? As it turns out, a very important one. According to Taylor, the individual self is the vehicle through which humans seek a meaningful life, and the material from which they fashion it. From this perspective, Western secularity social structures were born from the 'great disembedding of the individual from the sacred cosmos and from society' (Casanova 2010: 274). According to this narrative, human beings were shaken loose from the cosmic hierarchies discussed above, disaggregated, and coalesced into the 'direct-access' social structures discussed in the previous chapter.

This process produced a very specific kind of individual, which Taylor calls the 'buffered self'. A 'buffered' self is sealed off from external callings and demands—whether from the divine, or from other worldly beings. She may *choose* to respond to some of them, but she is not 'porous' in the way that her progenitors were—that is, constantly open to external influences, whether deities or demons. As the 'buffered self' developed, Taylor argues, she began to be driven by inner impulses, reasoning and reflection—an idea that found expression in the Kantian notion of the self. She also began to look inward rather than upward for her main sources of morality and guidance. As Taylor claims, for the buffered self, 'deeply felt personal insight [has] becom[e the] most precious spiritual resource' (2007: 489). So, in this sense, the self has become a source of guidance and value previously derived from transcendent sacred beliefs.

For Western secular people, the self is also 'sacred' in another sense: it is considered to be inviolable, and 'the subject's body, affections, beliefs, and speech are regarded as *personal property*' (Asad 2011: 283). The most familiar formulation of this concept is the idea that 'one's life is one's own'. According to Talal Asad, this belief contrasts starkly with transcendent religious accounts, in which one's life, body and soul were seen as the property of God, and later of the state, as an earthly proxy of divine authority. However, in a Western secular framework, one's life is considered to be fuller and more differentiated from those of others if it is 'more fully appropriated as [one's] own' (Taylor 1991: 74).

According to Talal Asad, the Western secular belief in ownership of the body translates into deep inhibitions against pain and suffering. According to Asad, pain hampers:

> The body's ability to act effectively in the 'real world' ... [but, on the other], it is also the most immediate sign of this-world, of the senses through which its materiality, external and internal, is felt.
>
> (2003: 68)

In other words, pain ties one to the immanent world, and to the embodied dimension of human being—including the natural and biological aspects which are central to human flourishing. Yet it also dampens one's ability to exercise individual agency, and may, as a result, thwart one's aspirations or plans for self-realization. This, claims Asad, is why people living within Western secular world-views express particular disgust at forms of violence which damage or remove parts of the body, such as dismemberment or mutilation. He suggests that the abhorrence of these acts stems not (only) from sympathy, but also from horror at the prospect that the integrity of one's 'own' body could be violated, or that one could be deprived of the opportunity for self-realization (Asad 2003: 149).[2]

In a Western secular framework, this is no small deprivation; the ability to produce one's 'own' self is central to Western secular ethics. Indeed, Taylor suggests that the desire to live 'one's own' life has led Western secular people to regard 'their' selves as projects to be worked on and, ultimately, perfected. In this regard, he shares with Foucault the idea that the appropriation of self is also an attempt to produce it. Indeed, he argues Western secularity demands and cultivates:

> A human agent who is able to remake himself by methodological and disciplined action. What this calls for is the ability to take an instrumental stance to one's given properties, desires, inclinations, tendencies, habits of thoughts and feeling, so that they can be *worked on*, doing away with some and strengthening others, until one meets the desired specifications.
>
> (Taylor 1989: 159–60)

Taylor argues that this expectation has created a culture in which people feel immense pressure to ensure that they 'get the most out of [themselves]' (2007: 477) and deeply fear failing at this task. This pressure is closely related to the ideal of high life discussed above. For the 'buffered self' of Western secularity, the meaning of life is not guaranteed. In the absence of immutable, transcendent frameworks of meaning, it is incumbent on the individual herself to find meaning in life—or not, as the case may be. Moreover, being 'buffered' or closed off to the callings of other beings means that the Western secular self is protected from external influences, but also deprived of the meaning they might give to her life. As Taylor puts it, being buffered leaves the Western secular self-vulnerable 'to the danger that not just evil spirits, cosmic forces or gods won't "get to" it, but that nothing significant at all will stand out for it' (2007: 303). In this context, making meaning out of one's own life (and self) is a high-stakes endeavour.

Taylor terms this striving for self-creation the ethics of 'authenticity'. 'Authenticity' refers to the desire to live a life in which:

> Each one of us finds his/her own way of realizing our humanity ... [in which] it is important to find and live out one's own [life], as against surrendering to conformity with a model imposed on us from outside, by society, or the previous generation, or religious or political authority.
>
> (Taylor 2007: 475)

In other words, authenticity is not only a product of the waning of belief in transcendent sources of meaning, but also an assertion of the human ability to make meaning. It is an expression of the human willingness and ability to confront meaninglessness, and to make something of it. As such, it is closely associated with an ideal of courage—to resist the 'comforts' associated with transcendent belief systems. For this reason, Taylor claims, the ethics of authenticity is closely associated with attaining maturity or full selfhood. The authentic individual, from this perspective is a 'courageous acknowledger of unpalatable truths, ready to eschew all easy comfort and consolation … capable of grasping and controlling the world' (Taylor 2007: 562–3).

Many people, Taylor claims, experience the aspiration to authenticity as a calling or a vocation. Indeed, the Western secular self is deafened to the callings of other, external beings, but her senses are finely tuned to those that originate within her. On first glance, it seems odd to characterize the ethics of authenticity as a vocation, as the term suggests a higher meaning or purpose. It has, Taylor claims, produced some of the less desirable aspects of Western culture: self-centredness, the instrumental treatment of others, a 'me-first' culture, and competitive obsession with professional success. However, Taylor argues that the draw of authenticity is analogous to a religious vocation, and to the sacrifices it demands. In pursuit of an authentic self, for instance, it is common for people to sacrifice time with their families in order to pursue their careers. But Taylor argues that this is not simply a symptom of arrogance—rather, 'many people feel *called* to do this, feel they ought to do this, feel their lives would be somehow wasted or unfulfilled if they didn't do it' (1991: 17). As discussed above, within a Western secular framework, work and economic productivity are viewed as ethical acts in so far as they promote human flourishing. The converse is also true: many Western secular people believe that work should not only help them to survive biologically, but also to be 'spiritually fulfilling, socially constructive, experientially diverse, emotionally enriching, self-esteem boosting, perpetually challenging, and eternally edifying' (Taylor 2007: 477). So, many of the life-enhancing and spiritually rewarding experiences offered by ritual and observance in transcendent systems are, in a Western secular context, sought through professional attainment. On top of this, as I have discussed above, Western secular individuals are vexed by the constant worry that they may 'waste their lives'—a prospect which cuts directly against the ideal of human flourishing. Authenticity, then, is not mere egotism; it is an attempt to live up to and maintain the ideal of high life.

It is not surprising, then, that the ethics of authenticity is closely related to humanitarianism. According to Luc Boltanski (1999) it is precisely the combination of altruism and the pursuit of authenticity that lends humanitarianism its driving force. Humanitarianism enables certain to people 'work on' themselves *by* contributing to human flourishing. It gives these people the ability to exercise their authenticity, and this enactment is central to self-realization. Indeed, Taylor states that some of the most potent sources of fulfilment in Western secular societies are situations in which 'you feel able to act, to do something to heal the world, when you can feel part of the solution and not simply part of the problem' (2007: 681). This idea is reflected in a video featuring the late Sergio Vieira de Mello, a high-ranking UN official (see also Chapter 6). The video, featured in a documentary charting his own career attainments in the field of humanitarianism, is intended to inspire young people to join the UN High Commission for Refugees. He states that this organization is the best opportunity you have in your life of achieving your dreams. Never forget the real challenges and that the real rewards of serving in the United Nations are out there in the field, where people are suffering, where people need you.

(BBC 2011b)

Here, a direct connection is drawn between attending to the suffering of others and attaining authenticity. Just as the Western secular individual is expected bravely to confront meaninglessness and oblivion with creative action, the viewers of this video are exhorted to 'do something' meaningful in the face of violence and suffering. On the one hand, Boltankski points out, this kind of dynamic may simply encourage would-be humanitarians to 'cultivate themselves through absorption in their own pity at the spectacle of someone else's suffering' (1999: xiv). On the other hand, the dynamic described here is actually a reflexive one. By attempting to redeem and re-empower the sufferer as an 'authentic' human being, the intervenor simultaneously seeks to realize herself as such—and by seeking her own authenticity, she attempts to realize (or redeem) the selves of others.

From this perspective, Western secularity provides a very distinct ideal of human life, oriented towards the goal of human flourishing, or high life, and pursued through the appropriation of the self. As I shall now argue, the violation of these ideals produces powerful images of bad death that haunt Western secular cosmology, and shape decisions on intervention.

Dead ends: Western secular notions of bad death

'War kills', states Michael Walzer, 'and that is why the argument about [it] is so intense' (2004: ix). But is it the simple facts of killing and death that render war controversial? In his study of suicide bombing, Asad (2007) attempts to tease out why this form of killing and dying is so viscerally disturbing to the Western secular mind. First of all, he points out that death and killing are not, in themselves, considered to be anathema in all cosmological frameworks. The incredible response of aversion to these acts is nonetheless is definitive of (if not strictly unique to) Western secular beliefs and ethics. Second, he concludes that 'what seems to matter is not the killing and dehumanization as such but how one kills and with what motive' (Asad 2007: 4). In other words, not all forms of killing and dying are the same, and some forms are more abhorrent than others for particular groups of people. I shall argue that this is the case in the context of contemporary intervention. Indeed, even the most vocal proponents of military intervention do not call for it in the face of every loss of human life. On the contrary, they seek to ration the coercive power, moral will and political capital required of military intervention for the very 'worst' or 'most shocking' forms of killing and dying (see Evans 2008). *Responsibility to Protect* outlines four of these: crimes against humanity, war crimes, large-scale systematic killing and genocide or ethnic cleansing. Each of these atrocities involves the systematic destruction of a human society, and thus its ability to live and flourish. The closely related concept of human security (see Chapter 5) frames the killing and injury of individuals, or the reduction of their chances to live a 'full' life as the most offensive kinds of harm. In both cases, what is at stake in these concepts of the 'worst' forms of violence are the Western secular ideals of high life discussed above.

Every cosmology contains images of death, and judgements about what constitutes a 'good' or a 'bad' death. However, dealing with death poses a distinct challenge within Western secularity (or any totally immanent cosmology). Although death remains inevitable for humans, there is very little place for it in a cosmology that prizes human life above all else. In fact, it is almost exclusively treated as a foil for the ideal of high life, and as a fundamental mark of the secular 'evil' described in the previous chapter. To the Western secular mind, death involves an absolute negation—quite literally, a dead end to life. According to John Keane:

> There are … lots of different ways of being killed, but only one result: you are dead, you are no more … For someone, somewhere, you may become a statistic; if you are lucky, your photograph and treasured belongings will be held in perpetuity by relatives, friends, colleagues or lovers. But the truth is that those who suffer violent death have been pushed over the edge … they are just blood-stained bodies covered in ants or flies, shallow graves dug up in parks or the practice grounds of sports stadiums, twisted heaps in the desert, motionless hulks on stone slabs. End of story.
>
> (1996: 70)

Death, from this perspective, is the diametric opposite of Hannah Arendt's concept of natality (1976, 1998), in which the appearance of each new person brings with it a new world. In a Western secular belief system, death is the reversal of this process, the erasure of the unique worlds that appear with every human birth and life (see also Bauman 1992).

This image of death contrasts starkly with those found in most transcendent cosmologies, including the Judeo-Christian one from which Western secularity is trans-forming. Within various currents of this tradition, death may be interpreted as the will of God or a chance to (re)unite oneself with the divine, as a rite of passage into the spiritual realm, or as the culmination of a life. As Achille Mbembe (2003) points out, death has also assumed different forms within strands of Western political philosophy not primarily oriented towards theology. For instance, he explores Hegel's view of death as a driving force of human history, and Georges Bataille's claim that it is both 'the source and the repulsive condition of life' (Mbembe 2003: 15). But these conceptions of death are effaced within mainstream Western secular thinking. Instead, death is framed as a perpetual threat, the external void against which existence and its meaning are pitched (see Badiou 2007). It is a horror to be limited, predicted, resisted and avoided—at least for as long as possible (Bauman

1992). This infuses Western secular cosmology with a strong sense of irony, and even of melancholy: the cost of enshrining life is that one must accept death, and the ultimate futility of attempting to eradicate it. Nonetheless, Western secular ethics demands that all of the energies of human civilization be channelled into this quixotic effort (see Bauman 1992).

The imperative to struggle against death has very specific implications for social and political action. As Bauman argues, it produces a strong desire to repulse death, and to segregate the dead from the spaces occupied with the living. This practice, in itself, does not constitute a sharp break with transcendent traditions; in many cosmological frameworks, people believe in drawing boundaries between the spaces of the living and of the dead. The difference in a Western secular society, Bauman suggests, is that this act of separation is not one in which the dead are sanctified, but rather in which they are expelled as a form of pollution. In such societies, Bauman claims:

> Death (alongside all other acts betraying the 'biological underside' of Homo *Sapiens*) [is viewed as] *indecent*—dirty and polluting. People blighted with such a shameful and repelling affliction [are] to be kept out of sight.
>
> (1992: 136)

From this viewpoint, death is an affront to life. It is not only offensive, but also dangerous; it is treated as an unpleasant, shameful—and possibly contagious—disease. It also undermines the crucial distinction between 'mere' life and the ideal of human high life. According to Julia Kristeva, 'The corpse represents fundamental pollution. A body without a soul, a non-body ... must not be displayed but immediately buried so as not to pollute the divine earth' (1982: 109). Here, Kristeva highlights yet another inversion performed by Western secular cosmology: the 'earth', or the space of everyday life, is framed as divine, and the dead are to be expelled from it rather than welcomed into it. According to Keane, these beliefs help to explain why violence is treated as anathema in Western societies:

> It violates the principle of the sanctity of human life, a presumption that in practice often dovetails with the belief that as far as possible violence should be hidden away from human eyes.
>
> (Keane 1996: 9)

Indeed, violence and its effects provide living (or, more accurately, dead) proof of the fragility of human life and the impotency of human agents against death. For these reasons, with Western secular cosmology it is deemed necessary to maintain sharp distinctions between those harmed and killed by violence, and those living in conditions of human flourishing. As I will illustrate in the following chapters, the same drive towards segregation is applied on the international scale—not only to those who are actually dead, but also to those people framed as imminently 'killable', or polluted by the presence of death. It is these very boundaries, in fact, that define and contain the category of 'humanity' within Western secular beliefs.

Death is the *bête noire* of Western secularity precisely because it undermines each of the ideals of high life discussed above. First, it extinguishes the 'sacred self'. This model of the self, as I have argued above, is premised on the integrity and functionality of the body. This makes it possible to exercise the particular form of individual agency which is deemed to be essential to the appropriation and realization of the authentic self. But, according to Kristeva, death converts the vital, empowered human being into 'a decaying body, lifeless, completely turned into dejection, blurred between the inanimate and the inorganic' (1982: 109). Death not only renders humans dead, but also *inhuman*.

In a belief system in which the self is considered sacred, the destruction of the body in which it is embedded is sacrilegious. To confront the dead human body—and particularly the *killed* human body—is to witness desecration, and to feel the meaningfulness of one's own life diminished by it. This is the exact opposite of the Western Christian tradition of pondering the memento mori, a symbolic image or object intended to remind one of the fleeting nature of life and the inevitability of death, and, in so doing, to confirm one's place in a transcendent cosmos. In contrast, Western secular beliefs demand that humans reject and avoid exposure to the evidence of death because encountering it fractures their cosmological foundations in the ideal of high life.

Violent killing and death

Contemplating her first-hand encounters with victims of violence in sub-Saharan Africa, the medical anthropologist Carolyn Nordstrom writes:

> [I have] seen bodies severely deformed by accidents, illness and microbes. And in these cases I feel compassion, sympathy and sadness … But I don't feel the world tilt on its axis. I don't want to escape from a world too ugly to contemplate living in. I don't suffer a crisis of existential proportions. It is the violence one individual wilfully does to another that causes this powerful reaction.
>
> (2004: 62)

For Nordstrom, violent killing is much worse than death from illness; it creates an existential crisis and makes the world seem too 'ugly' to inhabit. From a Western secular perspective, both of these forms of death lead to the same 'dead end', so why should one form seem so much more hideous than another?

The biological death of humans, of course, happens on a massive scale every day. However, it is *killing*, or violent forms of death, that tend to dominate the international social imaginary. This makes sense in a context in which not only collective human life, but also the individual self, are enshrined as ideals; large-scale killing negates both. First, violent killing entails a form of death as theft, or as the misappropriation of the self. According to Judith Butler:

> Violence is surely a touch of the worst order, a way a primary human vulnerability to other humans is exposed in its most terrifying way, a way in which we are given over, without control, to the will of another, a way in which life itself can be expunged by the wilful action of another.
>
> (2004: 29)

In other words, it is not simply the possibility of death or injury that renders violence so terrible. It is the fact that human lives can be 'given over without control' to the instrumental aims of other human beings. Butler's horror at this prospect evinces a belief that the opposite should be true—that is, that humans should have some control, some propriety over their own lives and the ways in which they are disposed of (or so to speak). Keane, too, highlights this aspect of violent killing. He argues that:

> Involuntary death by violence is a scandalous violation of the ground rules of any civil society, especially one that enjoys a maximum of democratic freedoms and equalizing solidarities.
>
> (Keane 1996: 70)

In other words, the threat of violent death is always shocking, but even more so in societies that value and seek to guarantee the integrity and individual agency of the self, as reflected in legal equality and democratic structures. Keane's comments also imply that this form of killing is a more grievous harm in a society in which one can expect to attain a degree of self-realization by virtue of these features.

Second, violent forms of death (killing) extinguish the ideal of human flourishing, and not only because they literally wipe out large communities of people. The fact that systematic killing is always done by humans[3] has several implications in this regard. It demonstrates that human life is not the primary ideal for all humans, and it shows how easily this ideal can be undermined through human action. Furthermore, systematic violent killing directly perverts the image of 'direct-access' social systems and the ethics of mutual benefit associated with them. In the case of genocide, massacres and other systematic forms of killing, the direct connections between people become an infrastructure for killing. It is precisely the directness of people's connections to one another, and to state or military structures, that render them vulnerable. This subversion recalls Elaine Scarry's (1985) claim that the horror of torture derives not only from the forms of suffering inflicted within it, but also from its ability to convert a place of shelter and comfort (the room) into a site of pain. Similarly, when social structures such as states, civil societies or even bureaucracies—all of which are expected to safeguard human lives and their flourishing—are converted into killing machines (see Mann 2005), a similar, vertiginous inversion occurs. The very structures, networks and laws that are expected to provide security become instruments for the efficient and brutal destruction of life.

Indeed, violence is understood as the negation of meaningful life itself. Any potential it might have to enhance human life is denied—except in a few specific cases, which I shall discuss shortly. As Taylor argues, in Western secular social systems, there is 'no place for violence and rage, but only for pacific mutual benefit' (2007: 649). This is something of an exaggeration; as I shall argue in Chapter 7, Western secular societies have their own forms of violence and 'cultures of death' (see Asad 2003), albeit very limited ones. However, Taylor is correct to point out that the disciplines of Western secularity's 'civilizing order' have sought to repress and marginalize violence such that it appears as a mere pathology, and is denied any 'numinous power' (2007: 649), or the capacity to endow higher meaning. This involves rejecting the 'warrior ethic', which valorizes killing and being killed violently as the ultimate form of 'good death'. This ethic, according to Michael Shapiro (1997) has been a feature of many societies, including the predecessors of currently Western secular states. However, according to Michael Ignatieff, within societies whose resources and energies are devoted largely to human flourishing, one can expect to live a relatively long civilian life, and high value is placed upon this. In such a society:

> Sacrifice in battle has become implausible or ironic … as peace has become a settled expectation of civilian populations, the idea of martial sacrifice and the nobility of death in combat have become ever more extreme destinies.
>
> (Ignatieff 2001: 186)

Within these societies, the meaningfulness of one's life is borne out in the sustained act of living—not in the moment of death. Death in battle no longer guarantees a 'good death'; on the contrary, it is much more likely to negate, or at least abridge, the meaning of one's life.

The impulse behind this denial of the meaning-making properties of violence is rooted in a desire to discourage violence. But it is, in fact, a risky premise in a world in which violence is a perennial problem. In short, if violence cannot enhance human life or its meaning, and always destroys it, then all deaths produced by violence are by this definition meaningless. This paradox is raised by Scarry (1985). She ponders the chilling and counter-intuitive possibilities of finding an alternative to killing as a means of waging war. What, she asks, would change if we substituted killing with a chess match or a singing competition? According to Scarry:

> If [the answer] is 'nothing', then another form of contest could perform the function of war just as well and far less painfully: though this would

of course necessitate the heartsickening recognition that all previous wars might have had a substitute.

(1985: 90–1)

This paradox captures the risk of attempting to remove the special meaning of violence: if it has no capacity to confer meaning (or at least a form of meaning recognized in Western secular social systems), then the lives instrumentalized to it are made meaningless. Scarry's thought exercise frames one of the most basic dilemmas confronted by intervenors: whether to acknowledge or deny the meaning-conferring properties of violence.

So, killing, or death by violence, creates a set of paradoxes within Western secular cosmology. However, even within this category, there are two forms of killing that are deemed particularly offensive.

Being killed for/as nothing

According to Scarry, 'the only thing more overwhelming than that a human community should have a use for death ... is that the community will then disown that use and designate those deaths useless' (1985: 73). In other words, it is bad enough that killing be used instrumentally to attain an end or confirm an ideal, but should these ends and ideals be removed, then the deaths are stripped of any meaning whatsoever. Similarly, Nordstrom states that 'to die at the hands of violent meaninglessness is the paramount paradox, the source of terror and ... existential absurdity' (1997: 133). For her, true terror arises from the obliteration of the meanings of lives for no discernible reason—or at least not one that resonates for the people who are killed. These two quotes refer to one of the most reviled forms of death within Western secularity: killing that takes lives without compensation, that leaves them destroyed, uncounted, disposed of as mere objects, and devoid of 'higher' meaning.

Stripping violence and death of their 'numinous' capacities may be an effective way to devalue killing and to deter violence. It directly resists cultures that valorize violence, in which killing and being killed may appear to offer the best chance of attaining meaning in one's life. But, on the other hand, being killed in the name of a purpose or ideal ensures that some meaning is conferred in the process. Even if it this meaning is not authentic for the person killed (that is, a meaning that she might have chosen for 'herself'), it is nonetheless a form of meaning that might be recognized by others. On the other hand, if violence negates meaning without conferring it, then those killed can only be treated as 'sacred lives' (Agamben 1995). A 'sacred life' (or *homo sacer*) is a life that is killed but not sacrificed; that is, it is destroyed but without attaining a higher meaning. Bare life is killed purely to realize its capacity to be killed, is not even offered the consolation prize of meaning imposed by others.

According to Giorgio Agamben, this kind of killing is the basis of sovereignty. The power of states, he claims, derives from the fact that all citizens may be treated as 'killable' at any time. When states or other institutions of sovereignty do kill, this does not confer any special meaning upon those killed. On the contrary, it simply constitutes these people as 'killable', and reproduces sovereign power structures. For this reason, Agamben rejects retroactive attempts to recuperate the meaning of the lives killed en masse by states, whether in concentration camps or legal wars. We feel the strong urge, he claims, to invest these lives with posthumous meaning as an act of mourning and empathy, or as a means of honouring them. However, doing so masks the true atrocity of the conditions of their deaths, and of the power structures responsible—in other words, it lets their killers off too easily. To truly comprehend the nature of mass killing, Agamben insists, we must see it not as a source of meaning, 'but simply [as] the actualization of a mere "capacity to be killed"' (1995: 114). And this, he suggests, is a capacity shared by all citizens of sovereign states. This image of 'bare' or 'sacred' life upends the ideal of high life. Rather than emphasizing human life, it exploits the human capacity for death in order to enshrine sovereign power.

The anti-ideal of being killed for/as nothing also has implications for the killer. Killers involved in mass violence tend to be presented not as psychopaths, but rather as cogs in uncontrollable social machines (see Mann 2005; Arendt 1963). From this perspective, they, too, are instrumentalized by sovereign power. Agamben explains this state of affairs by arguing that the Hobbesian state of nature, or the war of 'all against all', was not in fact abolished with the appearance of the sovereign state. Instead, he claims, it became embedded *within* the state itself, such that every human life became 'sacred' in relation to every other one. In such conditions, one kills and is killed as 'bare life'. Killing does not enhance the meaning of the killer's life, but only bolsters sovereign power, which renders her own life sacred.

We can also see this assumption reflected in accounts of the 'uncivil wars' of the late twentieth and early twenty-first century. In such wars, Keane states:

> Th[e] acts of violence are random and mindless. The killers' faces are blank ... they are often no-hopers who believe in nothing but their own private fantasies. Their senses are attuned only to violence. Unafraid of being shot or injured, they are ... self-destructive gangsters driven by 'anger at anything undamaged'.
>
> (1996: 140–1)

Here, the killers are depicted as a being almost as inhuman as the corpses they produce. Indeed, one of the central critical points made by proponents of the 'new wars' theory (see Kaldor 2006; Keen 2008) is that contemporary (un)civil wars are oriented towards profit or power alone, and have no 'higher' meaning. This argument is ambiguous, ethically speaking. Although it is intended to criticize and oppose war, it presumes a hierarchy of kinds of killing. Specifically, by treating the banality of these deaths as a marker of their enormity, it seems to imply that the deaths in question might have been slightly 'less bad' had they been 'for' a normative or transcendent purpose. For instance, Keane's description seems to suggest that had the killing been less 'mindless', the killer 'more human', the purposes more lofty, then the deaths would have been less abominable. This logic, as I shall argue in Chapter 7, lies at the heart of a dilemma faced by intervenors. On the one hand, in order to uphold the ideal of high life in the face of mass violence, they must imbue killing with some capacity for meaning-making. However, this is thwarted by the second central image of bad death in Western secular cosmology: killing or dying 'for something'.

Killing or dying 'for something'

Just as Western secular ethics abhor forms of killing that deny the intrinsic meaning of human life, it is also threatened by forms of killing that instrumentalize human lives to transcendent ideals. In other words, it rejects the more traditional concept of sacrifice just as powerfully as it repels Agamben's inverted version. Taylor suggests that, in societies dominated by Western secularity, it is taken for granted that 'people are no longer sacrificed to the demands of supposedly sacred orders that transcend them' (1991: 2). Sacrificial killing undermines the idea that human life is the highest ideal in itself, and subjects it to a 'higher' register of meaning—whether 'democracy', 'communism' or the will of God. Indeed, according to Taylor, the rejection of a sacrificial ethic was one of the most formative elements of contemporary Western secularity. It has intensified, he suggests, in the contemporary era as a direct response to the large-scale violence experienced in the twentieth century. Taylor contends that:

> Millions of people were dragooned in the last century in the name of impossible ideals of social transformation. They longed to return to what they saw as the normal, the ordinary, the satisfactions of unmobilized human life.
>
> (2007: 628)

In other words, the emphasis on the value of mundane, everyday life is a reaction against the logic of sacrificial killing in the name of 'higher', more abstract ideals. According to Slavoj Žižek, this ethos has become so embedded in Western secular societies that the taste for sacrifice has been eradicated almost completely. He reflects on this trend in the aftermath of the World Trade Center attacks of 2001:

> Witness the surprise of the average American: 'how is it possible that these people [terrorists] display and practice such a disregard for their own lives?' Is not the obverse of this surprise the rather sad fact that we, in First World countries, find it more and more difficult even to imagine a

public or universal Cause for which we would be ready to sacrifice our life [sic]?

(2002: 40)

For Žižek, the impulse towards sacrificial violence that shaped the history of all modern, Western states (see Žižek 2009) has been transmuted into disgust. The horror that citizens of these states feel when contemplating an act of sacrificial violence is one of abjection: the act undermines their deepest beliefs, yet resonates with a disowned aspect of their own characters. It also, from Žižek's perspective, underscores the weakness of their own belief systems, which fail to provide ideals grand enough to incite people to such extreme acts. Contemporary acts of terrorism oriented towards transcendent ideals evoke all of these disturbing feelings simultaneously within the Western secular mind.

Horror at sacrificial violence is also related to the emphasis on bodily integrity discussed above. The notion of self-ownership produces a deep-seated aversion to the use of human bodies as mere material for embodying the beliefs of others. Scarry's (1985) analysis of war highlights this problem. She suggests that killing in warfare is a strategy used to solve the 'crisis of transubstantiation' that comes with the pursuit of transcendent ideals. Simply put, big, universal ideas such as 'freedom' or 'divine will' have no tangible expression in the material world, and must be literally embodied in order to appear in this world. In war, the damaging and destruction of human bodies is a means of making 'real' the abstract norms to which the violence in question is oriented. From this perspective, war is quite literally a form of human sacrifice on a large scale—an idea that unsettles Western secular minds (and stomachs).

Sacrifice and bad death in the context of intervention

Western secular notions of bad death, as I have discussed above, are the diametric opposite of the ideal of high life. They involve forms of killing and dying that extinguish human flourishing and violate the sanctity of the self. While all forms of death trouble Western secular beliefs, violent killing— whether 'for nothing' or 'for something'—raise the ultimate challenge to this framework. With very specific exceptions (which I shall explore in Chapter 6), these images set the ethical parameters of international intervention. They lie at the root of intervenors' assumptions about which kinds of killing are 'urgent' or worthy of particular kinds of responses. Moreover, they help to determine what kinds of killing—and dying—intervenors are themselves willing to engage in.

To illustrate this, I shall now discuss how Western secular conceptions of high life and corresponding notions of bad death help to explain one of the most troublesome paradoxes of intervention: the reluctance to risk the lives of intervenors in order to 'save' those of others. As I shall argue in the following chapters, intervention is an attempt to assert the primacy of high life in the face of bad death, and to bolster faith in the capacity of human institutions to uphold this ideal. Understandings of bad death, then, help to determine in which cases the impulse to intervene emerges and is acted upon. However, the same beliefs cause intervenors to baulk at the prospect of relinquishing their own lives in order to 'save strangers' (see Wheeler 2000), or at the possibility of dying an 'unnecessary' death in 'someone else's war'. Within a Western secular perspective, intervenors are placed in a bind: in order to save others from bad death, they may have to expose themselves to it. The converse is also true: if they are unwilling to die 'bad deaths' or consign members of their 'own' citizenry to this fate, then they may leave others to it.

This problem is at the centre of one of the most explicit (and, indeed, one of the few) debates about death in the discourses surrounding intervention: the impact of the death of intervenors on states' willingness to intervene. Often referred to as the 'body-bag argument',[4] this interpretation suggests that heads of state demur from committing troops to military interventions if they believe that the risk of casualties is substantial. Wheeler (2000) traces the rise of this argument throughout the interventions of the 1990s. During this period, Western states, freshly triumphant in the wake of the Cold War, were eager to be seen as custodians of international law and, more broadly, of humanity. However, the simultaneous rise of 24-hour news reporting by journalists embedded at sites of violence (often known as the 'CNN effect') created a problem for intervening states. It made it possible for publics to see, often in real time, the dangerous conditions into which intervenors were deployed. In some cases, it also allowed them to witness the deaths of intervenors. As a result of such dynamics, Wheeler claims, decisions on intervention became increasingly responsive to public demands for the reduction in casualties of intervening troops. Perhaps the most seminal example of this was the doomed excursion into Somalia in 1993, in which American troops were dispatched into the midst of a brutal civil war to ensure the delivery of humanitarian aid. However, due largely to tactical miscalculations by the American command, a series of attacks on intervening troops culminated in the violent, public killing of eighteen US infantrymen. This caused a substantial popular backlash within the US, one that recalled civic outrage at the Vietnam war—another distant country whose war was deemed to have little relevance to the everyday lives of Americans (see Khong 1992). This backlash threatened to undermine the popularity of the Clinton administration; indeed, it is widely believed to be the source of that administration's reluctance to engage more fully in intervention in Rwanda's genocide the following year.

This perspective suggests that the desire to avoid 'unnecessary' deaths is a direct outcome of public demand and its implications for domestic electoral politics. This is a plausible *functional* explanation of how public reactions affect the political decision-making process. But what it fails to explain is the source of the public disgust at the return of intervenors in 'body bags'. As I have argued above, it cannot simply be taken for granted that the mere death of intervenors is sufficient to evoke this kind of response. Indeed, the US has a long tradition of venerating those killed in wars, whether this is expressed in annual ceremonies to commemorate soldiers who fought in the two World Wars, or in patriotic displays of flags to honour those killed in more recent wars in Afghanistan and Iraq. The idea that the deaths of intervenors could be 'bad'—and in particular, that they might be 'needless' or 'wasteful'—reflects a distinctly Western secular understanding of death.

First, it is deeply influenced by the presumption that death itself, in any circumstances, is to be avoided. The fact that there is still a strong culture in Western countries of honouring soldiers who have died in battle does not mean that there is a public taste for death in battle. While they may be remembered as 'heroic', these deaths are, for the most part, framed as regrettable and tragic—that is, as necessary evils to be avoided wherever possible. Indeed, as Wheeler argues, 'no Western government … intervened to defend human rights in the 1990s unless it [was] very confident that the risks of casualties were almost zero' (2000: 300). From Ignatieff's (2001) perspective, this aversion to death arises from a popular belief within modern Western societies that death can, for the most part, be avoided through the use of technology and scientific advancements that remove the need for soldiers to engage in dangerous, ground-based combat. The demand for 'casualty-free' forms of combat (see Ignatieff 2001) is reflected in the use of air strikes as the predominant form of force in interventions such as NATO's interventions in Kosovo in 1999 and in Libya in 2011. More recently, the development and use of Unmanned Aerial Vehicles (UAVs) by the US, the UK and a range of other countries has made it possible quite literally to fight a war from thousands of miles away, with no risk whatsoever to the individuals controlling the machines (see Singer 2009; Sparrow 2007). The use of UAVs is a direct response to the Western secular image of death as an evil to be avoided at all costs.

The belief that it is *possible* to minimize the deaths of intervenors has converged with the Western secular drive to prioritize high life. According to Asad, this has produced a significant shift in the expectations surrounding humanitarian intervention, such that 'soldiers need no longer go to war expecting to die but only to kill' (2007: 35). He argues that this removes the conventional understanding of war as an *exchange* of killing and dying. This is underpinned, Asad contends, by the prevalence of neo-colonial attitudes among intervenors. There is, he states:

> A long-standing tradition of fighting against militarily and ethnically inferior peoples in which it is proper that the latter die in much larger numbers. Since they do not value human life as the civilized do, they will expose themselves to greater risks, even undertake suicidal operations, and therefore suffer more casualties.
>
> (Asad 2007: 35)

In other words, he argues that intervenors are willing to accept more casualties on the 'other side' when fighting against (and perhaps also for) people who are perceived to place less value on life, or to have fewer prohibitions against death. Conversely, the deaths of intervenors seems 'wasteful' in comparison precisely because they are thought to value their 'own' lives, or to 'mind dying' more. This logic may lead to perverse consequences. Western liberal states ostensibly minimize attacks on civilians, and the UN has explicitly condemned the planning of operations in which 'force protection' outweighs the humanitarian goals of the mission (see UN 2000). However, the desire to eliminate the deaths of intervenors may lead to the use of strategies that devalue the lives of civilians in relation both to the protection of intervenors' lives and the killing of 'high value' targets. The use of UAVs by the US in Pakistan and Yemen is a prime example of this. The capacities of these machines to target specific individuals may reduce the need for battle between ground troops and combatants, which is often costly in terms of human lives and injuries. However, so-called drone attacks may also harm civilians who are in the wrong place at the wrong time—for instance, in the case of communities gathering for the funerals of combatants, or living in houses shared by targets (see Luban 2012). In such situations, Asad claims, intervenors use the foggy element of motive—that is, of 'humanitarian' intentions, or the desire to 'liberate' a people—in order to distinguish what might otherwise appear to be war crimes as 'collateral damage'.

This desire to eliminate the deaths of intervenors is a direct reflection of the Western secular aversion to being killed 'for/as nothing', which finds its clearest expression in the idea of 'unnecessary' deaths. As Eyal Weizman (2011) argues, humanitarianism is driven less by the pursuit of the best possible good than by the desire to engage in the 'least possible evil'—that is, to minimize what are considered to be 'necessary' harms. In practice, this usually involves a calculation of how much killing is considered to be excessive. And, according to Walzer 'commonly, what we are calculating is *our* benefit (which we exaggerate) and *their* cost (which we minimize or disregard entirely)' (2004: 38–9). Weizman identifies this logic of calculation in the strategies used to plan and execute attacks associated with military intervention. For instance, he describes how, in the post-2003 intervention in Iraq, the Bush administration used sophisticated computing systems (called 'Bug Splat' during the Kosovo intervention, and later renamed 'Fast Collateral Damage') to design remote attacks. These systems used data such as the size and shape of a building, its construction materials and proportions and population density around the target site to determine how many civilians would be killed in attacks on 'high value targets'. The algorithms used by these systems made it possible for the US to ensure that it stayed precisely within the bounds of international law, in terms of the numbers of deaths produced by each attack. Indeed, in designing the attacks, thirty became the 'magic number' of civilian casualties that could be produced without executive permission; any more than this and an attack had to be signed off either by President Bush or Donald Rumsfeld. In this system, Weizman comments, US military lawyers decided that anything above the threshold constituted 'unlawful killing', but anything below it could be considered a 'necessary sacrifice' (2011: 132).

Weizman's analysis demonstrates how calculations of 'necessity' and 'excess' shape intervenors' willingness to kill. However, this logic also exerts a profound influence on intervenors' perceptions of when it is necessary for them to die, or at least to risk dying. While it may be possible only to minimize the deaths of civilians, as I have discussed above, Western intervenors believe that it is possible and desirable to avoid deaths on their own side 'completely'. By this logic, the deaths of *any* intervenors seems excessive and wasteful. Walzer argues that this approach is perfectly compatible with just war theory, which states that a military commander is 'bound to minimize the risks they must face, and to avoid wasting their lives' (2004: 16). From Walzer's perspective, the 'waste' of soldiers' lives occurs when the value of the benefits they seek are 'outweighed' by the loss of lives, or when victory is deemed to be unlikely. This, of course, makes implicit assumptions that the loss of life in itself is a hyper-good (see the previous chapter) that could, in itself, outweigh another good such as ending a civil war. Based on this reasoning, Walzer defends the calculus of 'necessary' killing, and the creation of a dynamic in which soldiers kill without risking their own lives. As he claims, 'so long as they can aim accurately at military targets, soldiers have every right to fight from a safe distance' (Walzer 2004: 16). He is not troubled, as Asad is, by the fact that fighting is not framed as an exchange of killing and dying. Instead, his approach demands that death be minimized wherever possible. In fact, he argues that a commander is morally remiss if she allows soldiers to be killed if it is at all possible to avoid it.

This logic of excess and necessity clearly reflects the aversion against killing and dying 'for nothing'. However, it is also intertwined with the Western secular rejection of sacrifice. Sacrifice, too, is treated as an evil that should be minimized at all cost, but which may in some cases be necessary. For instance, Wheeler excoriates Western democracies for their unwillingness to sacrifice troops in the face of escalating genocide in Rwanda in 1994. The term 'sacrifice' is appropriate since the humanitarian goals of intervenors provide a 'higher' good to which their lives might be consecrated. Wheeler suggests that the widespread fear of casualties among potential intervenors prevented Western states from upholding some of their most cherished values. In Wheeler's words:

> Putting out the inferno of genocide is in both the national and the global interest because failure to do so risks creating a contagion that will undermine the values of all civilized societies.
>
> (2000: 303)

This statement exemplifies an optimalist notion of sacrifice, which is framed as a necessary evil. Wheeler does not, like Žižek, frame sacrifice as a good in itself, or as an expression of human greatness. Nor does he appeal to states and publics to engage in sacrifice as an act of altruism. Rather, he implies that some level of sacrifice is necessary to upholding the values of 'civilized societies'—predominantly the ideals of human flourishing embedded in the ethos of humanitarianism. Wheeler's argument also points to a tension at the heart of Western secular notions of life and death: the failure to accept one form of bad death (sacrifice) might actually undermine the ideal of high life on a broader scale. Walzer makes a similar appeal, claiming that:

> It is very hard these days, in the Western democracies, to put soldiers at risk. But humanitarian interventions and peace-keeping operations are first of all military acts directed against people who are already using force, breaking the peace. They will be ineffective unless there is a willingness to accept the risks that naturally attach to military acts—to shed blood, to lose soldiers.
>
> (2004: 73)

Walzer's argument is more pragmatic than normative; he states that in most contemporary conflicts, peaceful peacekeeping is an oxymoron, and 'if it were possible, it wouldn't be necessary' (2004: 73). This is a more hard-nosed version of the argument put forward by Wheeler. Simply put, if intervenors are serious about the task of protecting the ideal of human life against the threat of bad death, then they must be willing, in some cases, to die for it. This does not contradict Walzer's claim that it is just to protect the lives of intervenors; he does not glorify their deaths or suggest that they should be sent recklessly into dangerous situations. Rather, he argues that a set of questions must be confronted:

> Is this a cause for which we are prepared to see [intervenors] die? If this question gets an affirmative answer, then we cannot panic when the first soldier or the first significant number of soldiers ... are killed in firefight.
>
> (Walzer 2004: 73)

According to Walzer, any military commander who chooses to 'sacrifice' his soldiers in this way is acting completely within his rights, 'so long as he does the best he can to minimize the sacrifice' (2004: 24–5). So, from this perspective, it is crucial to minimize the sacrifice of intervenors' lives where it is possible, and to embrace it as a necessary evil where it is not.

From this perspective, intervenors should accept *some* sacrifice, but only when it can be minimized, and only when it is deemed to be 'worth it'. As such, weighing up the value of humanitarian goals and the lives of intervenors relies on the kind of 'strong evaluation' discussed in the previous chapter. Decision-makers must assign relative value to a range of goods, deciding which ones qualify as 'hyper-goods' and which are to be given less priority. One way of making these calculations would be simply to weigh up the numbers of deaths accrued to either 'side'. Yet, as Neta Crawford argues, even if we are able to estimate the total number of deaths on all 'sides', such calculations are not straightforward:

> How are we to value the independence of a people, their right to live without fear of massacre, and against the cost of lives sent to preserve their rights? And what of the opportunity costs of action? Which things should we forgo at home so that others can live? How shall we measure the costs of inaction? Would we feel right letting others suffer if the material costs of action outweigh the benefits?
>
> (2002: 427)

In other words, decision-makers are often confronted by a range of incommensurable goods (or hyper-goods—see Chapter 2), along with a range of unknown, or unpredictable, outcomes. In such situations, no algorithm or computer program can help. Decisions about intervention come down to *judgements* about the relative value of human lives in relation to other ideals, and often these judgements are heavily biased. According to Wheeler, it is 'arbitrary in the extreme to put a figure on how many British, American, Canadian soldiers should have been sacrificed to save hundreds of thousands of Rwandans'—although he states that any such figures must be 'well above' the number of intervenors' lives lost in Somalia in 1993 (2000: 303). Perhaps, then, decisions on the necessity of sacrifice calls for a more explicit and frank discussion of the relative value assigned to lives, and precisely how these values are assigned. This, however, would shine a spotlight on the thinly veiled practices of calculation that underpin current practice, and expose the contradiction at the heart of universalist humanitarianism. The very idea that it may be 'worth it' to accept the deaths of intervenors in some cases but not in others directly negates the idea that all human life is equally valuable. In other words, an open acknowledgement of humanitarian's reliance on logics of necessity and calculation would cast doubt on its ability to uphold its own guiding ideals. This is one of the most perilous conditions of operating in a Western secular cosmology: without firm, transcendent ideals to determine action, the entire responsibility to decide on life and death falls into the hands of humans, who are invested in their own ideals of life and death.

Conclusions

Western secular cosmology revolves around the ideal of high life, which elevates everyday human life above everything else in the universe. This ideal is based on two key images. 'Human flourishing' enshrines everyday human life as a source of meaning, contrasting it firmly against the idea of 'mere' biological life. The notion of the 'sacred self' emphasizes reflexive, proprietary forms of agency: self-possession, self-development, self-realization and so on, which exhort individuals to assert their 'ownership' over their own bodies and lives. The forms of bad death that shape contemporary discourses on violence and intervention directly contravene this ideal. All violent death threatens to undermine the ideal of high life and to negate the ownership of the self. However, two forms of bad death in particular—dying 'for/as nothing' or dying 'for something'—create contradictions that complicate decisions on intervention. Specifically, the same forms of bad death that inspire intervention constrain and shape the strategies through which it is carried out. On the one hand, intervenors are driven by a strong impulse to prevent or halt the 'bad deaths' of others. But on the other hand, intervention in situations of large-scale violence often requires exposing intervenors to these forms of death. This has produced a logic of 'necessary' and 'unnecessary' killing and/or sacrifice, in which decision-makers must weigh up the competing hyper-goods of 'saving' the lives of embattled people and safeguarding those of intervenors. In the absence of transcendent norms, and under the immense pressure of Western secular prohibitions against death, the balance often tilts towards the latter.

This discussion sheds new light on debates about the pragmatics of decision-making about intervention. Most of these debates focus on the incentives and pressures placed on decision-makers by public (or personal) aversion to specific kinds of death and killing. I have argued, however, that it is not enough to understand how decision-makers respond to these pressures. We also need to understand the sources of their actions, and the beliefs about life and death that they reflect. This chapter has introduced the fundamental conceptions of life and death that shape Western secularity. Now, I shall argue that the same images of high life and bad death help to constitute the category of 'humanity', and to determine who is included within it.

Notes

1 I use the term 'high life' as shorthand to refer to the image of humanity that arises from the combination of these two ideas.
2 This belief is, of course, premised on a problematic assumption that self-realization (and agency, for that matter) requires a 'normal' or 'complete' human body—a premise that most theorists of disability would reject.
3 Some humans are killed by non-human animals, but rarely in a systematic way, and the devastation wrought by storms, viruses, bacteria or natural disaster are not generally considered to be 'violent' in the same sense because they lack instrumental intention. It is possible that developments in military robotics could lead to killing by autonomous machines or 'drones', but at the time of writing these machines still require human intentionality in order to carry out killing.
4 This phrase refers to the public distaste for seeing troops returned to their home countries in body bags.

4   Is nothing sacred?
Disenchantment and dehumanization

Without any divine guarantees, how can 'humanity' be made and kept sacred? In Western secular cosmology, human beings and their institutions must forge the category of humanity, demonstrate its uniquely 'higher' nature, and maintain its meaning in the face of the forms of bad death discussed in the previous chapter. The belief that allows humans to do this is, simultaneously, their Achilles heel and the basis of their unique cosmological status: disenchantment.

Disenchantment is a central concept within Western secularity, and is closely tied to secularization, but it is also an integral part of the trans-formation thesis (see Chapter 2). It suggests that the processes that helped bring about the trans-formation of secularity continuously strip the world of *intrinsic* meaning, replacing this with purely instrumental meaning. These processes reduce all non-humans to mere materials for human projects, or empty receptacles for meaning that humans project upon them. In traditional enchanted frameworks, human life is framed as one layer in a complex hierarchy of beings, all subsumed under some kind of divine force. Each kind of being—non-human animal, vegetal, mineral or spiritual—has a place, and intrinsic meaning of its own. In the trans-formation of Western secularity (or so the story goes) this meaning was gradually stripped from other beings until humans were the only ones that remained intrinsically valuable. Disenchantment is associated with a very specific kind of logic: instrumental rationality. According this logic, it is the capacity to be instrumentalized that renders a being disenchanted. Within Western secular ethics, all beings believed to be disenchanted—whether animate or inanimate, material or intangible—are regarded as 'raw materials' for the promotion of high life. The converse is also held to be true: treating a being as if it were an object converts it into one.

It is by dint of the belief in disenchantment that humans living in a Western secular framework can conceptualize themselves as unique, 'higher' forms of being. The intricate hierarchy of the enchanted cosmos is replaced by a binary, in which the high life of humans is contrasted sharply against a dull, meaningless universe awaiting instrumentalization. Indeed, the Western secular category of humanity is actually best understood in negative terms, as the residual effect of this process. In other words, it is the disenchantment of everything else that affords humanity its definition and elevated status.

However, this is an unstable foundation on which to stake the whole category of 'humanity'. If instrumental–rational processes can strip the intrinsic meaning from everything else in the universe, then it stands to reason that they can do the same to human life. Within this logic, when humans are instrumentalized as raw materials for the projects of other humans, they too can be interpreted as disenchanted objects. Indeed, the forms of bad death described in the previous chapter are considered abhorrent largely because they perform this function, instrumentalizing human lives either to 'higher' purposes or the exercise of pure power. By treating human beings as disenchanted objects, these forms of killing erode the boundary that separates 'enchanted' humans from the 'disenchanted' universe.

The logic of disenchantment, I shall argue, makes it possible to believe in 'dehumanization'. Dehumanization refers to acts or processes that, intentionally or otherwise, reduce human beings to a sub- or non-human status. It is considered integral to the logics and strategies of modern mass killing, as it is thought to remove the inhibitions of killers. By this account, people feel more able to dispose of the lives and bodies of others in an instrumental way if they *believe* these others to be nothing but 'mere' objects, non-human animals[1] or other kinds of 'disenchanted' beings. This logic, I shall argue, only makes sense against the background of Western secular cosmology and belief in the process of disenchantment. Within a transcendent framework of meaning, it is not in the gift of humans to grant or revoke intrinsic meaning. Moreover, in an enchanted world-view, comparing a human being to a non-human animal or an inanimate object would not necessarily, and certainly not automatically, reduce that being to a mere object. Indeed, non-human animals and inanimate objects can be deemed sacred (for instance, relics or sacred animals). Depending on the specific hierarchy in which it was embedded, a non-human animal or an inanimate object might demand much *less* ethical consideration than a human, but there would likely be significant rules guiding how it could be used or harmed. The binary of disenchantment–enchantment produces an all-or-nothing logic: a being is either human, or it can be treated as if it were nothing. I do not mean to argue, of course, that transcendent world-views produce less killing; on the contrary, for centuries people have destroyed other humans (and many other beings) in the name of transcendent ideals. Nor am I suggesting that Western secularity cosmology is inherently oriented towards violence, at least not more than any other belief system. What I am arguing is that belief in disenchantment makes possible the distinct concepts and logics of killing that underpin modern mass killing.

This chapter explores three ways in which belief in disenchantment 'makes dehumanization possible' (see Esmeir 2006). First, the narrative of disenchantment enables human beings to believe that the instrumental treatment of others is sufficient to disenchant them. I call this phenomenon 'direct dehumanization'. It posits a unidirectional exchange in which an intentional subject consciously attempts to dehumanize an unwilling object. This is the most common interpretation of dehumanization, and it can be found in many theories of genocide and mass killing. Second, I complicate this understanding of dehumanization, arguing that it is an intersubjective and multi-actor phenomenon, not the objective result of particular kinds of action. Dehumanization, I argue, can only be effective when one or more of the parties involved hold two beliefs: that dehumanization is possible, and that certain human actions are capable of producing it. From this perspective, dehumanization is not simply the product of the intentional actions of aggressors, but also of the acts of witnessing and response of (usually well-meaning) third parties— including intervenors. Third, I introduce the idea of 'categorical dehumanization'. This concept suggests that some humans are regarded as dehumanized objects as a result of shifts in the boundaries of human institutions that distribute instrumental meaning. This is a substantial risk in a totally immanent cosmology, in which all meaning is understood to be created, altered and revoked by humans. It is also one of the downsides of positing a binary between 'enchanted' humanity and a 'disenchanted' universe. In such a context, being cast out of the category of humanity condemns one to the status of a disenchanted object.

By identifying the link between Western secular cosmology, disenchantment and dehumanization, this chapter explains how certain ways of interpreting, analysing and, of course, engaging in violence undermine the category of humanity. This set of beliefs has helped to produce new logics of killing that are, ironically, anathema to the ideal of high life. In particular, it suggests that the beliefs employed to protect a *uniquely* enchanted category of humanity leaves those protected by this category constantly vulnerable to dehumanization. This highlights another contradiction at the heart of Western secular cosmology. Namely, the cost of enshrining humanity at the cost of all other beings may be that nothing is sacred—not even human life.

Disenchantment, human exceptionalism and 'anthropological machines'

The idea of disenchantment plays a pivotal role within Western secular cosmology and culture. Captured most seminally in the writings of Max Weber (1922), the concept of disenchantment is associated with the increasing rationalization of the world—in particular the rise of instrumental rationality, and the desire to remake the world to meet human specifications. Disenchantment is closely related to the processes of secularization discussed in Chapter 1—it is, in fact, one of the strategies through which secularization comes about. This does not mean that wherever one finds disenchantment, one has entered a totally secularized sphere, but rather that it its most extreme expression is found in that particular strand of Western secularity.

Disenchantment is, quite literally, the process through which the 'higher' or intrinsic meanings of beings are removed (or secularized). It derives largely from Weber's writings on the transformation of modern society and Christian belief. According to Weber, the mastery of the physical and natural world by rational, technical and scientific means has put paid to 'divine' explanations of worldly phenomena. In the aftermath of modernity, the world came to be regarded as largely inanimate. There are still some 'gods' remaining in the world after the advent of modernity, but these exist only in the fragments of grand theories and ruptured religious beliefs, in conflicts between 'value spheres' and the massive, impersonal forces that shape contemporary societies (for instance, economies and states) (Weber 1922). They are not 'divine' in a transcendent sense, or unified. They much more closely resemble the mêlée of 'resonances' and moments of 'mundane transcendence' described by Connolly (1999, 2011).

How did the grand theories and religious traditions of the Western world end up in this state? According to Weber, disenchantment arose through a series of revolutions in which transcendent values rationalized and devalued *themselves*. Like the proponents of the 'transformation thesis' discussed in Chapter 1, Weber contends that these changes emerged from sources internal to Christian beliefs. Specifically, he traces this change to the creation of Protestantism, which placed a heavy emphasis on the quest for 'rational knowledge' of God's purpose, and an understanding of the world. In a manner that mirrored the trans-formation of the totally immanent framework of Western secularity, Protestantism:

> Engendered its own demise, for it lent legitimacy to a secular science that in turn rejected and *devalued* all religious values ... In its attempt to prove its own intrinsic rationality through non-religious means it affirmed the value of science, and with this laid itself open to the charge of irration-alism and to attack from the outside from 'rational', secular forms of this-worldly legitimation.
>
> (Gane 2002: 21)

Overwhelmingly, these forms of legitimation are associated with scientific, or other instrumental–rational processes. From Weber's perspective, the aim of such processes is to make the world knowable, and open to manipulation. Indeed:

> In a disenchanted world everything becomes understandable and tame-able, even if not, for the moment, understood and tamed. Increasingly the world becomes human-centred and the universe—only apparently paradoxically—more impersonal.
>
> (Jenkins 2000:12)

In this quote, Richard Jenkins refers to an intriguing paradox: in order to make the world ever more in their own image, humans have found it neces-sary to make everything else in it less human (and, indeed, inhuman). This idea of 'human exceptionalism' involves denying the personality, spirit, soul or agency of anything that is not confirmed as a human being. It has become so deeply entrenched in Western secular discourses that the very suggestion that a non-human has agency, ethical status, or any degree of animation is often dismissed as 'anthropomorphism'—a term that is almost always used in a derogatory way (see Bennett 2010). A theological source of this idea can be found in the concept of '*deus deracinus*'—literally, the 'uprooting of God'. This term refers to the gradual loss of belief that God was embodied in material beings, or that the latter could serve as vehicles of a divine purpose (Bilgrami 2010: 147).

Jane Bennett's (2001) analysis of the Western secular narrative of disenchantment sheds light on this process. In pre-Renaissance Europe, she claims, human beings lived in a world in which plants, non-human animals and what we normally think of as inanimate 'objects' were assumed to have personalities, and to be infused with divine or magical qualities. In this context, humans relied heavily upon non-human beings as sources of meaning, in several ways. For instance, these other beings helped to form the complex hierarchies in which humans found their place, and the intrinsic meaning of all beings was interlinked. Moreover, humans looked to non-humans for transcendent forms of knowledge or potency. They believed that certain plants had magical powers to heal or aid in prognostication, or contemplated the sublime patterns of nature to detect evidence of the divine plan. In other words, the 'body' or material manifestation of the divine was not only human—it also included a range of other worldly beings. However, Bennett argues, as the Judeo-Christian God came gradually to be viewed through an anthropomorphic lens, the human body came to be regarded as the only material manifestation of the divine. Indeed, the fact that humans shared a form—the physical human body—with Jesus Christ led them to believe that they were uniquely linked to the divine. In the trans-formation of Western secularity, this belief was emphasized to the extent that the divine faded away, leaving the figure of the human as the closest approximation to god. It was this *human* image of the divine that was removed from the world in the transformation of Western secularity. Viewed through this lens, Western secularity and its category of humanity emerged from a process of dehumanization—the dehumanization of the cosmos.

If we follow Bennett's story, then the standard claim—that 'science' disenchanted the universe—falls apart. First, the universe needed to be regarded as inhuman, and only then could the instrumental–rational logic of science be used as a tool for subjecting it to human ends. Once humanity was understood to be at the centre of the universe, all of human energy was to be directed towards promoting it, and bolstering its 'higher' status. The demystification of natural phenomena through the use of taxonomies, abstract theories and experimentation made it necessary to view them in purely instrumental terms. This process also involved a reversal of the relationship between the divine and the material that gave humans the idea that they were exceptional. Whereas the materiality of Jesus Christ originally conferred a unique status upon humanity, in Western secular societies this status is defined by its separation from, and domination of, the material world in the absence of the divine.

In this framework, humans regard themselves as the only beings capable of 'enchantment'. This proposition has two different, intertwined meanings. First, it is understood that only human beings can be enchanted in themselves. This idea derives from the belief that only human beings have souls—or the closest approximation in Western secular cosmology, selves. It is another way of saying that, while other beings may be animated, or bear the values projected onto them by humans, only humans have intrinsic meaning. Second, it is believed that only humans can be *subjects* of enchantment—that is, only humans possess the powers of awareness or affective sensibilities to *be enchanted* by others. As Bennett (2001) argues, enchantment should not only be understood as an objective property of certain beings. Rather, it is an affective state of wonder, fascination, mystery, attachment and, ultimately, ethical responsiveness. From this perspective, a being is enchanted only in so far as it can produce these states in a human, and in so far as the person encountering it is open to enchantment and inclined to experiencing it as such. This (inter)subjective account of enchantment highlights a different dimension of disenchantment (which is central to the problem of dehumanization). Namely, disenchantment not only refers to the divestment of intrinsic meaning from specific beings, but also to the closure of human minds and bodies to the experience of being enchanted, and the dulling of their receptivity to sources of enchantment. Taylor's notion of the 'buffered self' (2007; see Chapter 3 in this volume), closed to external sources of meaning and driven by internal impulses, exemplifies this state. Even among critiques of standard narratives of disenchantment, the capacity to be enchanted (and thus to confer the status of 'enchantedness' on another being) is assumed to be an exclusively human property. For instance, Connolly (2011) offers a persuasive case that the complex assemblages and force-fields that shape the world—whether political movements or climate change—can offer moments of heightened experience that produces a state very much like enchantment. He argues that some of these phenomena may have agency or something akin to it. However, only humans—on the basis of their distinctive biological, physiological, neurological and cultural features—are considered as possible subjects of the experience of 'immanent transcendence'.[2]

This understanding of humans as the source and arbiters of enchantment lies at the heart of Western secularity's radically simplified cosmic hierarchy. Taylor (2004, 2007) argues that this cosmological structure is 'flat' in relation to the complex cosmological structures of the Judeo-Christian religion, but it is rather more like a bas relief. Humans living within this framework perceive themselves as standing out against the rest of the universe on the very basis of their uniquely enchanted status. Bennett suggests that this hierarchy is created by 'parsing the world into dull matter (it, things) and vibrant life' (2010: vii). However, even 'life' is subdivided into 'meaningful' (or metabiological, human life) and 'mere' biological life, or, in the ancient Greek terms preferred by Agamben (1995), *bios* and *zoe.*

The construction of the boundary between these kinds of being comes at a severe ethical cost to non-humans. Belief in the logic of disenchantment underwrites an ethical stance in which non-human beings can be seen, and treated, purely as resources for enhancing human life. As Taylor puts it:

> Once society no longer has a sacred structure, once social arrangements and modes of action are no longer grounded in the order of things or the will of God, they are in a sense up for grabs ... Similarly, once the creatures that surround us lose the significance that accrued to their place in the chain of being, they are open to being treated as raw materials or instruments for our projects.
>
> (1993: 5)

The process that Taylor refers to has produced a particularly narrow ethics, in which moral considerability—or the belief that a being warrants *some* degree of ethical treatment—is limited to humans. While some other beings may be considered indirectly, because of their value to humans, no other beings are viewed as being automatically worthy of ethical consideration. According to Thomas Birch (1993), this has constrained ethical responsiveness in a way that has, historically, cut off many groups of humans (along with myriad other beings) from moral consideration—women and slaves being prime examples.

However, it is by dint of this narrow range of ethical responsiveness that Western secular humans have become so efficient in maximizing the ideal of high life. According to Bilgrami, the ability to absolve oneself of ethical attachment to other kinds of beings removes the inhibitions to instrumentalizing them to the ideal of high life. He states that in a Western secular context:

> With no metaphysical obstacles remaining, the scale of taking from nature's bounty could be pursued with unthinking and unconstrained zeal. Nature, being brute, could not make demands or put constraints on us. Because it was brute, we did not need to respond to it on its terms. All the term-making came *from us.*
>
> (Bilgrami 2010: 149)

In a context in which humans call all the shots, Bilgrami contends, it is common for them to ignore the ethical callings of other beings. Indeed, to make a 'calling', one must have a voice; and in most Western secular accounts of agency, being able to 'speak' is predicated on the possession of human subjectivity (see Agamben 1995). Bruno Latour (1993) argues that beings which are often reduced to mere 'things' can actually speak—not in human language, but rather through the 'propositions' their bodies make, or their ability to stimulate human sensibilities (see also Bennett 2010). For instance,

Weizman's (2011) work demonstrates how objects such as a wall, a fragment of bone or the wreckage of a demolished house can be—and often are—used to testify in courts about violent events. But for these callings to be heard and responded to by humans, they must be *receptive*. This, in turn, requires a belief in the ability of non-humans to make callings, and a capacity to recognize them. Of course, human beings often make rational, instrumental calculations about the need to protect or restrict harms to non-humans. An example of this is the range of policies associated with 'environmental security' (see Dalby 2002; Barnett 2001), which is oriented towards protecting the environment for human consumption or use. In this context, non-human animals, plants and natural phenomena are securitized not because they are deemed to be 'owed' protection, but rather because doing so is seen to be in the interest of promoting high life.

Clearly, the ability to treat natural phenomena as disenchanted has offered many advantages in terms of the promotion of high life. It has transformed the world into a set of resources and enabled human beings to further their own sense of well-being and quality of life with little restraint. However, it has also placed the meaning of human life at risk, in two important ways. First, it has depleted the richness of meanings and experiences upon which humans can draw, as well as the depth of their ethical attachments. According to Connolly (2011), both transcendent frameworks and exclusive humanism privilege humanity too much. They do so to the extent that its connections with the world, and sense of belonging in and to it, are severely diluted. Taylor (1993), too, chronicles a 'loss of meaning' that has occurred with the trans-formation of Western secularity. He refers to the erosion of traditional sources of belief and repositories of meaning, but also to the vocabularies, repertoires of action—and, I would add, affective sensibilities—on which humans draw. These meanings still exist, and are exploited by Western secular people in their pursuit of authenticity, but they are subordinated to the dominant logic of instrumental rationality. Or, if they escape or exceed its dominion, they may only be detectable to the Western secular mind only in the sudden disruptions and intrusions—of 'religious' fervour, or natural dis-asters, or emergent crises—of which Connolly writes. So, by removing the intrinsic meaning of other beings, humans deplete the very sources upon which they can draw in order to pursue authenticity and high life. They may also experience a profound sense of alienation. As Bilgrami suggests:

> Disenchantment does not merely produce alienation in the loose sense of that term (as a depression, or a loss of interest in things, sometimes does), it produces an alienation in the quite strict sense of an absence of agency, reducing us to mere receptacles for our desires and their satisfaction.
>
> (2010: 155)

The image of humans as 'mere receptacles' for their own desires perfectly mirrors the framing of non-humans as vessels for human, instrumental meaning. This idea leads to the second major risk for humanity of disenchanting the universe.

Specifically, the attempt to erect and guard a strict boundary between human and non-human forms of being renders the former almost as vulnerable as the latter to instrumentalization. The binary between human and all of other forms of being is not simply a residue of the trans-formation of Western secularity. On the contrary, for Western secular people, it is utterly essential to the category of humanity, and preserving it is a matter of extreme priority. The logic behind this is simple: Western secular cosmology consists only of enchanted and disenchanted beings, and it offers no grey areas. If the boundary between human and any other form of being is removed, then there is nothing to protect the enchanted status of humanity. And, if this is the case, then there is nothing to stop humans from being instrumentalized in the same manner in which they have treated the 'natural' world. As Bennett puts it, this mindset insists that

> The *ontological* divide between persons and things must remain lest one have no *moral* grounds for privileging man over germ or for condemning pernicious forms of human-on-human instrumentalization (as when powerful humans exploit illegal, poor, young or otherwise weaker humans).
>
> (2010: 11–12)

Bennett specifically singles out the likening of human beings to germs—a common metaphor used in acts of deliberate dehumanization in the context of mass killing (see below). It suggests that the boundary between enchanted humanity and the universe it has disenchanted is frail at best, and can easily be breached. This is the nightmare that haunts Western secularity and propels the logics of modern mass killing. In these logics, human life is treated as if it were as disenchanted as the world it instrumentalizes.

Dehumanization and 'anthropological machines'

What makes a being human, and differentiates it from other forms of being? According to Agamben (2004), humanness is conferred on certain beings by 'anthropological machines'. These machines, constituted by social relations, forms of knowledge, norms and linguistic constructs, act like a series of mirrors. They reflect both the humanity and the animality of a being, and construct one against the other. In other words, they allow humans to see their humanity in contrast with animality of other beings, and vice versa. However, for Agamben, the boundary between these characteristics is fluid. 'Humanity' is 'suspended between a celestial and a terrestrial nature, between animal and human' (Agamben 2004: 29); it is neither one nor the other, but rather exists in the caesura between them. The status of humanity is continually 'decided' by the acts in which the human aspects of a being are recognized against its non-human animal characteristics. In this sense, anthropological machines reproduce the boundary between enchanted and disenchanted beings discussed above, but *within* an individual, separating the 'animal' and 'human' dimensions of a discrete person.

This leaves the human being in a precarious position. Anthropological machines frequently change form. They do so in response to shifting patterns of knowledge, norms, criteria and perceptions of 'human' and 'animal'. This means that the human being constantly hovers on the brink of inhumanity. Rather than an essential status, her humanity is only the exclusion of her non-human animal qualities. These qualities remain part of her and can override her human status, which exists only to the extent that the anthropological machines in question succeed in excluding them. This gives a new meaning to the term 'human exceptionalism'. Specifically, for Agamben, humanity is a 'a kind of state of exception, a zone of indeterminacy in which the outside is nothing but the exclusion of an inside and the inside is in turn only the inclusion of an outside' (2004: 37). The 'inside' (humanity) and the outside (non-human animality) constantly threaten to invert themselves, and a being that is human one moment can become inhuman the next.

This idea is reflected in the concept of dehumanization, which has become one of the key devices for interpreting and explaining large-scale violence in the modern era. The basic idea behind dehumanization is that the beings that we normally recognize as 'human' may also take a number of non-human forms: the non-human animal; the inanimate object; the machine; the monster; even, as I shall argue, the dead body. The logic of dehumanization depends entirely on the dichotomy between enchantment and disenchantment. It relies on the fact that, if human beings are treated as non-human beings, compunctions about instrumentalizing them will disappear. Its dark genius as a logic is that all humans are vulnerable to it because none of them are 'purely' human (see Latour 1993). Biologically, humans are animals; they live with, among and as part of machines (whether metal, social or cybernetic); they are subject to physical forces, and share their materiality with 'objects'; and so on. This does not suggest that there is nothing 'special' or distinct about humans—what is extraordinary about them is precisely their ability to possess all of these different features. However, the belief that humans are 'purely' human is both naïve and dangerous. It masks the complex affinities and vulnerabilities shared between human and other beings. In a context in which other beings are treated as mere objects, this means that various dimensions of humanity can also be treated as such. As long as the fantasy of a 'pure' human is upheld and staked *against* non-human forms of being, simply highlighting a person's non-human animal, machine or material aspects thrust this person into the realm of the disenchanted. This, according to the idea of dehumanization, is precisely what happens in situations of systematic violence.

I shall now argue that dehumanization is made thinkable and actionable by Western secular cosmology and its narrative of disenchantment. For the most part, dehumanization is treated as a fairly straightforward, linear process in which a human being is treated, and disposed of, as some kind of non-human being. However, as I shall now argue, this is only one dimension of dehumanization. To understand the others, it is necessary to look more closely at the anthropological machines that produce dehumanization, and the cosmological beliefs that fuel them.

Direct dehumanization

In February 2011, embattled Libyan leader Muammar Gaddafi urged his loyalists to attack 'rebel' groups that were staging violent protests across the country demanding his removal. To encourage a violent response among his loyalists, he referred to the protestors as 'cockroaches' and impelled his followers to 'cleanse Libya house by house',[3] as if disinfecting it of germs. According to a prominent humanitarian lobbying organization (ICRP 2011), this speech used language 'reminiscent of the genocide in Rwanda' and made clear his 'cruel objective' to engage in large-scale killing. The use of these metaphors, they claimed, was substantial evidence of Gaddafi's conscious intention to engage in crimes against humanity, and therefore part of a justification for military intervention.

This example illustrates a concept that I shall call 'direct' dehumanization. This is by far the most common interpretation of the term 'dehumanization'; indeed, the two ideas are usually conflated. However, as I shall argue, it represents a simplified model of what actually occurs when a person is perceived as 'dehumanized'. Its explanatory power resides in the connection it makes between the removal of 'human' status and the efficacy of systematic violence in modern states. Simply put, it frames dehumanization as a kind of expedient, which removes ethical, social or other qualms which might restrict large groups of 'normal' people from killing. Those who use this term tend to take for granted that dehumanization is 'real' or 'possible' through these means, focusing on its effects and how it can be prevented. I do not argue with the contention that direct disenchantment 'works' as a logic of killing; but the very basis on which it functions is rooted in specific cosmological assumptions. As I shall now demonstrate, the *belief* that direct dehumanization 'works'— underwritten by a belief in disenchantment—goes some way to making it possible.

In situations of direct dehumanization, it is assumed, the removal of one's 'human' status is relatively straightforward. According to this approach, once human beings are persuasively likened to non-human beings—and particularly 'low' forms of life deemed useless to, or predatory upon human life (hence the 'rats' and 'germs' of genocidal rhetoric)—'normal' human beings can be easily persuaded to kill them. A clear example of this logic can be found in the NGO Genocide Watch's 'Eight Stages of Genocide' handbook (Stanton 1999). This document presents dehumanization as a linear process which moves through a series of identifiable stages. It begins with the separation of different ethnic groups, which is expressed and entrenched through the use of publicly recognizable symbols. In this process, Kelman (1973) contends, certain groups of people are denied what are considered to be uniquely human qualities such as individuality and their belonging within a community. Once these groups are sufficiently separated, through the conscious efforts of leaders within a dominant group, they 'are equated with animals, vermin, insects or diseases' in a way that 'overcomes the normal human revulsion against murder' (Stanton 1999: 1). Finally, violence is routinized and channelled against these outgroups, who are branded as threatening forces. Through each of these steps, these authors suggest, the inhibitions against killing are gradually removed.

By this account, direct dehumanization re-enacts on a smaller scale the cosmological process discussed above, in which a binary is drawn between 'enchanted' and 'disenchanted' beings. In this case, one group of human beings constructs a collective anthropological machine in which its own humanity is staked against the animality (or other non-human features) of another group. This machine emphasizes the non-human animal (or other non-human) features of a group of beings until they are 'recognized' not as human but as inhuman. Crucially, the functionality of this anthropological machine as a killing machine depends entirely on the belief that all non-humans are disenchanted and unworthy of ethical consideration. Just as Western secular cosmology dulls human receptivity to the ethical demands of non-human animals, microbes or stones, direct dehumanization functions by equating humans with these beings. Simply by likening humans to 'disenchanted' beings, it becomes possible for leaders of dominant groups to deafen the ears of their members to the ethical 'callings' of victims.

Perhaps the most influential account of this strategy was developed by Hannah Arendt in *The Origins of Totalitarianism*. This study examines the role of direct dehumanization in several powerful historical strategies of domination, from colonialism to the mass killings and terroristic regimes of twentieth-century communism. Arendt begins her analysis by explaining how colonial strategies of government worked by producing hierarchies among 'higher' and 'lower' forms of life. These hierarchies were reproduced and embodied throughout the structures of government and social norms. Even the classic colonial strategy of encouraging 'natives' to preserve aspects of their indigenous cultures was oriented towards this goal. It provided the evidence needed by colonial governors to point out differences between their forms of life and those of the colonized, and to infer that these differences were inherent. This move, Arendt contends, produced a 'new imperialist consciousness of a fundamental, and not just a temporary, superiority of man over man, of the "higher" over the lower breeds' (1976: 130). From these hierarchies, she claims, it was a short step to creating discourses of 'race'. These discourses provided for colonizers an:

Emergency explanation of human beings whom no European or civilized man could understand and whose humanity so frightened and humiliated the immigrant [colonizers] that they no longer cared to belong to the same human species.

(Arendt 1976: 185)

In this encounter between the colonizer and colonized, Arendt describes a malfunction of the anthropological machines upon which the former relied. Specifically, they expected the machines to reflect an image of the animality of the other, which would confirm their own humanity, and superiority. Instead, they were greeted with an image of the humanity of the other, which emphasized their own likeness, and therefore their own animality. So frightening was this experience that colonizers redoubled their efforts to produce a distinction between themselves and their subjects. To this end, they turned to the binary offered by Western secular cosmology. Colonial subjects were constructed as 'natural' beings, likened to non-human animals and denied a 'specifically human character' (Arendt 1976: 192–4). They came to be viewed by colonizers as a kind of natural resource. Indeed, colonizers 'treated the natives as raw material and lived on them as one might live on the fruits of wild trees' (Arendt 1976: 194). In this manner, colonizers reproduced the binary of enchantment–disenchantment within the human species, instead of between very different species. The creation of this binary not only eased the process of instrumentalizing the colonized, but it also removed ethical impediments to doing so. As Arendt puts it, 'when European men massacred [their subjects] they somehow were not aware that they had committed murder' (Arendt 1976: 192).

The effectiveness of this strategy rests entirely on the belief that all non-human beings can be instrumentalized to meet the needs of 'high' forms of life. In other words, the effectiveness of dehumanization as a strategy does not lie in the separation of 'higher' and 'lower' forms of life alone. Rather, it relies on a belief in the distinction made between 'enchanted' and 'disenchanted' forms of being, and the assumption that only the former have an ethical status.

Each of these beliefs reflects the basic cosmological assumptions of Western secularity. First, the notion that any being can be 'reduced' into a lower form only requires a cosmology in which there are no overarching structures to guarantee its enchanted status. Second, direct dehumanization is based on the radically simplified hierarchy of being life that is central to narratives of disenchantment. Crucially, direct dehumanization can remove obstacles to violence only in so far as non-human life is deemed profane and destructible. The concept would seem implausible in a context in which all forms of life were deemed sacred, or at least worthy of ethical consideration.

Effective dehumanization

How could one human being do this to another? This is a question that is often asked in the wake of violence, particularly large-scale killing. Most often, it is used rhetorically; it expresses disgust and condemnation on the part of the observer. But we should take this question very literally. Specifically, we should ask what conditions make it possible for humans to disenchant one another. Moreover, we should tap into the note of disbelief that this question expresses, and ask ourselves why we *believe* that dehumanization is possible. To do so, we need to ask what makes us believe that the acts associated with dehumanization are effective—that is, why we think they are sufficient to strip a human being of this status.

The theory of direct dehumanization provides a simple and compelling argument: people are likened to non-human beings, and then they can be disposed of as such with much greater ease. The logic of disenchantment helps us to understand why the latter assumption is connected to the former. But a piece of the puzzle is still missing. Namely, what is it that enables people to believe in the transformation of a human into a 'lesser' being? To believe this, one must have a deeper investment in the *possibility* of disenchantment. Although disenchantment is often presented in empirical terms, as a 'fact' borne out by historical evidence, it is actually a very particular belief about the universe and the possibilities of human agency. Western secular cosmology takes for granted that human beings are the arbiters of meaning (see the pervious chapter) and that they possess the ability to strip other beings of their intrinsic meaning. This, in turn, is based on a belief that no external (that is, transcendent or divine) forces override this form of human action, or militate against it. In such a context, everything comes down to what humans believe—and what they can make other humans believe. If there is no overarching external guarantor of the meaning of a person's life, then beliefs must be rooted in evidence from this world. And if one can demonstrate evidence that a person is less than human by *treating her as such*, then it is likely that others will follow suit.

From this perspective, dehumanization is not a direct, linear exchange between a subject and an object. Instead, it is an intersubjective process that relies on multiple parties. Moreover, there are no inherently 'dehumanizing' acts; the ability of a particular act to dehumanize a person depends entirely on the extent to which it convinces others that the person is less than human. So, even overtly abusive acts—for instance, calling a person a non-human animal or a piece of garbage—is dehumanizing only if another party (perhaps even the victim herself) *believes* it to be true and acts as if it were. This means that dehumanization is carried out not only by the object and subject, but also by third parties who use the idea to explain what has occurred. In other words, calling something an act of 'dehumanization' presumes that the act has been sufficient to strip the victim of her humanity, and espouses a belief that this is possible. I call this the 'effective' dimension of dehumanization, or the belief in the efficacy of humans to disenchant the universe.

The key to effective dehumanization is recognition—specifically, the ability to make one human recognize another as a disenchanted being. This involves considerable cognitive work, both for the person attempting to dehumanize someone else, and for those confronted with her efforts. Agamben's analysis emphasizes the fact that human beings are simultaneously human and other, and it is only by highlighting the otherness that their humanity is subverted. In other words, a being must be human (at least on some level) in order to be *de*-humanized.[4] So, to recognize a person as 'dehumanized', one must not only exaggerate her non-human aspects; one must also acknowledge, then override, the humanity that one sees reflected in her. Take, for instance, the example of torture, which is in general considered to be a dehumanizing experience. In the torture room, the body and emotions that we identify as 'human' are not entirely obliterated. Rather, they are disfigured—temporarily through pain, or permanently through injury. When one sees a victim of torture and considers her to be dehumanized, one must first see her human-ness and then its distortion. So, dehumanization is never a total or complete process. The 'dehumanized' being is not so much *in*human or *non-human* as she is formerly human—and, perhaps, soon-to-be-remade human (see below). And this depends very much on how persuasively the perpetrator can construct her as such.

From this perspective, dehumanization is very much in the eyes of its beholders. This argument has gained ground in recent studies of the phe-nomenon within the field of social psychology. In particular, research on 'infra-dehumanization' can illustrate how it functions in practice. 'Infra-dehumanization' refers to subtle, everyday cognitive processes through which others are denied a 'fully human' status. It confounds the idea that dehuma-nization can only occur through conscious, directional, intended action, and suggests that it may take place on a very different register of experience. Rather than focusing on overtly 'dehumanizing' acts and their instrumental effects on the victim, this approach focuses on the processes that take place in the mind of the participant and/or observer of this dynamic. Crucially, it suggests that those responsible for dehumanizing others may not be aware that, let alone how, they are doing so. Indeed, as illustrated by Karen Stollznow's study of the use of 'dehumanizing' rhetoric in everyday language, many per-petrators of dehumanization do not recognize themselves as such (although third parties might). They might casually call a woman a 'cow' or a 'bitch', or refer to a domineering colleague as a 'force of nature', without recognizing these as speech acts which dehumanize another person.[5] By this account, dehumanization need not be driven by desire or intent, and even those who deeply oppose it on a conscious level may enact it on a subconscious one. All that is required is a set of ontological beliefs about the features that qualify one as a 'human', and about the conditions in which these are nullified.

According to the experiments conducted by Bastian *et al.* (2009) and Haslam (2006), human beings discriminate between 'humans' and 'non-humans' on the basis of specific sets of properties. The first, which these authors associate with 'human nature', are possessed by humans and by many other kinds of animals—such as warmth, responsiveness and autonomous agency. They represent the space of affinity and overlap between human and other forms of being. Because they are definitive of humans but not exclusive to them, these 'human nature' qualities deemed necessary but not sufficient in designating certain beings as 'human'. A second set of qualities refers to features that are thought to be unique to humans. These include refined emotions, self-control and moral responsibility. In contrast to 'human nature' properties, they reconstitute the Western secular boundary between human and non-human within the individual psyche by positing an inherent distinction. Once again, these qualities are considered to be necessary to humans, but not sufficient in themselves. However, in combination, these two sets of properties present an image of the 'full human'.

According to these authors, infra-dehumanization occurs when an individual picks up on more or fewer of the qualities discussed above. This interpretation suggests that dehumanization is not total or generic, but occurs in degrees and in different forms. Haslam (2006) argues that this depends very much on how each individual or group 'scores' on the basis of the features discussed above. For instance, a low assessment of the 'human uniqueness' qualities of a specific group of people is likely to produce an 'animalistic' image of dehumanization; Arendt's account of colonialism fits this bill. In contrast, a low assessment of a group's 'human nature' features is more likely to produce a 'mechanistic' understanding of dehumanization, in which the victim is treated like a machine or robot. Michael Mann's (2005) accounts of the mechanical ordering of genocidal societies seem to exemplify this.

There are limitations to the theory of 'infra-dehumanization'. Not least is the fact that the research in question was carried out among a relatively small group of young, Western university students, which raises questions about its applicability to human beings 'in general'. However, the philosophical implications of these studies are much more important; they suggest that we should be attentive to the inter- and intra-subjective processes through which people come to believe in, and act upon, dehumanization. Crucially, they encourage us to pay attention to the beliefs of multiple parties: the aggressor, who believes in her capacity to dehumanize and adopts this as an overt strategy; the accessory to the killing, who internalizes judgements about a particular group of people and expresses these through language or physical acts; in some cases, even the victim, who identifies herself as 'dehumanized', either because she has internalized this belief or (mis)recognized herself as such. I do not by any means wish to suggest that victims of dehumanization are to blame for it. Rather, my point is that the insidious logic of dehumanization can trap even its victims in the intersubjective processes that constitute it.

Ironically, even third parties who seek to bear witness to dehumanization and fight against it are part of this process. Simply by 'recognizing' certain people as 'dehumanized', they actually bear witness to the *efficacy* of dehumanization as a form of human agency, and bolster belief in it. In order to convince others that dehumanization is a terrible thing, they must first persuade them that it is real, possible and within the capabilities of humans. This problem presents itself in public and intellectual discourses that decry the 'dehumanization' of victims of genocide, torture or mass rape. Ironically, it is particularly pronounced in empathetic portraits of those who have *survived* violence. Many of these portraits emphasize the fluidity of the human body with the dead body. As Butler's work on the framing of warfare suggests, victims of violence are often portrayed as 'not quite living, that is, living in a state of suspension between life and death' (2004: 36). In a similar vein, Veena Das (2007) argues that victims of violence are portrayed as bearers of 'dangerous knowledge' because they have witnessed the degradation of human life. It is common to assume that people with this kind of knowledge 'fee[l] and se[e] death everywhere' (Tirman 2011: 6), or that they forever carry 'the sour smell of rotting corpses in their nostrils' (Keane 1996: 158). Although they are intended to draw attention to the horrors of war, these empathetic descriptions are powerfully dehumanizing. Along with the images of animals, machines and objects, dead bodies are another powerful image of the inhuman. In fact, in a cosmology that abhors death and contrasts it directly with human life, they are the *opposite* of human. They act as a constant reminder of the fragility of the border between humanity and inhumanity. Indeed, it might be a larger stretch to perceive a person as a non-human animal or a robot, but it does not take much imagination to see a person as a dead body. So, despite their normative commitments and good intentions, emphasizing the 'deadness' of a victim of violence contributes to her dehumanization by confirming the efficacy of killing to dehumanize.

This problem also rears its head in responses to 'dehumanization', particularly those that are oriented towards restoring the humanity of victims. Agamben sees this dynamic in the work of the UN's High Commission for Refugees. He claims that its employees:

> Can only grasp human life in the figure of bare or sacred life, and therefore, despite themselves, maintain a secret solidarity with the very powers they ought to fight ... here human life is exclusively considered (and there are certainly good reasons for this) as sacred life ... only as such is it made into the object of aid and protection.
>
> (Agamben 1995: 133)

In other words, categorizing the suffering of certain people as 'dehumanizing' in order to prioritize the resources and care directed to them has the ironic effect of affirming their 'non-human' status.

So far, I have argued that dehumanization is an inter- and intra-subjective process. Direct dehumanization of the kind discussed above can be effective only if we believe it to be possible. This belief is endemic (if not unique) to Western secular cosmology. In most transcendent frameworks, human beings do not have total control over the meaning attributed to particular beings. If a being's value is intrinsic, or guaranteed by an external force, no amount of harm, disfiguration, alienation or humiliation could displace this. However, dehumanization makes sense in Western secular cosmology, in which belief is derived from earthly experience rather than transcendent rules. In this context, human action can alter the meaning of life and the order of the universe. So, when one recognizes and treats another being as inhuman, this may be sufficient to make others believe that this is true. This analysis highlights an inherent paradox within theories of dehumanization, and their use as a normative tool for preventing or responding to violence. As Samera Esmeir puts it, opponents of dehumanization may efface the human 'subjects of violence, even while wishing to recognize the humanity of the dehumanized' (2006: 1548).

Categorical dehumanization

The responsibility to protect was developed in the early 2000s as a means of re-energizing the normative will to protect threatened groups of people when their own states failed to do so or, in fact, became aggressors. This task clearly weighed heavily on the shoulders of its proponents, including former UN Secretary General Kofi Annan. In a speech that was widely credited with inspiring *The Responsibility to Protect*, he asked how the UN could respond to 'a Rwanda, to a Srebrenica—to gross and systematic violations of human rights that affect every precept of our common humanity' (quoted in ICISS 2001: 2). Indeed, the acts of genocide and mass killing with which Annan conflates these two places are framed as threats to 'humanity itself'—that is, to the ontological category of humanity. According to Annan, the killing of large groups of human beings undercuts the very foundations of this category. The driving purpose of responsibility to protect is to bolster this category by ensuring that it is upheld consistently and universally. Indeed, the inconsistency with which human rights are upheld and human lives protected belies the universality on which the category of humanity is based. Annan argues that the genocide in Rwanda led to the impression that, 'for all the rhetoric about the universality of human rights, some human lives end up mattering a great deal less to the international community than others' (ICISS 2001: 1). The idea that some human lives might 'matter less' than others raises a significant problem for proponents of universal human rights: it suggests that the goalposts of 'humanity' can be moved. Moreover, it suggests that human action (violence in particular) is capable of moving them. When this happens, large groups of people may be left on the 'wrong' side of the human–inhuman boundary. I call this phenomenon 'categorical dehumanization' because it is produced by shifts in the boundaries of the category of humanity.

In some cases, categorical dehumanization is deliberate. In the examples of direct dehumanization discussed above, perpetrators deliberately move the boundaries of humanity in order to exclude certain groups and encourage their elimination. For instance, Hagan and Ryder-Richmond's (2008) account of dehumanization in Darfur traces decades of systematic efforts on the part of the Sudanese government to exclude black Sudanese citizens. The use of abusive public rhetoric and discriminatory policies by politicians and 'ethnic entrepreneurs' placed the black Sudanese 'outside the normative universe of moral protection, leaving them vulnerable to targeted genocidal victimization' (Hagan and Ryder-Richmond 2008: 876). From this perspective, categorical dehumanization is an integral—and intentional—element of direct dehumanization. However, as I shall now demonstrate, it may also arise from unintentional collective changes or systemic processes—including, ironically, the movement towards humanitarianism.

The problem of categorical dehumanization is one of the contradictions at the heart of Western secular ethics. On the one hand, this belief system places the well-being of humans above all other concerns, wresting control over human destiny and meaning from the divine and placing it in human hands. On the other hand, it renders human (and other beings) vulnerable precisely by leaving this task to human agency. Without external, transcendent forces to guarantee its enchanted status, the category of 'humanity' must be embodied in human laws, institutions or practices, which are as malleable as the bodies and objects they govern. Crucially, the shape and functionality of these phenomena is determined by *human* action and judgement. As Asad puts it:

> When it is endowed with legal force, the abstract concept of 'humanity' allows authorities to decide who, by virtue of being *not human*, can legitimately be treated 'inhumanly' by the state and its citizens.
>
> (2003:157)

Unlike transcendent repositories or guarantors of meaning, human institutions and forms of agency can be accessed, influenced, altered and subverted by intentional human action, errors or circumstance. This property has proved immensely beneficial for humans in certain circumstances. For instance, Neta Crawford's (2002) work on the global diffusion of anti-slavery and anti-colonial ethics demonstrates how human norms, actions and affect can alter the boundaries of the category of humanity. In this case, the malleability of the category of humanity allowed its expansion; by making slavery and colonialism unacceptable, it admitted millions of people into the category of the 'fully human'. Had it been embedded in immutable transcendent structures, such changes in the category of humanity might not have taken place.

The downside is that the reverse also holds: just as the category of humanity can be expanded, it can be retracted. Asad (2003) analyses this problem in the context of debates over the extension of human rights to other forms of life. Animal rights activists, for instance, often suggest that many forms of life, and not just human beings, are worthy of legal protection and moral status. This contention challenges the sharp division between 'human' and 'animal' that lies at the heart of Western secular cosmology, and suggests that the border can (and should) be moved. A similar problem arises within the human species and is found in debates over genetic research, abortion and euthanasia. These decisions about the point at which a being becomes or ceases to be human are determined by laws and conventions, which differ across historical and cultural contexts. For Asad, these examples demonstrate that the category of humanity is not universal or constant, but rather a status that can be attached to various kinds of beings. This, he argues, has important implications for human rights, which apply only to those beings that are considered human in a particular context. When the boundaries of 'humanity' constantly change, human rights are little more than 'floating signifiers that can be attached to or detached from various subjects and classes' (Asad 2003: 157).

Asad also points out that the law cannot offer absolute protection to those whom it designates as 'human'. In practice, the application of rights:

> Authorizes different patterns of pain and suffering. [In so doing] it defines, or ... tries to redefine the concept of the human—and protect the rights that belong essentially to the human and the damage that can be done to his or her essence.
>
> (Asad 2003: 256)

So, the function of rights is not to render human beings inviolable, but rather to set a limit to the violations that can take place before the 'human' status loses its special meaning. Violence is not, in itself, against the law; only those forms of violence that are deemed to violate existing norms and laws about its use are. Likewise, as Stollznow (2008) points out, dehumanization is not, in any formal sense, illegal. Only when it becomes the basis for *disallowed* forms of violence does it become legally relevant.[6] In other words, human rights are used to police dehumanization, but they are not designed to eliminate it fully.

Furthermore, depending on rights and legal structures to guarantee one's humanity is also a risky venture. Categorical dehumanization can occur when the structures that guarantee one's rights (and therefore, one's membership in the category of 'humanity') collapse. Arendt (1976) explores how this phenomenon helped to produce twentieth-century totalitarian killing.

The First World War, she suggests, produced large numbers of stateless refugees. Their home countries had either ceased to exist, no longer possessed institutions that could vouch for their legal personhood, or had revoked this status from them. In the context of the modern state, in which one's humanity is tied to one's citizenship, this left many people legally inhuman. According to Arendt, they came to be viewed as beings in excess of humanity, as superfluous life. Instead of individual, rights-bearing humans, they were seen as masses of undifferentiated life, simultaneously atomized and homogenized. Their sheer numbers and the weight of their needs threatened to overwhelm the war-weary states of Europe. However, their legal dehumanization offered a solution: because they were viewed as superfluous, it became possible for political leaders to believe that they could simply be eliminated without the 'disastrous results of depopulation' (Arendt 1976: 311). In other words, their destruction would not be counted as a loss of *human* lives. According to

Arendt, the dehumanization and destruction of life associated with twentieth-century totalitarianism was thoroughly legal in nature. Refugees could be viewed as 'excess' life only to the extent that their legally human status was revoked. Left without the protection of the law, 'the abstract nakedness of being nothing but human was their greatest danger' (Arendt 1976: 300).

However, categorical dehumanization does not only occur through changes in the law or the state. As Martin Coward (2006) argues, people can also be dehumanized when the material structures that help to enable them to be human are destroyed. Drawing on the worldly ethics of Heidegger, Arendt and Nancy, Coward contends that people can only realize themselves as human in specific material conditions: namely, those that allow them to live in pluralistic, heterogeneous collectives. For Coward, 'urban' space is the epitome of this, and 'urbicide', or the deliberate destruction of urban space, can literally be a fate worse than death. It not only destroys human lives, but also the conditions in which 'humanity' can be realized and restored. In this case, the literal, physical destruction of the conditions of humanity casts many people outside of this category and the protections that it offers.

The examples above suggest that categorical dehumanization occurs in extreme conditions, when the state and society are in crisis, or recovering from major shocks. However, it may also emerge through the benign or beneficient efforts of people seeking to respond to or prevent these crises. In particular, Esmeir (2006) argues that the promotion of human rights plays an integral role in 'making dehumanization possible' by framing certain people as beyond the 'legal pale' of rights-based protection. The efforts of human rights activists:

> Expose the radical evil that legitimated violence can institute, [but] they also establish an equation between the protection of the law and the constitution of humanity, effectively granting the former magical a power to endow the latter.
>
> (Esmeir 2006: 1544)

By highlighting situations in which human rights are not applied equally, proponents of this argument affirm the belief that rights and humanity are equivalent. In arguing that it is possible to be biologically human and to lack human rights, 'these critical assertions reproduce a particular conviction that humanity is a status to be conferred, or seized and taken away' (Esmeir 2006: 1544). From this perspective, linking humanity to human rights is a double-edged sword: it 'ensures recognition of [one's] (temporary) humanity and its (possible) suspension' (Esmeir 2006: 1546).

This occurs, Esmeir contends, because human rights do not treat the status of humanity as 'already-given', but rather as something which must be constructed. The regime of 'juridical humanity', as she calls it, presumes that a being is not human until it is legally constituted as such. The negative orientation of the law therefore precisely reflects the way in which beings are distinguished as 'enchanted' in Western secular cosmology: they are presumed to be disenchanted unless they can be established as 'human'. In this case, it is not necessary for laws to be changed or removed in order for categorical dehumanization to occur. Rather, it is sufficient simply for them not to be extended, to be applied unevenly or upheld inconsistently—that is, for groups of people to have *never been (legally) human*. This, Esmeir argues, underpins a widespread assumption that people living in regimes that do not guarantee human rights are passive, depoliticized victims, simply waiting to be made human. Indeed, as the last chapter suggested, being human involves possessing the agency to make oneself human, and to realize one's humanity in an authentic way. If, then, a group of people is framed as dehumanized, 'what political possibilities exist for them, aside from being victims awaiting humanitarian interventions?' (Esmeir 2006: 1548).

As Esmeir suggests, belief in categorical dehumanization provokes a strong desire to (re)humanize, an impulse which I will explore in the next chapter. For the present, it is important to focus on the ways in which Western secularity makes categorical dehumanization possible. Namely, it creates the binary between 'enchanted' and 'disenchanted' beings which forms the boundary of the category of humanity and determines the different ethical status of humans and non-humans. Shifting, human-made beliefs about the nature of these beings, and about the process of disenchantment, allow this boundary to be moved through human efforts. Indeed, the fact that the category of humanity is placed in human hands is one of the most profound sources of its precariousness.

Conclusions

Ironically, in a cosmology in which human beings take centre stage, it is surprisingly difficult to uphold the unique, special category of 'humanity'. This chapter has argued that Western secular cosmology and its central narrative of disenchantment make it possible to differentiate humans from all other forms of being. By treating all non-humans as 'disenchanted' beings, it is possible to claim that humans are uniquely 'enchanted'. However, as this chapter has argued, the construction of a binary between human–inhuman or enchanted–disenchanted has perverse consequences. Namely, the processes that are used to separate and hierarchize human and non-human forms of life can be applied *within and to* the category of humanity.

This logic underpins the phenomenon of 'dehumanization'—or, more to the point, the belief that it is possible and effective. 'Direct' dehumanization functions by equating human beings with disenchanted non-humans, and thus making it easier to instrumentalize them. However, this strategy can only work if one or more of the parties involved, or a third party, *believe* that the victim is a non-human, and that this status can be determined by human beings or institutions. Indeed, the investment of the status of 'humanity' in human institutions also creates vulnerabilities. Human institutions are malleable and subject to collapse. When they change, the boundaries of humanity may shift, leaving many beings on the 'wrong' side of the divide. In other words, the sharp divide between 'enchanted' humans and 'disenchanted' non-humans leaves all beings vulnerable to systematic destruction.

Throughout this chapter, I have emphasized that the logic of dehumanization is intertwined with Western secular cosmology. It is important, before moving on, to introduce a couple of caveats. First, I certainly do not mean to suggest that Western secularity is inherently oriented towards dehumanization. Instead, I wish to emphasize the risks and downsides of a cosmology that is ostensibly oriented entirely towards human well-being. Dehumanization is a *possibility* in the cosmological conditions created by Western secularity, not a certainty. Specific beliefs—in the possibility of disenchantment, the human capacity to enact it, and the lack of transcendent forces that could block it—create conditions in which dehumanization makes sense, regardless of how one feels about it normatively. Second, it is certainly not the case that *only* societies dominated by Western secular beliefs engage in dehumanization, or that it is always used for 'secular' ends. On the contrary, in several of the examples discussed in this chapter (for instance, Gaddafi's Libya, and Bashir's Sudan), the perpetrator of the violence in question overtly aligned himself with a transcendent belief system. However, these perpetrators are also embedded in modern state structures, which were born out of the trans-formations of Western secularity. As I discussed in Chapter 2, Western secularity has distinctive features, but it almost always appears in plural form, integrating elements of other belief systems. The logics that have produced mass killing since the last century are distinctly 'modern'—that is, instrumental–rational, mechanistic and systematic. What this chapter has argued is that beneath the machinery of the modern state pulses a powerful cosmology, one in which disenchantment and dehumanization are distinct possibilities. Now, I shall explore how international intervention is driven by the desire to reverse the process of disenchantment—that is, the impulse to re-enchant humanity.

Notes

1 I use the term 'non-human animal' in order to underscore the point that humans are one form of animal life, and to contest the binary between human and non-human animals—which, I argue in this chapter, helps to make dehumanization possible.

2 In fairness to Connolly, he does not broach the subject of whether or not a non-human could experience 'immanent transcendence'; his account of this specific phenomenon focuses on human experience, but his ontology and ethics clearly are not anthropocentric.

3 It is interesting to note that, in the same speech, Gaddafi expressed his willingness to 'die as a martyr'. In this manner, he invoked a very different idea of inhumanity: that of the human being consecrated by the divine.

4 Although, as Agamben and others point out, beings considered to be inhuman can be humanized. Indeed, Agamben argues that the category of humanity actually emerged through the humanization of apes.

5 Indeed, it is interesting how easily images of non-human animals ('dog', 'bitch', 'shark', 'bear', or even just the word 'animal') are used to describe people in everyday conversations in English whereas, in a setting of conflict or social strife, they might be interpreted much more darkly.

6 An exception might be hate speech. However, hate speech is defined in terms of the intentional desire to do harm to another person, which violates laws about the extent to which people can be harmed. Also, it is important to note that many uses of dehumanizing language (e.g. the example given above of casually calling a co-worker a 'cow') are not usually considered hate speech unless they are associated with a particular programme of racial, gender-based or other systematic abuse.

5   Re-enchanting humanity?

Disenchantment, re-enchantment and intervention

Being human is a precarious state in Western secular cosmology. As the last chapter showed, disenchantment—the very process through which the category of humanity is carved out of seemingly inert matter—can also undermine this category. However, disenchantment is not a one-way process, and human beings are not entirely helpless in the face of it. In fact, anxiety about disenchantment provokes a powerful and opposite response in the Western secular mind: the desire to re-enchant. What is often presented as an inexorable, linear process towards total disenchantment is, in fact, a dialectic of disenchantment–re-enchantment produced through human efforts. We can see this impulse at work in the efforts of intervenors who attempt to reverse the effects of dehumanization, to restore meaning to 'bad deaths', or simply to assert the ascendency of 'humanity' in the face of disaster. In order to do so, intervenors must reclaim lives they perceive to be disenchanted, enfolding them within recognized schemas of meaning. However, this produces a paradox: the attempt to re-enchant human beings contributes to their dehumanization. Why is this the case?

   The effort to re-enchant humanity through intervention relies on dominant source of meaning-making within Western secular cosmology: instrumental rationality. This form of meaning-making is a distinctive feature of Western secularity, and one of its most influential contributions. It is an overarching framework of meaning, which claims to be capable of encompassing the entire universe, and to which all other beliefs and rationalities are subordinated. However, ironically, it is also the driving force behind disenchantment (or at least the belief in disenchantment). This means that the most powerful tool available to intervenors for restoring meaning is also a force for its destruction. By measuring, explaining, predicting, targeting, symbolizing, counting and otherwise rationalizing 'bad deaths' or 'dehumanized' beings, intervenors contribute to their instrumentalization—and to their disenchantment. To illustrate this dynamic, I briefly explore how the dialectic of disenchantment–re-enchantment shapes international security, and in particular the norm of human security. Human security attempts to reclaim the meaningfulness of human lives by investing them with the attributes of high life: individuality, bodily integrity, self-realization and human flourishing. However, it does so precisely by instrumentalizing them to rational processes of liberal sovereignty, which critics identify as 'biopolitical'.

Next, I analyse statistical, verbal, visual, cartographical and symbolic materials produced by eighteen organizations of different sizes and levels of influence who seek to shape intervention by interpreting the effects of violence.[1] Although they tend to be paid less attention than the formal statements of intervenors (e.g. UN Security Council Resolutions or statements from foreign ministries), these 'grey materials'[2] are relied upon by intervenors, policy-makers, activists and academics as sources of 'what really happens' in situations of violence. In this chapter, I probe the ways in which these materials attempt to make meaning out of violence to enfold 'bad deaths' or 'dehumanized' beings within Western secular frameworks of meaning. However, at the same time, they construct specific groups of people as disenchanted and, quite often, dehumanized objects—as materials out of which meaning can be made. The dynamics of disenchantment–re-enchantment, therefore, are complex and often lead to ironic consequences. Understanding this dialectic is crucial to unlocking the cosmological beliefs that drive intervention and produce some of its most ambiguous consequences.

The dialectic of disenchantment–re-enchantment

Even for those who believe in its formative power, disenchantment is not a one-way process. Instead, it is one half of a dialectic; the other half consists of human efforts to resist its effects, negate its power, or restore meaning in its wake. For this reason, Western secularity is just as much shaped by the impulse towards re-enchantment as it is by the belief in disenchantment. As Jenkins argues, re-enchantment needs to be recognized as a feature of Western secular societies 'not just as a consequence, or a reaction, but right at the heart' of them (2000: 22).

Even Weber hints at this impulse in his treatment of disenchantment. In *Science as a Vocation*, he refers to the re-emergence of 'old gods' in modern societies; and in the *Protestant Ethic*, he speculates that 'perhaps new prophets will emerge, or powerful old ideas and ideals will be reborn at the end of this monstrous development' (see Lehman 2008). Weber refers to the incomplete nature of disenchantment, and the fragments of transcendent belief that circulate through its machinery. From this perspective, if re-enchantment occurs, it is as a remnant of, or a throwback to, previous forms of enchantment. In other words, it is a residual phenomenon rather than the result of concerted, instrumental human efforts. However, as I argued in the previous chapter, Western secular societies are characterized by a strong belief that disenchantment is a human-made process—and that humans can intentionally intervene in this process.

This argument is put forward by Taylor, who views re-enchantment it as a form of resistance against the encroachment of disenchantment into every aspect of life. He points out that many people living in societies dominated by

Western secular beliefs 'bridle at the idea that the universe in which we find ourselves is totally devoid of human meaning' (Taylor 2011a: 292). Their response to the experience of disenchantment is not always one of nihilism or anomie—or, indeed, 'disenchantment' in its more colloquial sense. On the contrary, Taylor claims, this experience is deeply ambivalent:

> We can be struck by the sense that we stand, as it were, before a normative abyss, that this blind, deaf, silent universe offers *no* guidance whatever; [but] we can [also] find here an exhilarating challenge, which inspires us, which can even awaken a sense of the strange beauty of this alien universe, in the face of which we stake our claim as legislators of meaning.
>
> (2007: 581)

In other words, instead of simply accepting meaninglessness, the experience of disenchantment can also galvanize one's impulse towards creativity and meaning-making. As discussed in previous chapters, the ability to act as 'legislators of meaning' is integral to the Western secular concept of high life. As such, this conception of humanity is produced at least in part by human responses to disenchantment.

One of the ways in which humans might respond to the threat of disenchantment is by attempting to (re)connect with the transcendent register of experience. For instance, they might try to recover 'an analogue of the original sensibility [of enchantment] … in the sense of the forces moving through nature … or in the contact with spirits of the dead' (Taylor 2010: 303), as in 'new age' movements. In a similar regard, Connolly (2011) suggests that phenomena as diverse as Christian evangelism, advertising campaigns and public support for wars engender these connections with the 'transcendent' register. It is possible that many of the events associated with the 'resurgence of religion' (see Chapter 1) are products of this impulse towards re-enchantment. I am not referring only to acts of 'religiously motivated' violence, protest or civil unrest, but also to the burgeoning of overtly Christian and Islamic modes of humanitarianism alongside the growth of their secular counterparts (see Barnett and Stein 2012; Lynch 2011).

However, the dominant, Western version of secularity offers its own strategy of re-enchantment, which does not rely on traditional 'religious' beliefs. Instead, it relies on the forms of meaning-making that define Western secular cosmology. The forms of meaning-making on which it relies are not transcendent in the usual sense; that is, they are believed to be the work of humans, and to emerge from the world rather than from an external source. Nor are they what Connolly refers to as 'mundane transcendence'—that is, fleeting moments or glimpses of forces that exceed human understanding. Instead, they emerge from a fascination precisely with human understanding, and the power of human rationality. In this sense, they resemble the secular notion of the sacred which, Barnett and Stein (2012; see also Chapter 2 in this volume) argue, inspires much of contemporary humanitarian action.

Specifically, the systems of logic, classification, ratiocination, prediction, pattern-making, analysis and representation are Western secularity's own distinctive contribution towards the arsenal available for the project of re-enchantment. Instead of drawing on transcendent frameworks, they offer a form of meaning-making that aligns with Western secular beliefs and assumptions about the world. At first glance, this assertion may appear absurd, but for Jenkins it makes perfect sense. He argues that:

> Formal–rational logics and processes can themselves be (re)enchanted from within, or become the vehicles of (re)enchantment. (Re)enchantment can be a thoroughly rationally-organized business.
>
> (Jenkins 2000: 13)

In other words, instrumental–rational process can, like any other source of meaning, be deployed as tools for investing, projecting and restoring meaning. They, too, can inspire the subjective responses associated with *being* enchanted, and, in this sense, they may be objects of enchantment. Jenkins lists a number of phenomena that are usually associated with rational or bureaucratic thinking, but which nonetheless can provoke enchantment: collective attachments such as ethnicity, sexualities, intoxications and ecstasies; consumerist cultural hedonism; the dreams of alterity inspired by tourism; the mundane daydreams of advertising and consumption; cinematic escapism; science fiction and fantasy; and even large-scale public events (2000: 18). Bennett (2001, 2010) adds to this list. She describes a highly instrumentalized contemporary world that nonetheless fosters a number of 'enchanting' beings: 'metamorphizing creatures' such as talking non-human animals or 'smart' computers, 'magical' technologies such as the internet; metals; food; and large-scale networks. Such beings, she argues, bear 'some resemblance to the wonderful, unlikely possibilities called miracles' (Bennett 2001: 28). She calls for the cultivation of sensibilities that would open humans to more robust connections with the world, and encourage them to embrace its multiple sources of meaning instead of succumbing to the narrative of disenchantment.

Such moments of enchantment, understood as fleeting encounters with the transcendent or awe-inspiring, most certainly occur within Western secular worlds. They fly like errant sparks from the moving parts of instrumental–rational forms of meaning, and burst unexpectedly from the processes of everyday life. However, this is not the dominant way in which the impulse towards re-enchantment is expressed within Western secularity. Instead, its dominant logics instrumentalize the phenomenon of enchantment, or, rather, conceptualize it in instrumental terms. That is, enchantment is treated as a more or less stable property that can be bestowed and removed. This form of re-enchantment is much more mechanical, deliberate and systematic than the fleeting, intense moments of enchantment discussed above. It is not so much an opening to the enchantments offered by Western secular artefacts and processes as an attempt to apply instrumental rationality to 'disenchanted' beings and to encompass them within this framework of meaning.

For this reason, it may be tempting to understand the processes of Western secular re-enchantment simply as an extension of the project of disenchantment. However, I shall argue that it should be understood as an effort towards *re*-enchantment because of the way it is used: to extend and bolster the category of humanity against the threat of disenchantment. Once the process of removing intrinsic meaning is set in motion, there is a constant struggle to maintain the boundaries of the category of humanity and to impose order on the beings that transgress them. This is the form that the impulse towards re-enchantment takes within a Western secular framework dominated by instrumental rationality.

As the previous chapter suggested, the extension of instrumental rationality is usually understood as a process that denudes the universe of meaning. However, disenchantment is a process of meaning-making in itself. Like transcendent cosmologies, it gives each being a place in the cosmos and assigns it a certain kind of meaning. Specifically, it replaces the intrinsic meaning of non-human beings with instrumental meaning measured in relation to human needs and desires. Indeed, this is the critical difference between the way in which transcendent and Western secular cosmologies organize the universe according to meaning: the meaning offered by transcendent cosmologies is regarded as intrinsic, immutable and possesses its own positive features. In contrast, the meaning conferred and removed by Western processes of meaning-making is revocable, mutable and defined negatively in relation to human needs.

This produces a distinct form of re-enchantment, in which meaning is forcefully made out of, or superimposed onto, non-human beings, and the intrinsic meaning of non-humans is converted into instrumental meaning. It is concerned mainly with the creation, distribution, exertion and regulation of meaning. Indeed, the focus of this particular project of re-enchantment is on deliberately, systematically and sometimes forcefully investing 'disenchanted' beings with instrumental–rational meaning. This kind of re-enchantment is an overt and agential attempt to *make* other beings meaningful. It emerges from a very different impulse than the forms of *enchantment* described by Bennett, who rejects the narrative of disenchantment and advocates attention to the enchantment of the world. The kind of re-enchantment I am describing fully embraces the linear narrative of disenchantment and attempts to reverse it in an equally instrumental manner.

Indeed, the kind of re-enchantment that is at stake in this Western secular project of meaning-making is not an experience of the transcendent, or of wonder, but simply the recognition that another being is the bearer of meaning intelligible to the beholder. Moreover, it is a kind of meaning that confirms the world-view of the beholder, and her own status as an 'enchanted' being. An example of this mechanical, linear understanding of re-enchantment can be found in the way that victims of 'humanitarian emergencies' are framed for distant spectators. As Bilgrami argues we may see a certain population from the detached, third-person point of view as having a certain average daily caloric count, but we may also see them from another perspective, which engages our practical agency, and describe the very same people as having needs to which our agency responds in one way or another—by sending funds, by joining political movements to improve the conditions of the poor and so forth … we experience *ourselves* as agents, experience ourselves as *generous* or *compassionate*.

(2010: 164)

In this description, the objects of humanitarian aid are not *just* 'bare life', reduced to a mere calorie count. But neither are they sources of enchantment, wonder or attachment in themselves, and there is no effort to cultivate such a response to them. Rather, they appeal to the Western secular desire to invest meaning in the lives of others by exercising one's own agency (see Chapter 3). The 'victim' is simultaneously placed outside of the category of humanity and identified as a target of human actions that will extend it. In the recognition of the 'victim' as a soon-to-be-made-human being, the spectator can exercise her own humanity and is reminded of the boundaries of this category. Likewise, the 'victim' is made meaningful by her proximity to this boundary, and by the spectator's ability to place her on either side of it. This affirms the immense creative power of the human being to constitute herself and her universe by deciding which beings are meaningful, and in what way—a central tenet of Western secularity. This reflexive instrumental encounter between the human spectator and the 'dehumanized' victim reproduces the belief in disenchantment, and in the human capacity to project meaning onto disenchanted beings.

The dialectic of disenchantment–re-enchantment is also clearly reflected in the discourses and practices of 'human security', which is increasingly invoked as a justification and a clarion call for intervention (see Khong and MacFarlane 2006). The basic premise behind human security is that individual humans and the flourishing of human communities should be the referent objects of security, rather than states. Within the large and varied literature on human security, there is a great deal of disagreement about which particular elements of human life most need securing, and which are legitimate and/or feasible aims for intervenors (see Paris 2001; Chandler 2004; Grayson 2008; Christie 2010). In particular, the field is divided between proponents of 'human protection' who suggest that human security should focus primarily on safeguarding individuals from physical harm, while advocates of 'human development' approaches suggest that the self-realization and emancipation of individuals is a fundamental part of this strategy (see CHS 2003; Sen 2008). I shall focus on the second conception of human security which has, arguably, come to the fore in contemporary discourses of intervention.

At first glance, the norms and practices of human security (and human development-oriented approaches in particular) are effective vehicles for promoting and extending the ideal of high life to people who are deemed to have been deprived of it. They promote an entirely immanent, anthropocentric ethic, framing the everyday life of human beings as the ultimate end. As the seminal document on human security, the 1994 UNDP Development Report, states:

> 'Security' refers to the legitimate concerns of ordinary people ... in their daily lives. For many of them, security symbolized protection from the threat of disease, hunger, unemployment, crime, social conflict, political repression and environmental hazards.
>
> (UNDP 1994: 22)

From this perspective, everyday life is not, or not only, a means to achieving a higher end; it constitutes an end in itself. It is not a matter of mere survival; rather, it offers the kinds of goods that Taylor describes as 'metabiological' (see Chapter 3), including quality of life, dignity, enjoyment, social justice and even emancipation. As Shahrbanou Tadjbaksh and Anuradha M. Chenoy succinctly put it, human security strategies are intended to ensure not only that humans survive, but also 'that our lives are worth living' (2007: 243). Moreover, human security discourses reflect the Western secular abhorrence of death, which, regardless of its form, is framed as the negation of human flourishing. As Anne Marie Slaughter puts it, 'from the perspective of human security, death, whether it be from violence or disease, is equally to be feared' (2005: 619). Discourses of human security also reproduce the boundary between humans and non-humans. Whenever non-humans enter discussions of human security, they do so only as means of satisfying the demands of human flourishing. So, for instance, calls for 'environmental security' do not advocate the protection of 'natural' beings in their own right. Rather, they are concerned with ensuring 'environmental security *for people*' (Barnett 2001: 122, italics mine), and with securing the environment *of* people. Likewise, 'food security' requires the cultivation, commodification and distribution of a range of non-human animals, plants and other living things. 'Health security' demands not only the production of non-human entities (food and medicine), but also the destruction of those beings (bacteria, viruses, parasites, and non-human animals, plants or substances that carry them) that threaten human health. By treating all non-humans as materials for producing human security, these discourses reproduce the exceptional status of humans discussed in the previous chapter.

Human security also promotes the ideals of individual propriety and self-realization that are central to Western secular belief. In this context, the individual is framed as both the 'ultimate actor' and the 'ultimate end' of security (Tadjbaksh and Chenoy 2007). Indeed what is deemed to be 'human' about human security is its focus on the *individual* (see UNDP 1994); individuality and 'humanity' are treated almost interchangeably. Rights, entitlements and forms of agency are attributed to individuals over collective groups (see Chandler 2004), whether states, nations, ethnic groups or more informal collective organizations. Moreover, in human security discourses, being fully human is associated directly with the ability to lead an individually fulfilling life and to act as an autonomous agent. In this context, the ability to have and to exercise choice is viewed as particularly salient. As the original framers of the concept put it:

> Human security … is concerned with how people live and breathe in a society, how freely they exercise their many choices, how much access they have to market and social opportunities.
>
> (UNDP 1994: 23)

Similarly, in Amartya Sen's (2008) seminal contributions to this discourse, human agency is understood in terms of the possibilities for attaining one's full social, economic and personal potential. Crucially, the autonomous agent idealized in human security discourses is an individual who is defined by her vulnerabilities and her ability to confront or combat them (Tadjbaksh and Chenoy 2007). This emphasis is closely related to the idea of authenticity and the Western secular imperative to 'work on' oneself; indeed, the 1994 UNDP report affirms the need to endow people with 'responsibility and opportunity for mastering their lives' (UNDP 1994: 24). A similar emphasis can be found in the demand for empowerment, which is conceptualized in various ways: as the capacity to exert control over one's destiny (Tadjbaksh and Chenoy 2007: 236), or to 'take control' of one's life (Khong and MacFarlane 2006); to develop and pursue aspirations (Large and Sisk 2006; Kaldor *et al.* 2007); to 'bring about positive changes' in one's life (Newman 2011:1750), or even to experience a heightened sense of self-esteem (Pupavac 2005: 170–1).

So, human security promotes and (re)produces the conditions associated with high life. It functions as a tool of re-enchantment by cultivating and extending high life to contexts in which it is perceived to have been destroyed, or prevented from emerging. Its focus on the promotion of immanent, everyday aspirations, authenticity (in the form of individual self-realization) and human flourishing makes it a powerful force for the promotion of high life. It also elevates these aspects of human life, not only by presenting them as ideals to be sought, but also by securitizing them—that is, presenting them as urgent and primary needs.

However, the very means through which human security is promoted may simultaneously contribute to the disenchantment of human lives. This process is illuminated by (mostly Foucaultian) critiques which human security as a project of 'biopolitics' (see Chapter 3). From a biopolitical perspective, the referent object of human security is a mere body whose life and death is to be regulated in order to ensure security. As the term 'human security' suggests, it is not only her body that is insecure, but also her 'humanity'. In this context, human security strategies functioning by deciding who is human, who is not human and who is to be made human through the regulation of her biological life and death.

In this vein, Mark Duffield's work focuses on strategies in which individuals and groups that have experienced categorical dehumanization are instrumentalized by large-scale processes of development and state-building. Drawing on Hannah Arendt's (1976) thinking, he contends that the processes of global capitalism generate 'human debris' or 'excess life' who cannot be absorbed within existing social and political systems. Instead, they generate competition over limited resources, leading to conflict and the rupture of governing structures.[3] According to Duffield, the projects discussed above are designed precisely to integrate 'excess life' within systems of sovereign power. As a result, they become the raw materials upon which this power is exercised, and through which it is extended.

This argument is extended by Michael Dillon and Julian Reid, who frame contemporary security and development strategies as attempts to engineer human life in order to ensure the well-being of the 'species'. Dehumanized beings or 'excess lives' threaten the integrity and stability of the liberal–capitalist order. So, according to these authors, they are subjected to processes of 'global triage' in which a 'treatment' is selected for them—and 'some of that treatment—a lot of that treatment—is directly and indirectly lethal' (Dillon and Reid 2009: 90). Specifically, these 'excess lives' become the target of what Dillon and Reid call 'killing to make life live': forms of killing that eliminate threats to 'fully human' beings and help to promote the flourishing of these beings. For instance, 'excess lives' might become the victims of bombs dropped in order to end a civil war that threatens to spill over into neighbouring states, or of 'drone' attacks intended to kill the leaders of terror cells. From this perspective, the logic that calls for the integration of 'dehumanized' beings into projects of development and state-building is the same one that underwrites the killing of these beings for the good of 'humanity'. For this reason, these authors suggest, 'liberal rule must be prepared to wage war not so much for the human, but on the human' (Dillon and Reid 2009: 20)—or, more specifically, on the dehumanized.

These arguments suggest that the strategies and technologies of human security reproduce the disenchanted status of people who have experienced categorical dehumanization. They *re*-instrumentalize these individuals by incorporating them within liberal–capitalist systems that produce sovereign power. Within these systems, the beings in question are reduced to the mere biological objects of power, and their lives and deaths are strictly regulated. In some cases, intervenors even kill these groups or members thereof in order to eliminate the threats that they raise to 'humanity' and to the flourishing of those beings deemed to be 'fully human'.

I want to argue that the two very different accounts of human security discussed above are not competing or mutually exclusive. Instead, they represent the two sides of the dialectics of disenchantment–re-enchantment, which are full of ricochets and twists, stitches and elisions. The attempt to re-enchant human life through the promotion of 'human security' involves practices that categorically dehumanize large groups of people. Moreover, strategies aimed at integrating these beings within the structures of human security—or indeed, at eliminating them—carry out direct dehumanization by treating them as disenchanted objects. So, the attempt to re-enchant humanity through international security strategies drives forward its re-enchantment. But, by the same token, what may appear to be a straightforward, biopolitical strategy of disenchantment may actually (also) be an attempt to secure the meaning of human life. In other words, intervenors attempt to re-enchant human lives through processes, logics and techniques that ultimately drive the processes of disenchantment. But, by the same token, what looks like a straightforward attempt to instrumentalize human beings to sovereign forms of power is actually an expression of the Western secular project of instrumental re-enchantment.

I shall now explore how this dialectic shapes the micro-processes through which intervenors make meaning out of violence. Although they are treated as mere auxiliaries to the practice of intervention, these techniques of meaning-making are fundamental to it. They help to shape the categories through which intervenors assess the urgency and severity of violence, and determine their responses to it. Just as in the examples above, these processes rely on the logic of instrumental rationality. As such, they (re)produce the victims of violence as disenchanted objects, even as they attempt to re-enchant them.

Making meaning out of violence

When an episode of violence occurs, how can international decision-makers, often thousands of miles away, understand what is taking place? More often than not, they rely on a vast stream of information—reports, graphs, charts, memos, maps and so on—to help them make meaning out of the events in question. These objects help international decision-makers to imagine the act of violence, to evaluate its importance and to formulate responses to it. The primary focus of these objects is almost always the same: deaths, or damage to the lives of humans. By quantifying, measuring, predicting, interpreting, visualizing and otherwise representing bad death or the threat thereof, they survey the boundaries of humanity and the places where it has been breached. Specifically, they highlight groups of beings that have been pushed beyond the category of humanity, whether by death itself, or through the denial of high life. Subjecting the lives of others to this kind of representation casts them as mere objects to be calculated and manipulated, and so it involves direct dehumanization. Moreover, by identifying certain beings as 'dehumanized', it enacts categorical dehumanization. And, by persuading decision-makers (and even publics) to regard certain people as dehumanized, it involves effective dehumanization. However, at the same time, they are the manifestations of a subtle but powerful process of re-enchantment. At the very instant that a bad death is captured, or a life categorized as 'dehumanized', it is embedded within Western secular structures of meaning. Indeed, these objects are artefacts of Western secular cosmology, forged through its central form of meaning-making: instrumental rationality. Moreover, by identifying groups of 'dehumanized' beings, these objects make it possible for intervenors to plan large-scale strategies for reclaiming the lives in question for 'humanity' (see Chapter 6). So, what might look like a straightforward process of disenchantment—the subjection of human lives to instrumental–rational processes—is in fact an effort to re-enchant them.

To explore this problem, I shall now discuss several artefacts produced by international organizations, NGOs, research institutes and scholars to shape international responses to large-scale violence. The examples on which I draw are not intended to reflect the 'international community' as a whole, or indeed to provide an exhaustive systematic analysis of the 'grey literature' (a name which is often used to describe such artefacts). They represent a small cross-section of this vast field, and of the actors who seek to make meaning out of violence—from governments and NGOs to scholars, consultants, experts, activists and publics. It is important to note that many of the artefacts here draw on shared sources of data, or refer to each other in a self-referential loop.[4] While this may raise issues of validity for the social scientist, it provides the anthropologist of the international with an interesting insight. In short, most mainstream sources of data on violence, dehumanization and bad death rely on the same forms of meaning-making, categories, semiotics, indicators and even raw data. For this reason, even a sample of artefacts as modest as the one discussed here provides good indications of how 'bad deaths' and dehumanization are imagined in the international sphere. By paying attention to these imaginaries, it is possible to see that dialectic of disenchantment–re-enchantment at work. I shall explore this in the context of two major tasks pursued by the producers of these artefacts: the documentation of 'bad deaths' and the identification of dehumanized (or 'killable') lives.

Documenting 'bad deaths' and 'killability'

Documenting deaths is one of the most central functions of contemporary conflict analysis and 'early warning' (prediction) systems. Such projects are concerned with counting and representing the instrumental deaths caused directly by violence, or, in some cases, indirect causes of death associated with violence such as disease or starvation in the wake of war (see HSRG 2010).

Quantitative measurements are quite literally used to 'make deaths count'. Specifically, they provide the building blocks of heuristic devices such as categories, continuums and rankings which shape how—and whether—international decision-makers apprehend violence. These processes of counting are directly linked with ontology, or the ways in which humans comprehend being; they literally bring new metaphysical categories into existence (see Chapters 6 and 7). For instance, the UCDP/PRIO database uses a quantitative figure (which has been widely adopted throughout the grey literature) as the determining factor in the category of 'armed conflict': 25 'battle-related deaths' (Themner 2013). Similarly, for the Center for Systemic Peace's (CSP) 'Conflict Trends Database', 'major armed conflicts [must] involve at least 500 fatalities' (CSP 2009). Both projects provide a basic threshold at which individual acts of violence and deaths assume a new status: the category of 'armed conflict' or 'major armed conflict'. The methodology used to determine these categories provides important clues as to the kinds of death which its framers consider to be most threatening to the category of humanity. The UCDP dataset is particular concerned with acute forms of violence—it counts only intensive bursts of killing that occur in the same locale and can be attributed to the same cause (Themner 2013). Likewise, the Political Terror Scale (PTS), which attempts to measure levels of authoritarian repression, also counts incidents of human rights abuses executed by members of security forces. However, as its authors acknowledge, it does not count similar acts of violence committed by criminal drug syndicates—which, in a case like Mexico, may be in numbers that rival those caused by state actors (Wood and Gibney 2010: 370). So, methods of counting deaths do not only create and sustain ontological categories. They also make judgements about what kinds of phenomena 'count' within these categories, and how much priority they are given.

Indeed, counting and categorizing deaths also makes it possible to assign them a place within a hierarchy. As I mentioned in the last chapter, Taylor's distinction between the 'hierarchical' world of Judeo-Christian belief and the 'flat' cosmology of Western secularity is rather too severe. Western secularity has its own very pronounced hierarchies and schemas, organized through the dominant logic of instrumental rationality. Through the processes of counting and documentation, the categories of deaths discussed above are assigned a particular place in a hierarchy determined by their numbers. Specifically, they are deemed to be of higher priority when they pass the thresholds discussed above, and move into a new category—for instance, from random killings to 'armed conflict', or perhaps from 'armed conflict' to 'war'. HIICR's 'Conflict Barometer', for instance, measures the 'escalation' and 'de-escalation' of episodes of violence longitudinally across the world. It reports that in 2010 '48 conflicts escalated. Among the escalating cases, 31 crossed the threshold to violence' (HIICR 2009: 3). In other words, as the number of deaths and violent acts rose, these 'conflicts' entered a new ontological category and demanded a different form of response—at least according to the framers of this project. This is why the quantification of deaths is so deeply interlinked with ontology: the perceived scale or magnitude[5] of an episode can determine how it is apprehended and reacted to. Whether or not an episode of violence is perceived as an issue of *international* importance depends upon this process to a large extent. Although there are no hard-and-fast rules to how the magnitude of a particular episode is determined or the precise thresholds which must be crossed, for any event to appear on the 'international plane' 'it must be a *grave* matter, a *serious* breach, cause *material* damage, result in *irrevocable* harm, *shock* the conscience' (Kennedy 2004: 134).

Quantitative measurements of 'bad deaths' make it seem possible to place deaths within different orders of magnitude and to determine whether they qualify as 'international issues'. This also allows potential intervenors to compare episodes of violence to determine whether a new event fits a precedent for which a protocol, guidelines or at least a history of response exists. It moves beyond analogical reasoning, through which international actors (mis)recognize a particular episode as the equivalent of a prior one and respond to it in the same manner (see Khong 1992). Instead of relying on subjective experience, quantifications of deaths seek to offer an objective means of comparing the magnitude of different events. It also enables potential intervenors to compare the severity of different events. For example, the PTS seeks to determine the relative magnitude of various forms of violence enacted by state forces on their citizens across a range of countries. Its authors give the following hypothetical example:

> Imagine that in Country A, security officials storm a labor rally and kill 100 labor union members. In Country B, however, 100 labor union members are arrested and imprisoned, tortured, and then killed. According to the approach of the PTS, the level of political violence in these two countries would essentially be the same.
>
> (Wood and Gibney 2010: 377)

In other words, according to this logic, it is possible not only to document the number of deaths but also to compare different kinds of harm and killing and make equivalencies between them. This way of organizing the deaths documented enables potential intervenors to make judgements about the relative urgency or priority of responses to particular events.

Many projects of this kind are oriented directly towards ranking episodes of violence—that is, in terms of determining which among the 'bad deaths' are the 'worst'. In some cases, implicit assumptions of this kind are stated in the text, glossaries or codebooks of the instruments in question. For instance, the CSP ranks various categories of violence by severity, on a scale from one to seven. To do so, it assesses the degree to which each episode of violence inflicts damage across a range of indicators: fatalities and casualties, resource depletion, destruction of infrastructure, and population dislocations, and perceived psycho-social damage. Similarly, the UCDP/PRIO Database converts its statistics on battle deaths into hierarchical categories: 'minor' designates an episode of violence involving 25–999 battle-related deaths per year; while 'war' (the word itself suggests increased severity) involves at least 1,000 battle-related deaths in a given year (Themner 2013: 7). Similarly, the Global Peace Index (GPI) examines a wide range of factors[6] in order to create a ranking of the most and least peaceful countries in the world. Although this instrument captures whole countries in a specific time period rather than particular episodes of violence, it is oriented towards comparing diverse forms and magnitudes of violence, partially on the basis of deaths and the capacity to cause them.

Another way of ensconcing 'bad deaths' within this framework of meaning is to embed them firmly within Western secular time. This enables intervenors to assess the scale of a particular act of violence in earthly, and specifically human, dimensions (that is, against the human population, or against human historical records). Rather than mythical events removed from the flux of history as part of divine time (see Taylor 2007), spokes in a cyclical wheel of time, or even mere flickers in geological time, episodes of violence are framed as events that punctuate human generations. In other words, they are dispersed across linear, sequential units of time (see Connolly 2011) measured against a human lifespan: for instance, the human generation, the year, day, month, decade or century, or historical epoch.

Conceptualizing violent events in terms of Western secular coordinates of time translates violent events into terms that can be computed by instrumental–rational thinking. Specifically, it allows decision-makers to identify patterns in violence and to predict possible future episodes within the range of human comprehension and response. As I argued in Chapter 1, this particular spatio-temporal framework is the foundation of 'direct access' social structures, on which contemporary intervention is based. So, interpreting episodes of violence in these terms makes it seem possible for humans to intervene in trajectories of violence (I shall return to this idea in the following chapter).

In order to translate 'bad deaths' into Western secular space and time, several projects aggregate numbers of 'bad deaths' longitudinally, measuring deaths each year in each country (that is in 'country years'). This produces a statistical overview of the 'total' amount of death-causing violence in the world at any time (see HSRG 2010). An example of this is the Center for Systemic Peace's longitudinal graphing of deaths caused by violence since 1945 (see Figure 5.1).

Placing 'bad deaths' into a Western secular spatio-temporal framework allows potential intervenors to do two important things. First, it offers them an image of the total quantity of 'bad deaths'—and therefore the magnitude of the threat to the category of humanity—in a comprehensible timeframe. Second, it enables them to make predictions about potential future threats, and to strategize about moments of possible intervention to stop them. To perform these tasks, intervenors require specific, sequential data about the incidence of particular events. Such data makes it appear possible to grasp and manipulate violence through understanding its temporal trajectories, processes and cycles. Indeed, the notion that conflict escalates (and de-escalates) in a cyclical manner is a central tenet of the literature on conflict analysis and transformation (see, for instance, Lederach 2003; Miall 2007). Conceptualizing conflict in linear and (to a certain extent) predictable patterns makes it seem possible to manipulate it. This is to be achieved by paying attention to cycles of conflict as they unfold through time and intervening at moments of transition, escalation or de-escalation to change their courses.

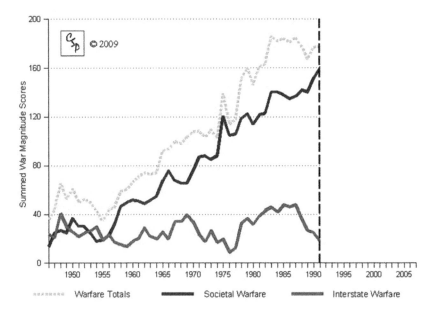

Figure 5.1 Global trends in armed conflict, 1946–1991
Source: Center for Systemic Peace, 2012.

Many sources in the grey literature focus on locating violence within linear, Western secular time. For example, the International Institute for Strategic Studies (IISS 2011) provides very detailed year-by-year timelines consisting of short summaries of events. These entries are placed in a vertical column, with the most recent events added at the top, making it appear as if the deaths in question occurred in a linear, causal trajectory. We can also see this technique at work in 'early warning' instruments and indicators, which are intended to aid in the prediction of episodes of violence. The concept of 'early warning' implies that 'there is no such a thing as a "sudden crisis"; only a lack of information or analysis' (SIPRI 2002: 1). In other words, this approach suggests, the omniscience of instrumental–rational thinking should make it possible to predict every episode of violence, as long as it is used properly. Early warning systems use statistical modelling and computational simulation to predict when and where specific types of large-scale killing may emerge. They aggregate a range of sources, including millions of news reports, the documented behaviours of particular leaders, and the relationship between socio-economic factors such as 'regime type' and gross domestic product (see O'Brien: 2010). For instance, the Continental Early Warning System developed by the African Union is designed to collect newspaper clippings and 'incident reports' across a range of regional offices, to be fed back to a central 'Situation Room' at the AU's headquarters in Addis Ababa. This data is analysed using software designed to assess risk and even map trajectories of violence in 'real time'. This data is then to be used by the chairperson of the Commission 'to advise the Peace and Security Council on potential conflicts and threats to peace and security in Africa and recommend the best course of action' (African Union 2012).

A closely related strategy of re-enchantment is to plot 'bad deaths' within immanent geography. This, along with their placement in Western secular time, places them within the scope of *possible* human action. For this reason, most if not all of the instruments designed to document 'bad deaths' use maps to show their concentration, magnitude, category and timeframe. Maps pull together all of these coordinates and pin them to a particular, earthly location. So, although they represent familiar shapes and names, these are not maps 'of' geographical space so much as they are maps 'of' bad deaths and the threats that these deaths raise to the category of humanity (see Debrix 2007; Shapiro 1997). By providing an 'intervenor's eye' view of the world and of 'bad deaths', these maps mark off the boundaries of 'meaningful' life and identify the points where it is most acutely threatened.

Clear semiotic signals are used to mark off the boundaries of these places. For instance, colour-coding is often used to designate places where 'bad deaths' have happened, or are expected to happen in the near future (see below). For instance, the UCDP provide a map which marks areas affected by 'armed conflict' in red, and countries not actively engaged in armed conflict in a 'neutral' beige tone, intensifying the tone of the colour in relation to the perceived degree of threat.[7] There is a surprising consistency between the chromatic signals used across different maps. Overwhelmingly, concentrations of bad death are shown in increasingly warm or intense colours (usually red, orange, or variations thereof). For example, the maps provided by the Global Peace Index (GPI)[8] and the Center for Systemic Peace (CSP)[9] use a chromatic continuum, with cooler or less intense colours representing more 'peaceful' places, and warmer colours and more dense pigmentation representing concentrations of killing or the threat thereof. Colour-coding taps into an instantly recognizable trope: the 'hotspot'. It also conveys in a simple, immediate way, the categories, comparisons and rankings discussed above. A blot of colour can represent a type of violence or its severity, make equivalencies between very different countries, or indicate the relative urgency of paying attention to different places—all in a single glance.

Embedding bad death in immanent geography and presenting it from an 'intervenor's eye' view also activates the viewer's sense of agency as part of the international social imaginary. As Kennedy puts it:

> On all these maps, the 'international community' is a large and real place ... from this vantage point, the sites of prior international engagement and disengagement loom large ... each stands for a 'lesson', has added or subtracted from the humanitarian policy maker's toolkit of possible solutions ... the map encourages policy makers to think of their

techniques as having shape, potential, potency abstracted from the context of their application.

(2004: 131)

Simply put, these maps place the viewer in the shoes (or control rooms) of intervenors, making it appear as if she can, at a glance, grasp the totality of the threat to humanity. Moreover, she can instantly imagine a range of possible responses and locate these in 'real' time and places. This makes the vast, abstract concept of intervention seem tangible and within human capabilities. So, even if the viewer is not an actual intervenor, these maps of bad death confirm her belief in the possibility of intervention.

Some maps even engage their viewers in the project of re-enchantment—that is, they mobilize them in the process of attributing new meaning to 'bad deaths'. Take, for instance, the interactive map produced by CNN, entitled 'Home and Away: Afghanistan War Casualties'.[10] This map is double-paned: on the left-hand side is a black-and-grey image of the US, and on the right-hand side, a similar image of Afghanistan. The exact location at which each death of a US or Coalition soldier took place is marked out in bright white, displaying the deaths like constellations of stars against a night sky. Along the bottom of the double-paned map are bar graphs which show the age and home state of the casualties, and the pattern of deaths by year. This map is interactive; by clicking on a dot on either the right or left-hand pane, the viewer may draw up personal details about the service people killed, including a photograph, age, information about how they were killed, their military history and a close-up map of the place in which they died. There is also a space for friends, relatives and others to share 'memories and messages' about the individual in question. This map places deaths into firm coordinates of Western secular time and space, individuating them with biographical data. Moreover, it invites its viewers to recognize and attribute these forms of meaning to each death and symbolically to restore meaning to it.

A similar example can be found in the Bosnian War Crimes Atlas (BWCA), a much lower-budget production which nonetheless performs the same function. It uses global positioning information technology (Google Earth) to mark out the individual and mass killings during the 1990s in Bosnia-Herzegovina. This project is intended to function both as a database for information on killings, injuries and violent act to aid in the analysis of conflict. However, it is also framed as 'digital memorial' to the people killed in these wars. On opening the online atlas, one is presented with a standard aerial map of the landscape and topography—including symbols pointing out places of interest related to travel, sightseeing and weather. However, once one clicks the button to zoom in, other symbols appear across the landscape like spatters of blood or bullet marks. Indeed, on zooming closer, one begins to discern their shapes: abstractions of bloodied bodies, skulls and the crosshairs of a sniper's rifle. Each denotes a particular kind of killing or harm: for instance, a black profile silhouetted against a red background refers to 'rape';

a pile of skulls to 'mass grave', and an image of white figures marred by red marks to 'mass murder'. When one clicks on a symbol, a photograph appears of the place of death/disappearance/grave, along with a list of the names of those killed/disappeared, including the surname, first name, name of father and place of birth. In some cases, short videos—including one of a sniper shooting at citizens of then-besieged Sarajevo—are also available. According to the founder and leader of this project, Mirsad Tokača, interviewed just after it was publicly launched:

> We listed all victims by name, we had more than 98 000 recorded deaths in Bosnia ... [the] problem was just to change model, to turn from numbers, into [the] *identity* of victims. Numbers are always something that can be manipulated ... You have, especially in the West, myths about number of killed. [sic] We want to free Bosnian society of these myths, and in turn provide identities, no matter who they are.
>
> (2010)

Tokača's explanation is interesting because it refers directly to the quantification of deaths discussed above, and to their instrumental use. When he claims that numbers can be manipulated, he suggests that they can be exaggerated or minimized in order to support the claims of particular interest groups. Only by restoring individualized coordinates—names, family, the places in which the person lived—is it possible to secure the meaning of these lives. Otherwise, he suggests, they continue to be instrumentalized to the abstract aims of others, not only in death but also long after it.

Both of these projects engage their viewers in the project of re-enchantment in a direct way. They interpellate the viewer as a virtual intervenor, urging her to 'do something' about these 'bad deaths'—if only by acknowledging them, or taking a few minutes to note the names and biographies of a few individuals. Moreover, they encourage the viewer to intervene virtually. As Tokača claims, 'you can use our Bosnian War Crime Atlas to trace around Bosnia, to create your own map of crimes' (2010) by selecting only one category, specific places or particular individuals to appear on the map. In other words, the viewer can make her own calculations of the deaths which she deems to be most interesting or important, then 'click to intervene'—that is, descend virtually to the places where these deaths occurred. The 'click to intervene' function is common to most of the maps I have discussed here; for instance, the GPI also allows viewers to click on a particular country or region in order instantly to draw up data on the deaths and violent acts that have occurred there. This function creates an uncanny simulacrum of 'virtual war' (Ignatieff 2001), in which targets are chosen and commands given through entirely electronic means. However, it also provides a striking visual image of the Western secular cosmos—the world, and specifically, 'humanity' viewed from the *human* intervenor's perspective—and allows individuals symbolically to enact the specific form of agency (intervention) that is central to this framework. In so doing, it not only presents an image of 'bad deaths' on an international scale, but also actively urges individuals to engage in the project of restoring meaning to them.

In some cases, the aim is not to document actual deaths, but rather possible future deaths. This is one of the main techniques through which dehumanization is represented. Indeed, although dehumanization is regularly referred to as a contributing factor to violence, there is no current framework for measuring dehumanization itself, and it does not appear as a factor in the methodologies of the projects discussed above. But these instruments undoubtedly show dehumanization, by demonstrating the vulnerability of certain people to be instrumentalized or killed. In short, they measure dehumanization by visualizing the 'killability' of a certain group of people.

One of the most common ways of imagining dehumanization is through the construction of stereotypes, each of which reduces a group of people to a particular vulnerability—for instance, starvation, rape or displacement. Take, for instance, Amnesty International's (AI) dossier on 'child soldiers'. It consists of a photo of a young, unidentified black child holding a gun and wearing a red military beret, accompanied by the following text:

> Boys and girls are used as soldiers to fight on the front line, as porters, messengers, guards or cooks. They are often seized and forcibly recruited by government forces, armed opposition groups and foreign forces, and are sent to military camps in preparation for armed combat. Conditions in the camps tend to be hard; and the children are often beaten, raped, tortured and deprived of food and sleep.
>
> (Amnesty International 2011)

The text does not relate specifically to the individual child shown in the picture; nor is it even made explicitly clear whether or not he is a 'child soldier' of the kind described above. Rather, the particular child in the picture stands in for a generic vulnerability—being abducted into child soldiering—and becomes a metonym for all of the individuals subjected to it. In this case, it is not the kind of killing or number of deaths that constitutes an ontological category (see above), but rather the possibility of future killing and death encapsulated in the figure of the child soldier, as victim and potential aggressor. Such stereotypes define whole groups of people precisely by the factors that are perceived to dehumanize them (see Kleinman and Kleinman 1996).

In many cases, this kind of stereotyping is applied to whole countries, societies or regime types. The NGO Saferworld, for instance, provides brief 'background' descriptions of the countries in which it works. Consider its briefing for the central Asia region:

> The five CIS countries in Central Asia constitute a distinct sub-region shaped by a shared Soviet legacy in the form of weak democratic institutions and poorly adapting economies, over-centralised and increasingly

authoritarian governments, arbitrary and often disputed borders, and a reliance on highly repressive law-enforcement agencies. These countries also lie strategically at the intersection between Europe and Asia, and consequently provide a transit corridor for various forms of trafficking including narcotics, small arms and migrants, as well as a strategic supply route in support of military operations in Afghanistan.

(Saferworld 2011)

This passage reduces the country in question to a range of structural and institutional factors—'weak democratic institutions and poorly adapting economies', 'authoritarian governments'—that render its citizens vulnerable. It also highlights opportunities for killing (the trade in small arms, the criminal gangs that are involved in narcotics and human trafficking, the supplies en route to Afghanistan). In this case, a whole country is reduced to its vulnerabilities and the killability of its population. Of course, this kind of stereotyping of countries is quite common in international discourses. It is reflected clearly in the statement by Kofi Annan that is credited with inspiring the norm of responsibility to protect. In the quote discussed in Chapter 3, he asks how the international community should respond to 'a Rwanda, to a Srebrenica', and to the 'gross and systematic violations' of human rights that happened in these places in the 1990s. In this sentence, places with rich and diverse peoples, histories and futures are reduced to single horrific acts of genocide and ethnic cleansing. In short, they are equated to 'gross and systematic violations of human rights that affect every precept of our common humanity'. When a place or society is converted into a metaphor for mass killing, it also becomes a comparator against which possible future deaths are measured (Khong 1992). So, whether or not a group of people is considered to be highly 'killable' by potential intervenors depends to a great extent on whether it is deemed to be like 'a Srebrenica' or 'a Rwanda'. Whether it resembles one of these places usually has little to do with its cultural, linguistic, material or natural features, and a great deal to do with the perceived exclusion of its citizens from the category of humanity.

In some cases, however, killability is measured through quantitative instruments similar to those used for documenting 'bad deaths'. It is often measured negatively, by identifying the absence of factors that guarantee high life and prevent dehumanization. The GPI, for instance, claims that 'peaceful' countries:

Have higher per capita income, higher levels of well-being, more freedom, perform better at sustainability, and appear to have a more equitable distribution of social spending ... a peaceful society also allows for a fuller expression of human potential, and in many diverse forms.

(GPI 2011: 5)

The likelihood of being killed or harmed by violence is, in this project, negatively correlated with the incidence of these factors. This is, of course, a rather tautological argument; it suggests that countries that possess these features are less likely to experience large-scale violence, but also that violence destroys these factors.

However, the 'killability' of a population is also measured positively by quantifying the factors that might facilitate large-scale violence. Indeed, although its explicit aim is to measure 'peacefulness' what the GPI actually quantifies is the capability for killing, along with factors that make certain populations more likely to be killed. For instance, it takes into account the number of refugees and displaced people as a percentage of the population, the number of homicides per 100,000 people and the number within each group of 100,000 people who are incarcerated (Institute for Economics and Peace 2010: 6). While the first two groups denote actual or potential victims of violence, the latter implies a connection between incarceration and the overall level of violence in a specific country. Similarly, the HSRG suggests that human security is at its lowest in situations with a high concentration of combatants (who are capable of engaging in violence), large numbers of displaced people (who are capable of being killed) and the lack of critical infrastructure (which might protect the former group from violence, or prevent their death from other causes) (HSRG 2010). Such measurements function by correlating vulnerability and the opportunity or capacity of certain groups (governments, extra-governmental groups or external actors) to kill. An example of this can be found on the online database of the Stockholm International Peace Research Institute (SIPRI 2011). This database allows the reader to search on the basis of indicators such as: armed forces, conventional weapons holdings and military activities; employment in arms production; planned notifiable military activities; arms embargos; arms control and disarmament agreements; and nuclear explosions. In short, this database provides information on each state's capacity to kill its or another state's citizens. It is particularly interesting because it also enables its readers to juxtapose these statistics with a range of qualitative indicators related to quality of life: general demographic statistics, perceptions of corruption, income and economic factors, life expectancy, education and voter turnout. By allowing readers to cross-reference these different categories of data, this source makes it possible to draw direct links between the capacity to kill and the perceived lack of high life—or, in other words, levels of dehumanization.

Through correlations of this kind, several projects attempt to pinpoint specific groups of people who are deemed to be most killable. In some cases, the focus is on regime types or particular features of a society. For instance, the Political Instability Task Force (PITF) model was developed to pinpoint accurately which countries are in imminent danger of violent, large-scale upheaval (Goldstone 2008). To do so, it uses just four variables: 'regime type', 'infant mortality', 'the presence or absence of high levels of discrimination' and 'the number of neighbouring countries with violent conflicts'. In other cases, particular groups of people are identified as future victims of violence— and as currently dehumanized beings. This is exemplified by a graph produced by the NGO Genocide Watch in its 'countries at risk' reports (Genocide Watch 2011),[11] which aims to identify the next victims and perpetrators of this crime. The graph lists groups of 'victims' either in general demographic terms (e.g. women, civilians) or with reference to specific cultural or national groups (e.g. Congo Tutsis, Darfurese). Next to this is a column which specifies 'killers' in the same way (e.g. ex-Rwandan genocidists, mineral warlords, government loyalists). Each country is ranked in terms of the severity of the threat, with seven referring to current massacres, six refers to potential massacres and five refers to the polarization of ethnic groups. The countries are listed in descending order, and each numerical stage is indicated by the ascending warmth of the colour of its background (e.g. seven is red, six is orange and five is yellow). This graph is intended to present to the reader an immediate image of the world's most 'killable' people. The perceived 'dehumanization' of these people is used explicitly as a measurement of the intensity of the threat. By combining stereotypes of vulnerability with measurements of the factors that enable and constrain killing, it frames these groups of people as (soon-to-be-) dehumanized beings. In so doing, it reproduces the effective dehumanization of these groups of people—even though its explicit intention is to help protect them and to affirm their humanity. This, I shall now argue, is a direct outcome of the dialectics of disenchantment–re-enchantment that shape this form of meaning-making.

Making meaning out of violence and the dialectic of disenchantment–re-enchantment

How does the documentation of 'bad deaths' and dehumanization (in the form of 'killability') relate to the dialectic of disenchantment–re-enchantment discussed above? Simply put, each of the forms of meaning-making discussed above is used instrumentally to bring dehumanized lives (back) across the boundary between enchanted and disenchanted beings. Furthermore, each technique involves the kind of instrumental re-enchantment discussed in the previous section—that is, intervenors attempt to invest meaning in beings that they perceive to be disenchanted. The techniques discussed above perform three tasks in this regard. First, they project instrumental–rational meaning onto the deaths in question which, second, allows intervenors to reclaim these lives as part of the Western secular cosmological structure. Third, the project of making meaning out of violence and the deaths it produces activates the specific kinds of agency associated with intervention: the ability to interpose oneself in processes of instrumentalization and dehumanization. Indeed, by making bad deaths and violent acts intelligible within Western secular frameworks of meaning, these instruments enhance their viewers' perceived ability to respond to threats to the category of humanity. As a result, they help to bolster faith in the capacity of human action to respond to secular evils and protect the special status of humanity. Maintaining and enhancing this kind of faith is, as I shall argue in the next chapter, fundamental to the project of intervention.

However, by the same token, the documentation of 'bad deaths' and violence instrumentalizes human lives and (unintentionally) contributes to dehumanization. The instrumental–rational techniques used to document, measure and analyse deaths treat human beings as raw materials for the production of meaning. This is the dark subtext of the phrase 'making meaning out of violence'—just as Western secular people are encouraged to make meaning 'out of' their own lives (see Chapter 3), they extend this principle to the lives of others. Specifically, the lives and deaths of others become fodder for (re)producing the boundary between human and inhuman life, between high life and bad death. Because they use human lives and deaths in this manner, the techniques in question promote direct and effective dehumanization. Direct dehumanization unfolds through the simple act of instrumentalizing 'bad deaths' to processes of meaning-making. As I argued in the previous chapter, it is only by framing certain human lives as disenchanted objects that it becomes possible to treat them instrumentally. I also suggested that the image of the dead body is one of the most powerful tropes of dehumanization. So, by representing millions of human beings as dead bodies (or body counts), these techniques reduce human life to a non-human status. Indeed, even by presenting the deaths in question as other non-human phenomena— numbers, symbols, categories of violence or places on a map, for instance—they produce a directly dehumanizing effect.

These instruments also promote effective dehumanization by encouraging their users to view the beings in question as dead bodies, statistics, symbols, hotspots and so on. This helps to explain why it appears so acceptable to do what might otherwise be considered a morbid or even disrespectful act: trawling through information about the dead, and calculating it in order to inform one's own actions. By reducing human beings to non-human phenomena and subjecting them to instrumental–rational processes, these techniques treat them *as if they were disenchanted*. This removes social inhibitions against instrumentalizing them further—whether for the purpose of planning future interventions to stop violence, for the purposes of education, or simply out of a dilettantish interest.

Moreover, techniques for measuring killability may constitute categorical dehumanization, even though their explicit purpose is usually to prevent it. As I discussed in Chapter 3, the act of 'recognizing' dehumanization is a double-edged sword: simply by identifying certain people as 'beyond the pale' of humanity, one may help to constitute them as such. The techniques discussed above—using stereotypes of people or places, positing correlations between killability and the potential to kill—frame particular groups of people as external to the protected category of humanity. It is crucial to note that they do so in empirical, not normative terms; that is, they represent what they believe to be the case, rather than what they think ought to be. Nonetheless, by defining certain groups of people as excluded from 'juridical humanity' (Esmeir 2006), they affirm the efficacy of this form of dehumanization.

It is also important to note that these instrumental processes of re-enchantment securitize (see Chapter 2) the meaning of human lives and deaths. This means that the project of re-enchantment instrumentalizes dead or 'dehumanized' beings in order to protect the 'fully human' living. Disenchantment is, in a Western secular context, a security threat. Within this framework of belief, being disenchanted makes people vulnerable to violence, which in turn undermines security and order. According to the logic of disenchantment, those beings characterized as mere objects are obvious and easy targets for violence. Moreover, the experience of being treated as a disenchanted object, or of being subjected to instrumentalizing forces beyond their control, may cause people to devalue their own lives. Indeed, the 'no-hopes' discussed by Keane (1996; and see Chapter 1 in this volume) are framed as dehumanized, soulless shells devoid of hope and attachments. Similarly, Taylor argues that young men are particularly drawn to violence:

> When they are unemployed, just hanging around, see no meaningful future for themselves, as in the refugee camps of Palestine. It is the matrices of meaning that their lives are embedded in which offer them the sense of vibrant purpose, which can galvanize them and give significance to their lives.
>
> (2011a: 190)

Taylor's comment is not a simple reiteration of the claim that people living in poverty are more likely to engage in violence because they have 'less to lose'. Rather, it suggests that these individuals have become disenchanted with *themselves*. Because, the argument goes, they believe that their own lives have little meaning, they place less value on them. As a result, the implication is, they are more likely to use their bodies against others in an instrumental way. A similar argument suggests that if one is removed from the structures that make one's life meaningful, or indeed if these structures are removed, one's sense of humanity is lessened (see Coward 2008). As Nordstrom suggests:

> Terror-warfare is predicated on the assumption that if all the supports that make people's lives meaningful are taken away from them, they will be incapacitated by the ensuing disorder ... shorn of political agency.
>
> (1997: 14)

From this perspective, denuded of meaning, the human being becomes a powerless object of systematic violence, stripped of agency and the means to resist. In all of these examples, the basic understanding is that being disenchanted leaves one more vulnerable to violence. Projecting meaning onto dehumanized beings and reclaiming lives 'lost' to violence seems to offer a means of neutralizing this threat. It is aimed at removing or reducing the targets of violence and the conditions of dehumanization that are believed to expedite it. For this reason, it should be understood as part of a broader project of ensuring the security of the 'fully human' living—one which relies on the instrumentalization of the dead and 'dehumanized'.

So, the efforts made to document 'bad deaths', 'killability' and the forms of violence that cause them epitomize the dialectic of disenchantment–re-enchantment, and the way in which this dialectic twists back and redounds upon itself. The apprehension of certain lives as disenchanted prompts a powerful impulse to restore their meaning, but the tools available to intervenors for re-enchantment drive forward the process of disenchantment.

Conclusions

Even if one accepts its basic logic, disenchantment is not a one-way street. On the contrary, just as Western secularity is distinguished by a belief in the possibility of disenchantment, it is also characterized by the powerful impulse to reverse this trend. Indeed, people living within Western secular frameworks abhor the loss of meaning caused by bad death, and seek to close the gaps it tears in the category of humanity. To do so, however, they rely upon a form of meaning-making—instrumental rationality—that has ambiguous implications. Although it is used directly as an instrument for projecting meaning onto disenchanted beings, this form of meaning-making is also the engine of disenchantment. As a result, it drives forward the process of disenchantment that it is intended to combat. The discourses and practices of human security exemplify this dynamic. On the one hand, they embody and promote high life, but the means through which they do so contribute to dehumanization.

We can also see these dynamics at work in the various techniques that are used to make meaning out of violence and to influence the actions of potential intervenors. In this chapter, I examined how the quantification and interpretation of bad deaths and 'killability' constitute a powerful attempt to reclaim lives 'lost' to violence within Western secular schemas of meaning. However, on the other hand, these processes of meaning-making perform direct, effective and categorical dehumanization. The same dynamics occur on a larger and different scale: in practices of security, and the norm of human security in particular. On the one hand, this norm orients security practices towards extending the ideal of high life. But, on the other, it promotes security strategies that reduce human beings to 'mere' biological lives and instrumentalize them thoroughly. Both of these examples, I have argued, are reflections of the dialectic of disenchantment–re-enchantment—or, more simply, of the impulse to re-enchant humanity through Western secular forms of meaning-making. I shall now explore how this dialectic shapes the coercive aspects of intervention—often with deadly results.

Notes

1 African Union Continental Early Warning System; Amnesty International; Bosnian War Crimes Atlas; Center for Systemic Peace; CNN's Database of Battle Deaths

(Iraq and Afghanistan); Fund for Peace/Global Peace Index; Heidelberg Institute for International Conflict Research; Genocide Watch; International Institute for Strategic Studies; Human Security Research Group; Ministry of Defence (UK); North Atlantic Treaty Organization; Political Terror Scale; Saferworld; Stockholm International Peace Research Institute; United Nations High Commission for Refugees; Uppsala Conflict Data Program Encyclopedia; UCDP/PRIO Database of Armed Conflict.

2 The term refers to literature which is neither peer-reviewed academic research nor journalism. It tends to include policy-oriented reports, recommendations, working papers and other sources produced by policy 'experts' or organizations purporting to possess expertise.

3 In this regard, Duffield's work provides a fourth argument for the securitization of the meaning of life. It suggests that wherever life is deemed to be 'excess' and, by virtue of, this 'mere life', it may have destabilizing effects on entire polities.

4 For instance, a surprising number of databases use data produced by the Economist's Intelligence Unit, or by other, similar databases (for instance, the UCDP database is used as a source for several other databases, as are the UN's human development reports and indicators).

5 The exception to this, of course, are the terrorist attacks or assassinations that are considered to be of 'international' concern because of the persons harmed or the country in which they take place, despite killing relatively few people in comparison to wars. However, I am concerned here with the way that violence is triaged in the grey literature rather than in media or government reports.

6 Perceived criminality in society; security and police; homicide; jailed population; access to weapons; organized conflict; violent demonstrations; violent crime; political instability; political terror; weapons imports; terrorist acts; deaths from internal conflict; military expenditure; armed services personnel; UN peacekeeping funding; heavy weapons; weapons imports; military capability; displaced people; neighbouring country relations; conflicts fought; deaths from conflict (external).

7 To view this map, visit: www.ucdp.uu.se/gpdatabase/search.php (accessed 8 August 2013).

8 To view this map, visit: www.visionofhumanity.org/#/page/indexes/global-peace-index (accessed 8 August 2013).

9 To view this map, visit: www.systemicpeace.org/CTfig19.htm (accessed 8 August 2013).

10 Due to the prohibitive costs for reproducing this image levied by CNN, I am unable to reproduce the image here. However, it is freely available at: http://edition.cnn.com/SPECIALS/war.casualties/index.html

11 Due to the prohibitive costs levied by Genocide Watch for permissions to reprint the graph, I am unable to reproduce it here. However, it is freely available on their website at www.genocidewatch.org/images/Countries_at_ Risk_Report_2012.pdf.

6 Angels of death
Logics of killing and letting die in military intervention

When interposing themselves into situations of mass violence, intervenors often assume the role of secular 'angels of death'. They act as agents of death, making decisions from 'on high' (sometimes literally) about who can be killed, who should be allowed to die, and in what circumstances. But they also act as arbiters of the meaning of death, distinguishing between bad death and the exceptions to it. This seems to present a contradiction: how is it possible that there are exceptions to bad death in Western secular cosmology? Death is, on the whole, abhorred by this framework. However, just like all cosmologies, Western secularity has 'its own culture of death' (Asad 2007: 50), which includes a narrow set of circumstances in which killing and dying can be tolerated, and even, in very rare cases, celebrated. These forms of death are tolerated in so far as they confirm the category of humanity, strengthen its boundaries, or ensure that human beings remain on the 'right' side of them.

The determination of which kinds of killing and dying are acceptable has a great deal to do with Western secular *ontology*. In the absence of transcendent explanations of being—for instance, belief in a divine plan, in fate, magic or providence—Western secularity relies entirely on its own immanent ontology. This means that it hinges on the way in which human beings understand the nature of being and act in response to their understandings. Ontology is not just a matter of beliefs about how the world is, or the specific ways in which it manifests itself; these perceptions refer to the *ontic*.[1] Rather, ontology is concerned with the *categories of being* that underlie (or overarch) these ways of being. In a Western secular framework, the power to determine ontology, and the responsibility to do so, is placed entirely in human hands, minds, institutions and forms of meaning-making. The previous two chapters have explored a number of ways in which intervenors engage in ontological projects: by constructing a unique category of humanity through processes of disenchantment; by categorizing 'human' and 'dehumanized' beings; and by maintaining the distinction between high life and bad death. Now, I shall explore how they use ontological strategies to make decisions about who should live, die and be killed. The converse is also true: these decisions help to constitute the ontological categories which they seek to sustain.

In this chapter, I outline four circumstances in which intervenors act as secular angels of death by determining who should die and how. I begin by rethinking the logic of 'letting die' that is so often criticized by proponents of humanitarian intervention. Intervenors often abstain from coercive forms of intervention even when they believe that it might 'save' a substantial number of human lives. This decision is almost always attributed to realist calculations of national interest, the scarcity of resources, will or public support. However, I shall argue that such decisions are shaped by the ontological categories discussed in the previous chapter. Specifically, an episode of violence must cross a particular threshold and enter into specific categories of bad death before it is deemed to be eligible for this kind of response. These categories, in turn, are constituted by the production of a certain number of dead or 'dehumanized' bodies. So, ironically, it is necessary for a certain number of deaths to occur before the kinds of agency associated with military intervention are activated. Moreover, reluctance to intervene is linked to the Western secular belief that human institutions and actors are solely responsible for constituting and protecting the category of humanity. When they fail in this task, there is no resort to theodicy, the anger of deities or the fluctuations of fate; the failure is final and damning. In this context, intervenors cannot be *seen to fail* lest they reduce faith in the ability of human institutions to uphold the category of humanity and belief in its special status. So, in situations where failure is likely, they may place the sustenance of this faith above the protection of individual human lives.

Next, I discuss two situations in which killing is considered 'good' to the extent that it promotes the ideal of high life and bolsters the category of humanity. The first case relates to perpetrators of violence. These individuals are framed as what Agamben (1995) calls 'wolfmen' or 'bandits'. In dehumanizing others, they are understood to have dehumanized themselves, and are placed outside the protected category of humanity. According to Agamben's account, they become 'killable' because they are considered to be 'already dead'. In other words, they are disenchanted beings and so, according to Western secular ethics, there is no absolute prohibition against killing them. However, this logic also encompasses the broader group of beings dehumanized by violence—those deemed to be 'killable' or soon-to-be-dehumanized by large-scale violence (see Chapter 5). They, too, are framed as 'already dead' because they have been pushed outside the boundaries of the category of humanity, or deprived of high life. This leads to rather chilling calculations: the killing of these beings is generally tolerated if it is thought likely to produce a future outcome that supports the ideal of high life. So, for instance, civilian casualties are likely to be tolerated (if not strictly allowed) when the outcome is expected to be the preservation of more lives, or the promotion of a form of government that promotes high life. The deaths of 'dehumanized' beings are understood to be a sunk cost, and so they are often framed as a 'savings' or 'economy' in deaths. Through this logic, the direct killing of perpetrators and victims of violence can be reconciled with Western secular ethics.

Finally, I explore the ethics of killing to 'make life meaningful'. Decisions by intervenors to kill or let die are variously described as biopolitical, necro-political (Mbembe 2003) or 'thanatopolitical' (Agamben 1995). Each of these concepts refers to the attempt to exercise sovereign power by controlling the conditions of death. They help to explain conditions in which Western secular prohibitions against death are overridden. However, there is one exception in which violent death can be understood as a source of positive meaning. This occurs in acts of violence that are understood as expressions of the ideal of human flourishing or authenticity. Such acts are linked to what Walter Benjamin calls 'divine violence'—a form of violence that is a pure expression of human life and its needs and which occupies a grey area between the prohibition of sacrifice and its acceptance. According to Benjamin, divine violence is not a celebration of, or an exhortation to, sacrifice. However, it tolerates a certain amount of sacrifice, just so long as the deaths or harms it produces express the needs of human life. Building on this concept, I examine the circumstances in which intervenors frame their own acts of instrumental violence as ontologically continuous with acts of divine violence carried out by others.

Each of these forms of killing and dying is integral to the Western secular project of re-enchanting humanity through instrumental–rational means, and it reflects the irony of the dialectic discussed in the previous chapter. In short, within Western secular cosmology, it is often deemed necessary to kill or let die precisely in order to uphold the unique meaning of human life. Understanding these exceptions to the rule, therefore, is necessary if we are to appreciate the sources of the contradictions at the heart of contemporary intervention.

Live and let die? Ontological categories, the logic of 'letting die' and 'responsibility to protect'

Decisions on who should be allowed to live and to die are intimately linked with the exertion of power. From Achille Mbembe's perspective, 'the ultimate expression of sovereignty resides, to a large degree, in the power and the capacity to dictate who may live and who *must* die' (2003: 11–12, italics mine). Agamben, on the other hand, suggests that this dictum is reversed in biopolitical forms of sovereignty. He argues that the ability to *make* live and *let* die is the defining expression of power in such conditions. In both cases, the efficacy of the sovereign and its ability to constitute the polity is based on the regulation of death. Building on these ideas, I shall argue that decisions to let die are part of the ceaseless processes through which the category of humanity is forged, redefined and protected. Biopolitical accounts are effective in explaining the dynamics of this process, but they offer little insight into what makes it seem possible and necessary. An understanding of Western secular cosmology provides this missing piece of the puzzle. In a Western secular cosmos, human beings alone are invested with the task of deciding on death—not only who dies, but who can kill, and how. The category of humanity depends on their ability to do so.

This approach helps us to rethink one of the most controversial questions regarding military intervention: why do international actors allow people to die in circumstances in which this kind of intervention might be, or have been, possible? The imperative placed on international organizations to 'do something' in the face of mass violence has produced a powerful but seemingly contradictory amalgam of humanitarianism and militarism (see Rieff 2002; Kennedy 2004). Paradoxically, its proponents demand the use of force to end violence.[2] Yet although the demand for intervention has increased dramatically in the post-Cold War period (see Chapter 1), full-scale military interventions are heavily constrained and relatively infrequent, and it is presumed that states are unlikely to intervene to save the lives of others.

Why is this the case? I shall explore this problem by examining the role of ontological categories and thresholds in the responsibility to protect. I do not wish to overstate the efficacy of this norm; responsibility to protect is not formally embedded in international law, and, despite frequent references to its rhetoric in the media it is difficult to prove whether or not it has had any concrete effect on interventions since the early 2000s. It is also important to note that the thresholds indicated in responsibility to protect are not novel in themselves; rather, they are recent instantiations of a long line of frequently changing thresholds for intervention, at least within Western European states (see MacFarlane and Khong 2006; Chesterman 2001). However, this norm reflects both the continuity of the use of ontological thresholds of violence throughout the history of IR and the current Zeitgeist surrounding how these categories are defined. In addition, the influence and appeal of responsibility to protect lies in its powerful rhetoric of refusal to allow large numbers of people to be killed in episodes of mass violence. Therefore, it is crucial to understand that, and why, this norm and the logic behind it *demands* that large numbers of people must die before military intervention can be contemplated.

If we accept the realist[3] logic of the framers of responsibility to protect, states refuse to intervene to save their own citizens or those of other countries for straightforward reasons. Specifically, they contend, international politics remains dominated by a brand of realism in which states rarely act 'altruistically'; they will engage in costly action only if it furthers their own national interests or ambitions for dominance. Conversely, there is great concern among critics of military intervention that it is an instrument for extending the power of dominant states under the thin guise of 'humanitarian' intentions (see, for instance, Ayoob 2004; Chandler 2003, 2004). However, according to the assumptions of the norm's founders, it also comes down to a calculation of resources—financial, human and moral. Political will, resources—and of course the willingness to die in 'someone else's war' (see Chapter 3)—are scarce commodities, and states competing for survival and dominance are unlikely to spend them generously. Setting the thresholds for intervention too widely, they reasoned, would enable states either to complain that the norm required far too much of them, or to use it as a specious excuse for military adventurism. From this perspective, maintaining the efficacy of the norm required constraining it quite narrowly. As one of the ICISS commissioners, Gareth Evans, puts it:

> If R2P is to be about protecting everybody from everything, it will end up protecting nobody from anything. The whole point of embracing the new language of the 'responsibility to protect' is that it is capable of generating an effective, consensual response in extreme, conscience-shocking cases … we need to preserve the focus and bite of R2P as a rallying cry in the face of mass atrocities.
>
> (2008: 294)

In other words, military responses should be reserved for those situations of 'extreme' violence, 'mass atrocities', and 'conscience shocking' cases in which 'humanity itself' is deemed to be at stake. These are cases in which not 'just' specific human lives, but the *ontological* status of humanity, is threatened by violence.

But how can one determine when an episode of violence qualifies as 'shocking' (and to whose conscience)? For many reasons—including the difficulty of formulating firm definitions and attaining agreement upon them (see Bellamy 2010)—the framers of responsibility to protect do not provide criteria for determining such cases. Beyond the pragmatic obstacles to setting such criteria, the framers of responsibility to protect confronted two fears related to the creation of unambiguous criteria. On the one hand, these criteria might be used as 'triggers'—that is, as soon as a certain number of deaths occur, intervenors might interpret this as licence to engage in military intervention (perhaps even without UN Security Council approval, which might become redundant if such criteria were set). Alternatively, certain states might then be compelled to intervene against the wishes of their leaders or electorate. The potential for criteria to act as a 'trigger' would preclude the normative debate and pragmatic strategizing which is considered necessary to international decision-making. On the other hand, setting a specific numerical boundary might exclude the possibility of intervention in cases of 'serious' violence that nonetheless did not meet the criteria. This hypothesis sheds new light on the curious category of 'large-scale ethnic cleansing' specified as a '*responsibility to protect* crime'. Surely the enormity of ethnic cleansing lies in the intent forcibly to separate or remove members of a minority ethnic group from a particular place, not in the scale at which this is carried out. In other words, the crime should be considered to be equal whether it is plotted against a group numbering 100 or a group numbering in the millions. Yet, as I have discussed above, perceptions of scale are deeply embedded in the categorization and prioritization of particular kinds of violence. This means that, if a particular numerical threshold were set, there would be no scope for extending the norm to cover acts of ethnic cleansing against a smaller group of people, or carried out on a less ambitious scale. So, there are good reasons not to set hard-and-fast criteria for the thresholds in question. But at the end of the day, this means that whether a situation poses a threat to 'humanity itself' is largely down to collective perception and judgement.

The categories discussed in Chapter 4 play a crucial role in this context. They provide ontological thresholds at which a certain number of deaths 'become' a war, a genocide or a crime against humanity in the eyes of possible intervenors. Moreover, they determine the order of magnitude of a particular violent event, enabling intervenors to discriminate between those which threaten the category of humanity as a whole. These ontological categories, I shall now argue, play an important role in determining decisions on military intervention, along with conscious calculations of national interest. They condition responses to events happening at the level of the ontic—that is, the level in which humans perceive what is 'out there' in the world—before rational deliberation even comes into play.

Responsibility to protect offers four 'threshold' concepts—war crimes, crimes against humanity, genocide and 'large-scale ethnic cleansing'. Its framers take pains to emphasize that the occurrence of these events is not a 'green light' for military action; it simply marks the threshold at which this kind of intervention should be considered as a matter of urgency. Indeed, these categories were deliberately selected for their capacity to provoke an immediate response. According to Evans, the function of the responsibility to protect is to condition the responses of potential intervenors such that:

> When the next conscience-shocking case of large-scale killing, or ethnic cleansing, or other war crimes or crimes against humanity come along … the immediate reflex response of the whole international community will be not to ask *whether* action is necessary, but *what* action is required, by whom, when and where.
>
> (2008: 289)

The categories on which responsibility to protect is based, then, are designed to act as automatic stimuli of a desire to respond. From this perspective, they are a valuable expedient for action intended to 'save' human lives. However, at the same time, the stimuli on which they rely are the deaths of, or harms to, humans. So, ironically, the thresholds created to spur possible intervenors to action are rooted in the logic of 'letting die'.

To understand why, it is necessary to delve deeper into the ontological work done by the processes of counting discussed in the previous chapter. Alain Badiou's (2007) account of ontology is useful in this regard. For Badiou, ontology is quite literally a matter of counting. He argues that the human world is composed of metaphysical machines which count every phenomena (or 'multiple') that 'presents' itself in the realm of human perception. Some of these phenomena are 'represented'—that is, they are recognized and reproduced as 'real things' within human institutions, perceptions, language and forms of action. Because this process is based on repetition and oriented towards stability, Badiou argues that those phenomena which are already represented in the world are more likely to be represented again; in other words, ontological novelty and change are rare and difficult to bring about. However, at the same time, ontology is always in formation and never entirely completed. The constant process of counting allows for the stability on which human life is based, but also the *possibility* of multiple futures and radical change (which I shall discuss in the following chapter).

For the present argument, the important thing to take from Badiou's approach is that counting is an ontological act: what is represented is real for humans, and what is not exists only as a disruption or an anomaly. This account mirrors the process, discussed in Chapter 4, in which categories of bad death and 'dehumanization' are formed. As I argued, the simple act of counting dead or injured human bodies literally brings into being categories such as 'armed conflict' or 'genocide'. In this context, a certain number of dead or harmed bodies must be 'presented' *and* 'represented' within the social imaginary of the international as evidence of 'armed conflict' or genocide' in order for them to come into being as such.

The circumstances in which these categories are formed poses an ontological problem for intervenors. Specifically, the process of becoming is diachronic, or unfurls over time, while the categories themselves are synchronic, or based on a particular 'snapshot' of time. Take, for example, the threshold concept of 'war crimes', which, according to the Geneva Conventions, involves acts of 'wilful killing, torture or inhumane treatment' that might occur through unlawful deportation, transfer, expropriation and other offences. Whether or not these crimes have occurred depends on their being enacted. Similarly, in order to punish a criminal for genocide, it is necessary to demonstrate both the 'mental' intention to destroy a group in whole or in part, *and* actions taken to *realize* this aim.[4] In other words, the existence of genocide requires the *completion* of an intentional act, whether the act is killing, rape, psychological torture, the forcible removal of children or the destruction of the conditions of a group's reproduction or the planning or incitement of these acts. Moreover, the formal definition of genocide refers to attempts to destroy a particular kind of group (national, ethnic, racial or religious) 'in whole or in part'. The concept of 'in part' presents a particular difficulty in this context— at what point can it be determined that a 'part' of a group has been destroyed, and how much of the group constitutes a 'part'? In other words, how many people have to be harmed or killed before this threshold has been reached?

When an episode of violence is unfolding, determinations about such thresholds must be made in real-time if intervention is to be effective. Yet legal principles like these are designed to work in two temporal contexts: either before an act occurs, to prohibit specific actions, or after they have occurred, to punish them. They are less useful in the middle of an episode, in which it is unclear (in an ontological sense) whether what is taking place is,

say, a 'low-intensity conflict' or an 'atrocity'. Because the categories to which
they respond emerge from the diachronic 'presentation' of violence and its
'representation' in categories, intervenors can never be precisely sure of when
an act may cross a threshold into a different category. This may lead to a
failure among some potential intervenors to appreciate the severity of the
harm in question, or to disagreement about whether a particular kind of
event has taken place. As Evans points out, the urgency or severity of a
particular episode of violence is 'always harder to convey at the crucial stage
of prevention than it is after some actual horror has occurred' (2008: 71).
Because the process of counting and the creation of categories of violence is
diachronic, potential intervenors are constantly re-calibrating their counts to
different categories. But the decisions, calculations and legal judgements they
must make are diachronic—that is, they must determine when the line
between one category and another has been crossed in conditions that are
constantly shifting. Moreover, they must try to anticipate whether and when a
threshold might be crossed that would move an act of violence into a different
order of magnitude.

   The logic of letting die operates in this gap between synchronic categories of
violence and the diachronic process of counting in which these categories
emerge. Norms such as responsibility to protect and legal documents such as
the Geneva Conventions demand certainty that a particular act has occurred,
and that it is sufficiently severe to warrant international action, before a
military response could be legitimately considered. As Weiss argues, the
threshold of 'seriousness' that must be crossed before intervenors can consider
taking military action under the rubric of responsibility to protect is quite
high (2004). While previous iterations of the norm suggested that murder,
slavery, imprisonment or the overthrowing of democratic regimes might constitute such threats, the final version of responsibility to protect restricted its
thresholds to direct and very large-scale forms of killing. Even in cases where
widespread suffering and abuse is evident, the framers of this norm demand a
high degree of certainty that one of the crimes it specifies will take place. For
example, Evans claims that prior to the US intervention in 2003, Iraq would
have been 'on anybody's [responsibility to protect] *watchlist*' (2008: 295, italics
mine) due to the strong evidence of systematic abuse of citizens by the
Baathist state. However, he claims, Iraq was not experiencing any of the four
'responsibility to protect crimes' at the time of intervention:

> Although there were clearly significant human rights violations continuing
> to occur … such crimes were neither actually occurring nor apprehended
> as being likely to occur when the coalition invaded the country in early
> 2003.
>
> (Evans 2008: 295)

This suggests that a strong burden of proof—and of certainty—is placed
upon intervenors if they wish to take action that is considered to be legitimate

within the 'international community'. As a result of this logic, intervenors must 'let' a certain number of people die or be harmed before they can make the persuasive claim that a particular threshold has been crossed (although this number, too, is not predetermined). Although a person can be retroactively tried simply for planning or inciting genocide even before any killing takes place, there is no parallel norm that suggests that pre-emptive military intervention can be justified unless genocide is very likely to be *realized*.

Moreover, because there are no hard-and-fast rules for defining the categories in question (or, indeed, for counting), different actors may arrive at the perception that a particular category of violence has emerged before others do. This may have contributed to the UN's foot-dragging over its response to escalating killing in Rwanda in 1994. Several high-profile actors and advocates labelled the acts in question as 'genocide' relatively early in its trajectory, but the categorization of the violence was fiercely debated in the public forums and backrooms of the UN. Barnett (2010) suggests that this was, for the US at any rate, a deliberate and very political choice. Admitting that a genocide was under way would have committed it to another costly and potential deadly intervention, which they sought to avoid after the previous year's doomed excursion into Somalia. From this perspective, it seems obvious that this misinterpretation of the situation was an act of outright denial. However, the argument outlined above suggests that there might also have been a genuine disjuncture between the beliefs of different actors, some of whom believed the threshold of 'genocide' to have been crossed at a much earlier point in time than others. The ambiguity of these thresholds in question not only allows for inconsistencies of this kind, but may also be exploited by states or organizations opposed to intervention.

So, reliance on human-made ontological categories places intervenors in a bind. In order to uphold the norms of the international community, they must abstain from military action until they have a degree of certainty that a particularly horrible act is taking place, or is imminent. However, as Ramesh Thakur points out, in cases of emergent violence, 'if [they] wait until [they] have] certainty ... then irreversible damage may already have been caused' (2002: 336).

This analysis is not intended to discount the power of national interest or the politics of isolationism in deterring intervention. It is certainly not intended to let any state or international organization off the hook for its (in) actions in the face of violence. What it suggests is that even in an ideal situation in which realist calculations and political factors did not come into play, intervenors would still most likely allow many people to die before taking action. The reasons for this are embedded deeply in Western secular cosmology—specifically, the idea that human institutions and forms of meaning determine ontology, and the processes through which this occurs. The lack of transcendent ontological categories and means for determining them means that intervenors are constantly engaged in the project of deciding on the thresholds of these categories. In a totally immanent framework, human actions—such as large-scale violence—can alter these categories rapidly, and intervenors must try to respond in real time. Given the legal and moral constraints placed on military intervention in particular, there is strong pressure for intervenors to wait for ontological certainty that might never arrive. So, rather than lapsing into realist explanations or apologias for inaction, this argument suggests that we need to pay attention to the ontological conditions in which decisions to let die take place if this problem is to be addressed.

Killing and letting die in the name of 'humanity'

In the wake of the Rwandan genocide, Michael Barnett, who had worked for the US Mission to the UN during that time, began to question his own actions. During the period in which he held this post, he was initiated into its norms and protocols, and became deeply invested in the UN as a source of meaning and value. According to Barnett, his sense of self became so bound up with that of the UN that he ultimately became 'more committed to the survival of the UN than [he] was to the Rwandans' (2010: 134) and found himself advocating policies that militated against a larger and more timely intervention by the United States. But Barnett was not alone. He:

> Began to question why [he], along with so many others ... had so quickly concluded that the needs of the UN overrode the needs of those who were the targets of genocide. Why, for instance, had neither the Secretariat nor any member state vigorously petitioned the Security Council to assemble an intervention force? Why were most member states apparently more exercised by the need to restrain the UN from any further involvement than they were by the need to dispatch assistance? How did the desire to protect the UN's reputation become a justification for not intervening?
>
> (Barnett 2010: 121–2)

These questions cut to the core of the logic of killing and letting die in the name of 'humanity'. Barnett's reflective response to these questions suggests that this kind of perverse outcome occurs as the result of acculturation into bureaucratic modes of reasoning and identification with an organization. This certainly seems to explain *how* a committed humanitarian might arrive at this state. However, I want to argue that there is also a deeper motivation for prioritizing the survival of the UN (or other major international actors) above the lives of particular people—whether this occurs through the failure to intervene, or the readiness to do so. This reason is directly linked to Western secular ontology, and the need to maintain faith in human organizations.

So far, I have argued that the logic of letting die has a great deal to do with Western secular ontology, and in the way that categories of violence are produced through human, instrumental–rational means. I have argued that, in

Western secular cosmology, human actors and institutions are responsible for creating and sustaining the unique category of humanity (see Chapter 1). They are not mere agents of divine will, but rather the sole arbiters of the meaning of life, and the only source of resistance against total disenchantment. However, because it is purely immanent and makes no references to divinity, Western secularity relies entirely on people perceiving its tenets as real and true, and acting on this basis.[5] In a totally immanent context, where there is no recourse to the mysteries of the transcendent, theodicy or fate, what happens on earth determines people's belief. So, those tasked with protecting the category of humanity must sustain popular belief in this category, and in their ability to define and protect it, through their own actions. In order to generate and maintain belief, these actions must be—and be seen to be—effective.

In these circumstances, potential intervenors often deem it necessary to let some people die in order to protect the category of humanity and secular 'faith' in the institutions that seek to protect it. Specifically, intervenors feel compelled to choose between protecting the category of humanity and safeguarding the lives of individual members thereof. Although it is usually left implicit, this distinction is deeply embedded within discussions of intervention. It is reflected in Walzer's (2004) work, which makes a subtle distinction between human lives, and human ways of life, or modes of being. If they fail in the latter task, he avers:

> We face a loss that is greater than any we can imagine, except for the destruction of humanity itself. We face moral as well as physical extinction, the end of a way of life as well as a set of particular lives, the disappearance of people like us.
>
> (Walzer 2004: 43)

This short passage highlights the ontological challenge faced by intervenors working within a Western secular belief system. Walzer refers to a number of nested categories, each of which represents a different order of magnitude: from 'a set of particular lives', to a 'way of life' or a 'people like us', to 'humanity itself'. His statement also illustrates the perceived distinction between threats at the level of the ontic and the ontological. Threats at the *ontic* level place particular people and social configurations in danger (and I would argue that 'ways of life' also fits within this category).[6] Meanwhile, threats at the level of *ontology* jeopardize whole categories of being. The loss of the latter is quite literally, according to Walzer, the worst thing that can be imagined, and all other losses must, by definition, be lesser in magnitude. Walzer presents this statement as a matter of fact and feels no need to elaborate it. Throughout the literature and public discourses on intervention, similar statements can be found—nothing is deemed to be worse than the loss of the unique category of humanity, and all other harms are assumed to be lesser. This argument can be a powerful means of overcoming aversion to military forms of intervention. Indeed, Walzer contends that, when confronted with the ultimate ontological threat—the loss of 'humanity itself', or a subcategory thereof—'we may be driven to break through the moral limits that people like us normally attend to and respect' (2004: 43).

In other words, the threat of ontological destruction produces a space of exception, in which actions that directly contravene Western secular beliefs about life and death (not to mention laws and conventions) may be acceptable. In order to create this space, intervenors must establish that threats to a particular group of people constitute threats to an overarching ontological category. This can be done in several ways. Perhaps most commonly, intervenors frame the referent object as 'humanity itself', or make explicit linkages between the destruction of some people, or a way of life, and the category of humanity. In this vein, the ICISS report (2001) argues that it is not states or specific ethnic, cultural or demographic groups that are at stake if large-scale killing is 'allowed' to unfold unopposed, but the entire category of humanity. This logic also suggests that protecting one subset of the category of 'humanity' has implications for the broader category.

Crucially, if threats to a particular group of people at the ontic level can be reconstituted as ontological threats to humanity, the task of protection becomes a reflexive one. This idea is expressed in the following quote from Henry Kissinger in the wake of the failed 1994 US-led intervention in Somalia:

> 'Humanitarian intervention' asserts that moral and humane concerns are so much a part of American life that not only treasure but *lives* must be risked to vindicate them; in their absence, American life would have lost some meaning.
>
> (quoted in Wheeler 2000: 203)

On first glance, this statement appears to express solidarity with the lives of the individuals killed in Somalia, or with Somalis as a group of people. The notion that American lives would 'lose meaning' if protective action were not taken seems to emphasize the equality of these lives. On closer inspection, however, the logic of this statement is far less altruistic, and it is certainly not a deontological argument. Somali lives are valued not in themselves, but because the threat to them has been (at least for Kissinger) successfully constituted as an ontological threat to humanity. By this reasoning, giving American lives to protect Somalis is an act of *self-protection*: Americans must protect the category of humanity, threatened by the deaths of Somalis, in order to protect the meaning of their own lives. In order to activate this kind of response, it is necessary for *ontic* threats to a specific group of people to be constituted as evidence of an *ontological* threat to 'humanity itself'. So, the powerful compulsion to protect the category of humanity can either spur on military intervention or preclude it. The deciding factor is whether or not the threat to a group has been constituted as an ontological threat to 'humanity itself', or an ontic threat to a specific group of people.

What Walzer's account does not reflect is the potential for conflict between the ontic and ontological—that is, between the desire to protect particular groups of people and the impulse to protect 'humanity itself'. Indeed, in some cases, the need to protect the latter produces powerful disincentives for intervention.

The reason for this is closely related to the problem of secular faith. An important way in which intervenors invoke the idea of 'humanity itself' is to posit themselves as its agents, collective embodiments and guardians. The actions taken by these entities are, therefore, framed as actions of, or on behalf of, 'humanity'. This idea has exerted a powerful influence on contemporary discourses of intervention. Indeed, according to Vivienne Jabri, the current ethical climate suggests that 'the wars of the future, the only wars that can be fought legitimately, are those that may clearly and unambiguously claim humanity as their ultimate purpose' (2007: 80). By acting ostentatiously (and effectively) in the name of 'humanity', these organizations constitute themselves as its ontological guarantors. This helps to explain the desire of international organizations to take decisive action in response to large-scale violence. According to Chandler (2004), military intervention offers states and international organizations opportunities to justify their existence and empower themselves. This drive, too, could be explained away by the realist dictum that actors in a competitive system will always seek to maximize their power and attain dominance. But it is also reflective of the need of these organizations to generate and sustain belief in their ability to act on an ontological level to safeguard 'humanity itself'.

The stakes of assuming this role are high. Acting efficaciously confirms both the category of humanity and the power of human agency—particularly the ability to intervene in trajectories of violence. But failure to prevent or reverse the disenchanting effects of violence can undermine secular faith (see Chapter 2) in both of these entities. For this reason, intervenors must maximize the situations in which they can intervene in a way that successfully upholds the category of humanity. However, they must also minimize the situations in which their efforts or capabilities are shown to be unequal to this task.

This logic can help to explain decisions for and against military intervention. The first case arises when states or international actors successfully equate threats to a particular group of people as threats to humanity, and feel confident of their ability to address them. Consider the now-famous comments of former British Prime Minister Tony Blair in relation to the decision to bomb Kosovo in 1999:

> The moral purpose was very simple. A gross injustice had been done to people, right on the doorstep of the European Union, which we were in a position to prevent and reverse … The bottom line was we couldn't lose. If we lost, it's not just that we would have failed in our strategic objective … [we would have] failed in terms of the moral purpose—we would

have dealt a devastating blow to the credibility of NATO and the world would have been less safe as a result of that.

(BBC 2002)

In this quote, Blair clearly emphasizes the degree to which he felt NATO was acting 'in the name of humanity' (or, in his terminology, in the name of 'people'). But he does not frame this as a good in itself. Rather, he argues that doing so was necessary if the 'credibility' of NATO and the moral structures for which it claimed to be fighting were to be upheld. In other words, intervening in this context (in which NATO's victory was quite decisive) helped to increase secular 'faith' not only in NATO, but also in its status as a moral actor and agent of 'humanity'.

However, this kind of reasoning can also work the other way—it can help to explain what Chesterman (2001: 163) calls 'inhumanitarian non-intervention'. This term refers to cases in which potential intervenors abstain from decisive action even when it appears to contravene their guiding principles or commitment. This is not entirely reducible to hypocrisy, inconsistency, or realist calculations. It may also occur in cases in which the likelihood of unsuccessful intervention threatens to diminish belief in the agency of intervenors, and faith in the robustness of the category of humanity. Barnett's account of the debates among UN decision-makers during the Rwandan genocide (see above) offers an example of such a case. He suggests that these debates were coloured by an intense fear that an *ineffective* military intervention might undermine the credibility of the UN. The case of Rwanda seemed to raise a double threat in this regard: it was possible, particularly from the US perspective, that a large military intervention might fail to protect Rwandan victims *and* result in the deaths of US citizens. From Barnett's perspective, the UN was leery of intervening in a decisive way lest it undermine its own credibility. In the case of the UN—more so, perhaps, than in the case of states or military organizations such as NATO—this credibility relies on the ability to embody and uphold the value of human life and the category of humanity. So, issues of shame, fear of failure and political costs almost certainly entered into the process of decision-making. Prohibitions against bad death, the desire to avoid 'body bags' for domestic political purposes, economic constraints and the hubris of international organizations all play their part. But, just as I argued above, even in hypothetical, ideal conditions in which these factors played no role, the same logic of letting die would most likely emerge. This is because intervenors may perceive a conflict between protecting 'humanity itself' and safeguarding particular people, and opt for the former.

The analysis presented here does not explain why particular episodes of violence are constituted as ontological threats while others are not in every case, nor the specific conditions in which certain course of action are deemed necessary to maintaining secular faith in intervenors. However, it does suggest that Western secular ontology plays a very important role in determining situations in which military intervention takes place or does not. Beneath all of the pragmatic considerations and realist politics surrounding intervention lurks the fear that humanity might lose faith in intervenors—and therefore in itself. And, if this happened, then whom or what would protect the category of humanity, or differentiate it from a 'disenchanted' universe? Within a Western secular framework, there is little willingness to find out.

Necessary evils: calculations of necessity and economies of death

For the most part, dying and killing are anathema within Western secular cosmology. However, there are a few very particular circumstances in which killing is accepted, if not welcomed or lauded. One of these is the killing of beings deemed to be 'dehumanized'. These beings fall through a loophole: the Western secular prohibition against killing applies to human beings, but dehumanized beings are, by definition, not considered to be fully 'human'. As such, killing them does not quite add up to killing 'full' human beings, at least within the Western secular logic of killing and letting die. 'Dehumanized' beings are considered to be, in an important sense, 'already dead' (see Butler 2009); that is, it is understood that if nothing were done, they would most likely die or be killed imminently. So, their deaths are treated as 'sunk costs'— costs which may be offset by actions that could protect other lives or move them onto the 'right' side of the human–non-human divide. As a result, casualties produced by military intervention are calculated as net 'savings' in deaths, rather than excesses. This exception to the prohibition against killing does not condone the systematic elimination of 'dehumanized' beings. But it does not condemn the incidental killing of some 'dehumanized' beings if this is deemed to be necessary in order to protect or produce 'fully human' beings.

Justifications of 'humanitarian violence' are often calculated terms of *necessity*—that is, the degree to which intervenors are compelled to act violently in order to protect the category of humanity. They are also shaped by understandings of *proportionality*, which suggests that the force used should not exceed what is 'necessary' in order to halt the harms in question (see Walzer 2004). This principle presumes that a certain amount of force is required, and that the harms it causes must be measured against the possible gains it might achieve. It presumes that different kinds of harms are commensurable and substitutable: that is, that harms of one kind can be offset by goods of another kind. Together, these principles create a logic in which 'humanitarian violence' and the harming of victims of dehumanization are framed as a 'necessary evil' (Weizman 2011).

The logic of the 'necessary evil' plays a central role in decisions on intervention. Asad argues that 'the humanitarian discourse that denounces unnecessary suffering rests on assumptions both of what is unnecessary and of what constitutes suffering' (2007: 32). Some of these are viewed as 'an affront to humanity', and their elimination is sought. These forms of suffering, he argues, are 'distinguished from the kind of suffering that was *necessary* to the process of realizing one's humanity—that is, pain that was adequate to its end, not *wasteful* pain' (Asad 2003: 111). Treating pain as a quantifiable substance, he avers, makes possible to think about human suffering in relation to the proportionality of means and ends. In other words, it enables inter-venors to consider precisely how much suffering of one kind they are willing to cause in order to prevent suffering of another kind. If the latter kind of suffering is deemed wasteful and harmful to the category of humanity as a whole, then the former kind may be deemed justifiable as long as it is deemed to be lesser. This is the kind of logic that underpins the notion of 'pro-portionality' in just war theory—that is, the idea that the use of violence is justifiable as long as it does not exceed the amount of harm that it is intended to prevent. This approach also implies that certain kinds of harms can be offset by gains—that is, that the killing of *some* civilians might be offset by the protection of a larger group of lives.

This logic of killing is often applied to the harms that occur in the course of 'humanitarian' military intervention. The violence used to carry out this kind of intervention is deemed 'necessary' in so far as it is used to halt or reverse episodes which threaten the category of humanity (see above). In this regard, harms to *some* people are deemed to be offset by the protection of broader categories of people, and of the category of humanity itself. Moreover, these casualties can be more easily justified in the calculation of 'necessity' because they appear to be 'cost neutral', and therefore cannot be considered 'wasteful' or 'excessive'. This occurs because killing or harming those groups of people identified as 'dehumanized' or 'killable' are framed as lives already lost; while saving them is ideal, losing *some* of them does not necessarily undermine the aims of the intervention. Indeed, the goal of intervenors is to minimize the loss of these lives, not to prevent it entirely. Therefore, inter-vention is a matter of deciding who *can* die or be killed, and in what numbers, before the aims of intervention become moot.

For instance, responsibility to protect identifies categories of people whom they deem to have been rendered 'killable' by the structural conditions in which they live. The framers of this norm exhort intervenors to 'protect the villager from murder, the woman from rape, and the child from starvation or being orphaned' (Thakur 2002: 328). The strong presumption here is that, in the absence of international action, these specific groups of people would certainly succumb to the fates assigned to them (rape, murder and starvation). This framing makes it possible to underwrite the potential killing or harming of members of these groups as the collateral damage of military intervention. The reasoning is as follows: had nothing been done to save these *categories* of people, then they would all have died/been raped/starved anyway. If an action might harm specific *subsets* of this category, but can preserve the category as a whole, then it is considered justifiable (even if not desirable). This logic is alluded to by Thakur:

> Intervention for human-protection purposes is carried out so that those condemned to die in fear may be rescued to live in hope instead. Even so,

military intervention, even for humanitarian purposes, is just a nicer way of referring to the use of deadly force on a massive scale.

(2002: 333)

In other words, the 'deadly force' required by humanitarian intervention is accepted because it promises to protect at least some of those 'condemned to die in fear' and to restore meaning and 'hope' to their lives. That is, by this account, a certain amount of coercive force is tolerable because it may move a large group of people to the 'right' side of the boundary between the human and the non-human. So, the secular 'evil' of violence is tolerated here because it is believed to be proportional to the good that it can achieve, and necessary in order to achieve this goal.

I most certainly do not mean to suggest that intervenors deliberately attempt to kill members of these groups, or view their deaths as desirable. Nor, once again, do I mean to justify the killing of civilians that attends military action of any kind. My aim is to shed light on the logic that enables intervenors to kill 'in the name of humanity' without viewing their actions as hopelessly contradictory. As Weizman (2011) articulately argues, military intervention is not a matter of choosing the 'best possible world', but rather the 'least possible evil'. In other words, it is not a matter of eliminating deaths and harms, but rather of economizing on them, and of deciding which are 'necessary'. Since 'dehumanized' beings are considered to be sunk costs, it is *possible* (if not desirable) for intervenors to kill them without undermining the basic Western secular prohibition against bad death. This helps to explain why the concept of 'humanitarian violence' is paradoxical, but not impossible, in a Western secular framework. Now, I shall examine two of the ways in which this kind of violence is used.

'Killing to make life meaningful': 'divine violence' and 'good death'

Above, I have discussed the context in which *incidental* or indirect deaths in the course of military intervention are tolerated. However, in some cases, the violence of intervenors is actually lauded, even if it involves killing. How is this possible in a Western secular framework, which abhors sacrifice? There is an exception to this prohibition. Specifically, violence on the part of intervenors is often celebrated if it is framed as a positive expression of the ideal of high life, or as an effort to constitute or bolster the category of humanity. In the context of military intervention, Jabri argues, violence 'comes to form the constitutive basis of a cosmopolitan law that binds humanity' (2007: 80). In other words, the act of killing itself is constitutive of the category that differentiates humanity from the 'disenchanted' universe and guarantees its unique meaning. This is not just 'killing to make life live' (Dillon and Reid 2009), but rather 'killing to make life meaningful'. In these circumstances, violence and re-enchantment converge.

There are several circumstances in which killing on the part of intervenors may be framed in this way. First, intervenors may kill actors who are deemed to be perpetrators of dehumanization, and therefore direct threats to the integrity of the category of humanity. This kind of killing overlaps with the calculation of 'economies of death' discussed above. Specifically, perpetrators of dehumanization are viewed as 'sunk costs' by virtue of their exclusion from the category of humanity; because they are deemed to be inhuman, killing them raises few ethical qualms. Moreover, because they constitute overt threats to the category of humanity, their killings are celebrated as triumphs of human intervention and affirmations of the category of humanity. Second, forms of killing or dying that affirm the ideals of high life (see Chapter 3)—that is, the collective ideal of human flourishing or the individual ethics of authenticity—may be tolerated and even lauded.

This first logic is invoked most explicitly in justifications for killing those held responsible for dehumanizing others. Agamben argues that these individuals fit into a special category: that of the 'wolfman' or 'bandit'. This category is composed of those beings who pose the most overt and vital threats to the ideal of high life: combatants, war criminals, terrorists, tyrants and other actors who violently instrumentalize the lives of others. In so doing, they flout and weaken the boundary between human and non-human life. They do so not only by directly dehumanizing other beings, but also through their very existence. The 'wolfman' or 'bandit' inhabits the space of the inhuman; by virtue of her crimes, she is cast out of the category of the human. Agamben's metaphor of the 'wolfman' illustrates this—the being in question has recognizably human features, but is undeniably non-human. Specifically, she is defined by her animal characteristics, and illustrates the ease with which the human can cross over the boundary into a non-human animal state—and bring others along with her. By dehumanizing others, the 'wolfman'/ 'bandit' dehumanizes herself and becomes killable. Indeed, killing the 'wolfman' or 'bandit' is not only acceptable; it is deemed *necessary* in order to restore the boundary between human–non-human and close the gap made evident by her existence. As Agamben argues, destroying a source and manifestation of dehumanization is a means of purifying the category of humanity, of purging the non-human features of human beings (see Chapter 4). As such, killing dehumanizers is a means of constituting and affirming the humanity of those beings captured within this category.

This line of reasoning is expressed aptly in Žižek's call for the killing of Nazi war criminals. He states that:

> *Out of our very love for humanity,* including (whatever remains of) the humanity of the Nazis themselves, we should fight them in an absolutely ruthless and disrespectful way ... when somebody kills just one true enemy of humanity, he (not kills, but) *saves* the whole of humanity. The true ethical test is not only the readiness to save victims but also, even

more perhaps—the ruthless dedication to annihilating those who made them victims.

(2002: 68)

In this quote, killing the perpetrators of mass dehumanization is construed as an act of 'love' for humanity. It is intended not only to restore the humanity of the victims dehumanized by mass killing, but also of the perpetrators. In this sense, it is a form of symbolic killing that restores both parties to the 'right' side of the human–non-human divide. This is a prime example of killing as re-enchantment.

We can see this logic at work in two high-profile killings that took place in 2011: that of al-Qaeda founder Osama Bin Laden in the spring, and of Libyan leader Muammar Gaddafi in the autumn. Bin Laden was the ultimate 'wolfman' or 'bandit'—in the decade between the 9/11 attacks and his killing, he was regarded as a monster to be 'hunted' by the US government. The murky circumstances of his killing by US special forces, including a burial at sea that directly contradicted his religious beliefs, were expressive acts of disrespect of the kind described by Žižek above. Gruesome images of his dead body were greeted with jubilation by crowds of people who gathered on the streets to celebrate in the US. To sense the triumph that attended his death, one need only glance at the now famous photo of key members of the Obama administration watching, rapt, as he was killed in real time. Similarly, Gaddafi was killed in the streets by a group of rebels armed and supported from the air by the UN-sanctioned NATO operation Unified Protector.[7] Graphic pictures of Gaddafi's bloodied, dead body were shown on the front covers of major Western media outlets, and the event was declared by the newly instated National Transitional Council of Libya as the moment marking the official liberation of Libya. The fact that he was ultimately killed by a group of his 'own' citizens allowed NATO and the UN to keep their hands formally clean. However, Gaddafi's killing was framed as a triumph of human intervention in violence—that is, as an act of violence that expressed the popular desire for high life in the form of democracy, human rights and human flourishing. These reactions are not, in fact, deviations from Western secular beliefs about life and death; they are entirely consistent with this belief system. For those celebrating, the deaths of these two individuals were not murders or acts of war, but rather the closure of holes torn in the category of humanity by their dehumanizing acts. The ontological categories discussed above also play an important role in these cases. Specifically, the killing of an individual was deemed acceptable and necessary if it affirmed the ideal of high life and the inviolability of humanity.

The second kind of 'killing to make life meaningful' is reflected in cases in which the deaths of certain people affirm the specific ideals of high life. On an individual level, this is exemplified by deaths that express and embody human authenticity and self-realization. According to Keane, an ideal death serves as the point from which individuals evaluate their lives unencumbered by the pressures of the world; they can reflect upon what they have or have not achieved, what they have become and what might be in store for them. In this sense, death is the same as birth, for it is precisely in death that life reaches its apogee.

(1996: 69)

For Keane, an ideal death is one in which dying is an act of self-expression, and the moment in which a meaningful life reaches fruition. Even this very final act becomes, for the individual, a means of grasping and shaping her 'own' self. In some cases, the individual may even choose the means or conditions of her death, and, in this way, shape her end just as she has fashioned her life. This is not the exact opposite of 'death as theft': instead, death is framed as the ultimate form of self-possession.

According to Keane, this kind of death occurs in very specific circumstances. He gives the example of the self-immolation of political activist Jan Palach in Prague in 1969, shortly after the Soviet invasion of the city. For Keane, this public suicide functions as a statement that 'noble death is better than ignoble life' (1996: 74). In other words, he lauds Palach's decision to end his own fully human life—and the individual agency that this provided—before it could be reduced to an inhuman life under Soviet occupation. More recently, a similar frame has been applied to the story of Mohamed Bouazizi, a Tunisian street vendor who, in late 2010, also burned himself to death in protest against harassment by municipal officials. Instead of a public suicide or even an act of terrorism, this act has widely been regarded as the catalyst of the 'Arab spring', the series of populist uprisings across North Africa in late 2010 and early 2011. Although both of these examples involve instrumental forms of killing, they appear to pass through the two horns of bad death. By killing oneself for a 'higher' cause, these individuals escape the charge of 'meaningless' death, or being killed 'for/as nothing'. However, the cause to which they sacrificed themselves was not transcendent, but rather related to the flourishing human beings in their earthly lives.

It is instructive to contrast these examples of 'good death' with the interpretation of suicide bombing which, 'for many non-Muslims in the United States, Western Europe and Israel ... quickly became the icon for an "Islamic culture of death"' after 9/11 (Asad 2007: 11). According to Asad, suicide bombing evokes a particular horror within Western secular societies:

Not simply because [the bomber] killed innocents or was prepared to die (that's common enough in war) or simply because he killed himself (that's not uncommon in peace) but because he killed himself in order to kill innocents.

(2007: 41)

Suicide bombing involves the obliteration of the self in order to harm others and subjugate their lives to a 'higher' cause. In contrast, the act of death-as-self-realization described above involves using a violent act of self-expression in order to affirm the ideal of human flourishing. In this manner, it is framed as the exact inverse of suicide bombing; it directly subverts the de-individualizing, transcendent violence associated with suicide bombing. So, although the physical acts in question are quite similar (with the exception that self-immolations are usually limited to harming the actor in question), the meaning attributed to them is very different.

The third form of 'killing to make life meaningful' is found in situations where violence is used to express the ideal of high life and popular desire for it. This occurs when groups of people are harmed or killed as an expression of the demands of humanity. We can see this framing of 'humanitarian violence' in discourses surrounding the 2011 intervention into Libya, which gained UN Security Council approval and was framed in the rubric of the responsibility to protect. The UN's justification of this intervention was based largely on the statement that conditions in Libya were repressive, violent and likely to lead to dehumanization and bad death on a large scale. In other words, intervention was intended to 'preclaim' many lives that were deemed to be imminently vulnerable to dehumanization. As Ban Ki-Moon argues, the intervention:

> Saved thousands of lives. When the air strikes began, government forces were poised to enter Benghazi. A bloodbath appeared to be inevitable. For now, we have prevented a humanitarian catastrophe.
>
> (2011)

Although NATO aimed to minimize civilian casualties in all cases, the intervention was far from bloodless. Over 9,700 airstrikes were carried out by NATO, which resulted in a large number of civilian casualties.[8] However, these deaths were differentiated from those caused by Gaddafi's regime, or indeed by ground-fighting between government loyalists and rebels. They were designated not as casualties of a brutal internecine war, but rather as side effects of a legal military intervention intended to protect 'humanity'. In this manner, the lives of civilians killed by NATO's intervention were directly claimed in the name of the human (or of human flourishing) *before* they could succumb to bad death at the hands of the Gaddafi regime and its loyalists. The lives in question were instrumentalized, but to the ideal of high life rather than a transcendent ideal or the pure exercise of sovereignty.

Moreover, this intervention was not intended simply to end an episode of violence or prevent 'bad deaths'. Rather, it was framed as a catalyst for the 'Arab spring'. Specifically, it was intended to expedite the destruction of authoritarian regimes and the creation of democratic, rights-based states. As Ban Ki-Moon stated near the outset of the operation:

> Air operations, alone, will not resolve the crisis. Nor will it bring about a political solution that meets the aspirations of the Libyan people ... our

long-term interest is to help them do so, focusing on the establishment of transitional arrangements that would meet the democratic aspirations of the Libyan people.

(2011)

In Ban's quote, the air strikes in question are framed as the prelude to a series of processes that will allow the 'Libyan people' to achieve their 'aspirations'. In this sense, the coercive, external intervention of NATO is, ironically, portrayed as a catalyst for the *self*-realization of the Libyan people.

In this regard, 'humanitarian violence' appears to be an ironic appropriation of the concept of 'divine violence' developed by Walter Benjamin. According to Benjamin, divine violence is an expression of 'pure power over all life for the sake of the living' (1986: 297). This is not biopolitical violence, through which individuals are killed for/as nothing (see Chapter 3) for an important reason: the 'life' to which they are sacrificed is elevated to an ideal, not a 'bare' necessity. Nor does this kind of violence constitute sacrifice (in its traditional sense) because the lives in question are not consecrated to an external deity, but rather to an immanent force. If human life can be said to be 'sacrificed' in such circumstances, then it is sacrificed to itself.

From Benjamin's perspective, divine violence cannot be an instrumental strategy used by sovereigns to control the lives of their subjects. It is a force that emerges 'from nowhere' as a direct expression of human energy, aspiration or anger. This term is usually applied to violence used in the context of spontaneous social uprisings (Žižek 2009), and the uprisings of the 'Arab spring' fit the bill precisely. However, in the example above, intervenors also invoked and appropriated the spirit of divine violence in justifying their action in Libya. Specifically, NATO's intervention was framed as a catalyst for revolution—that is, as a means of removing the obstacles to the divine violence carried out by protestors, and a means of expediting the expression and realization of their needs. In this manner, NATO's violence was made ontologically continuous with the divine violence carried out on the ground; although it did not constitute divine violence in itself, the intervention seemed to enable it. So, although NATO's action contrasts with Benjamin's concept (it was highly instrumental, planned and external), it appropriated the image and ethos of divine violence. This enabled intervenors to frame their violence as an expression of the ideal humanity. In so doing, they were able to avoid committing the ultimate Western secular sin: producing 'bad deaths' through meaningless killing or sacrifice to the divine. Instead, they took part in the sacrifice of a segment of humanity to itself.

Conclusions

Western secular cosmology abhors death, and violent killing in particular— but not in every instance. In some cases, intervenors act as secular 'angels of death', making decisions on who should live and die, and how this should happen. In this chapter, I have highlighted four exceptions in which killing and letting die are deemed acceptable, necessary or even laudable. These forms of killing and letting die are not at odds with Western secular cosmology, but in fact expressions of its underlying logic, ethics and beliefs. First, the ontological production of categories of bad death and 'dehumanization' demand that intervenors allow a certain number of people to be harmed or killed before the agency of intervenors can be activated. Second, the compulsion to maintain belief in the category of humanity, and in the ability of human institutions to uphold it, sometimes demands that certain groups of people are allowed to die in order to protect 'humanity itself'. Third, the instrumental–rational logics of proportionality and necessity allow intervenors to treat the deaths of 'dehumanized' beings as 'economies' of death rather than excesses. This enables them to kill some of the people whom they intend to protect without undermining their own beliefs and values. Fourth, in very specific cases, killing and death can be framed as affirmations of the category of humanity—for instance, when agents of dehumanization are killed, or when killing is viewed as a catalyst for divine violence that promotes human flourishing.

Together, these four exceptions to the prohibition against bad death constitute the closest approximation of Western secular notions of 'good death'. They demonstrate that Western secularity has its own 'culture of death' rooted in instrumental–rational reasoning and ontology. It also has its own human 'angels of death', who decide which beings can, or must die if the category of humanity is to be sustained. Now, I shall examine another strategy through which intervenors seek to deal with death: by offering a secular version of life after death.

Notes

1 The two concepts are frequently conflated, but the distinction is important. Whereas the *ontic* refers to the concrete, usually material ways in which being expresses itself to the human senses, *ontology* refers to the nature of being and the metaphysical categories in which it is expressed. Humans often engage with questions of ontology through the ontic—e.g. they might experience a particular mountain as the instantiation of the *category* of mountains—but the two levels of analysis are very different.

2 This is one of the reasons why, as detailed in the ICISS (2001) report, many organizations prefer to distance themselves from the idea of 'humanitarian intervention' and its militaristic connotations.

3 Responsibility to protect is often considered to be an example of liberal institutionalism, or even idealism. However, its grounding assumptions reproduce the basic tenets of realism: that states act only in ways that maximize their chances of survival in conditions of anarchy, and that the desire to attain national security (or dominance) is given priority over solidaristic or cosmopolitan commitments. It is important to be clear that its founders may, to greater or lesser degrees, oppose this model of international politics in a normative sense—but they reproduce it in the logic with which they approach the problem of intervention.

4 Or, alternatively, the planning, incitement of, complicity in, or attempt to commit genocide.

5 In most transcendent belief systems, it is understood that a deity exists whether or not people believe in it; hence the idea that non-believers may be punished or excluded from rewards by a deity in which they do not believe. Western secularity differs in that it is acknowledged to be a human construction, and that belief in it is rooted in empirical evidence rather than acceptance of transcendent will. In this context, a being exists when it presents itself to the human senses or aligns with human rationality; in the absence of this, it cannot exist.

6 That is, unless one considers a way of life to be constitutive of a metaphysical category of being in itself.

7 The primary task of the NATO mission was to aid rebel forces in overthrowing Gaddafi's regime, which had engaged in severe violence against citizens protesting against it. However, many of the aerial bombings focused on targets where Gaddafi, his family members or close supporters were believed to live.

8 At the time of writing, no official estimate of casualties had been produced by a recognized international body (see BBC 2011a). Indeed, for a sustained period after the interventions, the only formal count available was that compiled by various journalists and commentators on *Wikipedia*, which estimated (based on media reports) that 1,108 civilians were killed and 4,500 wounded by NATO strikes by 13 July 2011 (*Wikipedia* 2011; Dardagan 2011).

7 Life after death

Intervention, immortality strategies and rituals of re-enchantment

> Survival is targeted on others, not on the self. Though we never live through our own death, we do live through the deaths of others, and their deaths give meaning to our success: we have not died, *we* are *still* alive ... [we] *outlive* others.
>
> (Bauman 1992: 34)

So far, this book has focused on the darker sides of Western secular influences on intervention—its pitfalls and paradoxes, its perverse and unintended consequences. But Western secularity, like most belief systems, also offers meaning, hope and a sense of agency in the face of the most difficult challenges that face human beings. This chapter will explore one of the more poignant impulses within contemporary intervention: the desire to offer an immanent form of 'life after death' to those killed or harmed by violence. Yet, as the epigraph above suggests, restoring meaning to deaths is not only a matter of showing respect to those who have been killed. It is also a powerful means of affirming the ideal of high life in the face of violence, and of securing the meaning of the lives still being lived in its wake. On a broader level, it is an integral part of the global project of re-enchantment through which the entire category of humanity is forged and protected.

The transformative processes used by intervenors in the wake of violence—peace-building, conflict transformation, post-conflict reconstruction and related practices—are prime examples of this project of re-enchantment. They translate the processes of meaning-making discussed in Chapter 5 into concrete forms, and seek to 'reclaim' lives from violence by reconstituting them as part of the category of humanity. Processes of this kind are overwhelmingly analysed in practical or ideological terms. That is, they are treated exclusively as tools for bringing closure to violence, preventing future eruptions or (re)building a specific kind of polity. But viewed through an anthropological lens, they are also, unmistakably, a collective response to death. This is not just any response, but one that reflects Western secular beliefs about death, the primacy of human life and the need to assert the dominance of the latter over the former.

This chapter explores two ways in which intervenors use transformative processes as tools of re-enchantment. First, I discuss how intervenors use what Bauman calls 'immortality strategies' to offer a totally immanent version of life after death to those that have been killed in episodes of violence. In lieu of immortality or another transcendent reward, immortality strategies offer the ability to 'live on' in human institutions, memory, practices and objects. Like the creation of categories of violence discussed in the previous chapters, immortality strategies unfold at the ontological level. They are ontological interventions which sever deaths from the trajectories of violence that produced them, and re-instrumentalize these deaths towards a 'higher end'. In this regard, they share much in common with the idea of sacrifice, which is abhorrent to Western secular beliefs. But there is a crucial difference: these strategies re-instrumentalize deaths not to a transcendent aim, but to human life itself. By 'making something good come out of violence', they recuperate the meaning of deaths 'lost' to violence, and affirm the dominance of human life over death. So, these strategies do not only provide posthumous meaning to those who die in violence; they also seek to reverse the trajectories of violence that threaten the category of humanity. These are strategies of *survival* in its most literal sense: life is literally lived *over and against* death, and the meaninglessness it threatens.

Second, I explore the various rituals of re-enchantment that intervenors use to bring closure to an episode of violence. These rituals are used to carry out the division of life and death that Western secular beliefs demand (see Chapter 3): they put the dead in their place, insulate the living from their presence, and seal off the ontological holes that violence has created in the category of humanity. In addition, they often involve quite literal attempts at re-enchantment—that is, they appropriate elements of transcendent belief systems in order to restore meaning to a community recovering from violence. However, Western secularity also offers its own death rituals, which include public processes of 'self-transformation', cathartic practices of 'healing', and even rituals of transmutation, in which enemies are expected to embody one another in order to overcome their enmity. These rituals may sound wildly divergent from Western secularity, with its profound belief in instrumental–rationality and immanence. However, I shall argue that they are actually expressions of Western secular cosmology and beliefs, intended to redeem 'lost lives' by enfolding them into this framework of meaning.

However, the Western secular project of re-enchantment, which relies on instrumental–rational forms of meaning-making, is inherently dialectical. So, just like the projects discussed in the previous chapters, the immortality strategies and rituals of re-enchantment used by intervenors reproduce the problem of disenchantment. They perform effective disenchantment by treating deaths produced by violence as meaningless, and by using them as fodder for their own ontological projects. Furthermore, by subjecting these deaths to instrumental–rational processes of meaning-making, and by instrumentally appropriating fragments of transcendent belief systems, these strategies may desacralize other beliefs. They might also 'crowd out' or commandeer other, non-Western secular rituals of grief and mourning. For these reasons, they may have a profoundly disenchanting effect on the societies in which they unfold. So, the transformative processes used by intervenors offer strategies for recuperating deaths from violence and re-enchanting humanity—but at what cost?

Life after death: intervention and Western secular responses to bad death

All human societies face mortality, and each one must find a way to respond—to reconcile death with beliefs about life and its meaning, to cope with the grief of loss and the fear of endings, to confront the mystery of what (if anything) happens when a life is extinguished. Unlike its transcendent counterparts, Western secularity does not offer a comprehensive vision of life after death. On the contrary, in a framework that invests all meaning in *living* human life, death is a dead end. Death is understood not as part of life, but as an affront to it, an anti-ideal (see Chapter 3).

However, this does not mean that societies which fear and reject death are passive in the face of it. On the contrary, as Bauman argues, such societies are dominated by the project of rejecting and forestalling death. Advances in medicine, security and practices of consumption have made it possible for people in many societies dominated by Western secularity to bracket off death from their everyday lives. This makes it possible for them to imagine that they are immune to it (or at least that they should be). In this context, evidence of death on a large scale—particularly if it is deemed to be 'avoidable' through human efforts—is not just a shock or a horror, but an *embarrassment*. As I discussed in the previous chapter, it is crucial for Western secular institutions to prove their ability to uphold the ideal of high life in the face of death and disenchantment. Failure to do so may be interpreted not simply as a practical shortcoming but also as a moral failing. As Bauman puts it:

> If fate can be changed, the world can be made into a safer and more agreeable place, and if it is human practice, guided by human reason, which can secure that change ... [death's] persistence is now a reproof and a challenge ... it has been only by the dint of human sloth, wrongdoing or ineptitude that it is allowed to remain ... [it represents] the hard, irreducible core of human impotence in a world increasingly subject to human will and acumen.
>
> (1992: 134)

From this perspective, death is a problem that should fall within the scope of human control. This belief underpins the desire to confront—to prevent it, and where this proves impossible, to reverse its effects and, in so doing, to erase evidence of the failures of human agency. Indeed, as Jabri suggests, 'violent conflict preoccupies precisely because of its seeming persistence irrespective of the very modern idea that we have the capacity to eradicate it' (2007: 32).

Because it is caused by humans and therefore deemed to be within the realm of human control (see Chapters 2 and 3), it serves as a constant reminder of the inadequacy of human institutions to protect the category of humanity. So, intervenors working within a Western secular framework face immense pressure to 'do something about death'. To this end, they use two important strategies: reversing the ontological trajectory of violence, and enacting death rituals.

Immortality strategies

If there is no recourse to a transcendent form of life after death, human beings search for ways to secure their immortality on earth. Hannah Arendt (1998) argues that this impulse has long been a feature of Western political life, stretching back at least as far as the ancient Greeks. They understood themselves to be the only mortal beings in a universe in which everything else was immortal—not only their gods, but also the non-human features of the world. The immortality of non-humans was linked to their permanence, their durability in the face of time and change. Humans, embodied in fragile and vulnerable forms, could only attain this status vicariously, by extending themselves into the world. As Arendt puts it:

> The task and potential greatness of mortals [lay] in their ability to produce things—works and deeds and words—which would deserve to be and, at least to a degree, are at home in everlastingness, so that through them mortals could find their place in a cosmos where everything is immortal except themselves.
>
> (1998: 19)

To this end, they constructed buildings, spaces, artefacts and monuments which would testify to the greatness of the people who built them, and secure their place in an immortal universe. But these material beings were merely the stage for acts that would confirm one's immortality. To do so, one needed to live a *vita activa*—a public life, witnessed by one's peers, and marked by great acts that would resonate within collective memory for generations to follow.

The pursuit of worldly immortality, Arendt argues, was transformed by the rise and eclipse of Christianity, which first annexed immortality to the transcendent realm, then removed it altogether. Within this world-view:

> Political activity, which up to then had derived its greatest inspiration from the aspiration toward worldly immortality, now sank to the low level of an activity subject to necessity, destined to remedy the consequences of human sinfulness on one hand and to cater to the legitimate wants and interests of earthly life on the other.
>
> (Arendt 1998: 314)

In other words, the worldly acts which once forged one's permanent place in the universe became mere instruments for meeting the demands of survival or subordinating oneself to the divine. Immortality could no longer be made by humans; it could only be bestowed by God. The only role of earthly action in this regard was to demonstrate piety, follow the will of God, and, in so doing, attempt to increase the chances of being granted eternal life. Similarly, material objects and social structures were reduced to instruments for sustaining human life and regulating behaviour. Then, according to Arendt, the advent of modernization brought with it secular*izing* processes (see Chapter 1) that stripped away belief in a transcendent afterlife. All that was left in the wake was the life process itself, and humans became *animal laborans*—animals driven entirely by the need for survival. So, according to Arendt, the transformations that ushered Christianity in and out of dominance 'deprived individual life of its immortality, or at least the certainty of immortality' (1998: 320). In the wake of secularization, she avers, immortality could be attained neither through earthly activities nor divine will.

Arendt's narrative leads to a rather nihilistic conclusion: that, through its reduction to *animal laborans*, humanity has been irreversibly stripped of its capacity to confer immortality, and of the belief in its possibility. However, I shall argue that the latter assertion, at least, is unwarranted. Western secular social imaginaries—and the practice of intervention in particular—express a profound desire to attain earthly forms of immortality. Arendt argues that the rise to dominance of the 'life process' has extinguished the possibility of immortality by reducing the realm of human action to the pursuit of biological survival. But as I argued in Chapter 3, the concept of human life produced by Western secular belief is not purely biological, nor is it construed as a denigration of human life. On the contrary, the processes of everyday life have been elevated to an ideal, to the ultimate expression of meaning. From this perspective, the twists and turns that Arendt describes have come full circle. For the ancient Greeks, human beings were the only mortal beings in an immortal universe; for Christians, they were the only spiritually immortal beings in a perishable world. In contrast, Western secular cosmology frames human beings as the only beings capable of making durable meaning out of a transitive and impermanent world. So, instead of attempting to attain immortality by being 'like' gods or immortal objects, human beings seek immortality by being themselves. They assert the immortality of humanity by affirming the ideal of everyday, collective human life—not through great acts or monuments, but through the everyday practices of human communities.

Zygmunt Bauman's work helps to clarify this idea. According to Bauman, modern human societies have developed specific means for securing immortality. They may use 'immortality strategies', which allow individuals or groups to 'live on' in collective memory. Individual immortality strategies are similar to the ancient Greek notion of immortality discussed by Arendt; they are available only to those who have attained exceptional public recognition— for instance, 'kings and generals ... statesmen and revolutionaries' (Bauman

2006: 34–5). However, most people are only eligible for collective immortality strategies, in which their immortality derives from having been part of a broader event or purpose—not from individual achievements but rather the surrender of their individuality. These strategies can be observed in public monuments or narratives—for instance, of 'those who fought bravely in the war' or 'gave their lives for their country'. Although these strategies do not offer individual greatness, for many people, they:

> Make their death[s] instrumental in bringing forth something much more solid, lasting, trustworthy and significant than their uneventful, drab and unprepossessing individual li[ves].
>
> (Bauman 2006: 36)

Both kinds of immortality strategies can be observed in a memorial speech given to the UN General Assembly by then Secretary General Kofi Annan for the victims of the bombing of the UN's Baghdad headquarters in 2003 (see BBC 2011b). Annan first reads out a list of names of all of the UN personnel killed in the bombing, embedding their deaths within a collective structure of meaning. He then devotes a long postscript to Sergio Vieira de Mello, a high-ranking official who had held numerous posts within the UN—including the restructuring and trusteeship of Timor Leste. Annan emphasizes that 'Sergio', was the 'only top official in the UN known to everyone by his first name', singling him out for individual recognition within the UN's system of signification. The first act constitutes a collective immortality strategy, while the second fits the description of an individual one.

These strategies may be used to offer earthly immortality to specific individuals or groups of people. However, the very practices, processes and structures in which humans live can offer a form of immortality to human beings. According to Bauman, the processes of creating and sustaining everyday life assert the collective sur-vival of human life over death. Indeed, as he puts it, 'it is because we know that we must *die* that we are so busy *making* life … *im*mortality is something we must build ourselves' (1992: 7). From this perspective, 'making life' is the most powerful guarantor of immortality. Ensuring the continuation of human life does not only assert its power to triumph over death, but also its permanence. In this context, everyday processes through which modern societies attempt to live against death offer a form of earthly immortality—not in greatness or legend, but in the permanence of human life as a whole. Although they may avoid talking about death or engaging with it explicitly, the structures and cultures that constitute these societies embody their struggle against it. According to Bauman, the defining features of modern societies are produced by the constant attempt to assert human life against death. He argues that:

> Death (more exactly, awareness of mortality) is the ultimate condition of cultural creativity as such. It makes permanence into a task, into an

urgent task, into a paramount task ... and so it makes culture, that huge and never stopping factory of permanence.

(Bauman 1992: 4)

In other words, the cultural achievements, institutions, artefacts, social structures and other defining features of these societies emerge from the desire to affirm the primacy of human life and its flourishing over the imperative of death. From this perspective, these phenomena can all be understood as part of a large-scale collective immortality strategy—not for one group of people, but for 'humanity itself'.

I shall now argue that intervenors use this kind of immortality strategy in the wake of large-scale violence. They do so in order to secure the meaning of the deaths of others, but also to ensure their own immortality. Indeed, as the epigraph at the beginning of this chapter suggests, securing the immortality of others makes it possible for one to aspire to immortality oneself.

'Making something good come out of violence'

Why do intervenors seek to make 'peace', 'harmony' or 'prosperity' in the aftermath of large-scale violence? This might seem like an obvious strategy but, as I shall argue shortly, that attitude reflects a particular moment in the development of intervention. Indeed, it should not be taken for granted that the most obvious response to violence is to re-create a society 'for the better'. This impulse embodies the need of intervenors to respond to—indeed to resist—the power of death to constitute human societies. The 'transformative' strategies that have become central to contemporary forms intervention express the primacy of high life. By 'making something good come out of violence', they attempt to reverse and subvert the negation of human flourishing that large-scale violence entails. At the same time, they seek to create conditions in which those killed in violence can 'live on' in the structures, acts, practices and artefacts that confirm human flourishing. In this way, transformative strategies allow intervenors to close off trajectories of violence and to offer collective immortality strategies in their wake.

Intervenors carry out this task through simple but profound ontological work. Specifically, they interpose themselves in trajectories of violence and sever them from their instrumental ends. Then, they suture them to new ends: the creation of 'peace', 'stability' or 'emancipation', for instance. To do so, intervenors redirect the momentum and productive power of trajectories of violence, maintaining the instrumental rational logic of violence but changing its outcomes. This enables them to recuperate the deaths caused by violence, making them productive not of the ends of aggressors, but rather of the immortality strategies discussed above.

To make sense of this argument, I shall return to Badiou's ontology, which I introduced in the previous chapter. Badiou's ontology is deeply Western secular, and fundamentally anthropocentric. It suggests that human forms of meaning-making—counting, representing, and creative action—constitute the world. Humans can, and must, constitute and alter their own ontological conditions. However, they cannot bring about novelty from nothing. Rather, they alter the world by making strategic interventions into situations of radical contingency—that is, moments whose futures are indeterminate, and which could produce multiple trajectories and outcomes. Ontological intervenors—or 'militants',[1] in Badiou's language—create and sustain a world by 'closing' these trajectories around their own aims, and channelling them in a specific direction.

Violence creates radical contingency by destroying the material social and ontological foundations of the world. It involves the emergence into the world of what Badiou calls 'the void'. The void is, simply put, the realm of non-being. According to Badiou, it underlies all of the features of the 'existing' world like a negative mirror image. However, it is not only the antithesis of the existing world; it also contains all of the possibilities of being that might ever present themselves in the world, and thus is the source of genuine novelty. Periodically, the void extrudes into the represented human world, unsettling its foundations and opening the possibility of genuinely new phenomena. Human systems of meaning-making and social structures produce the world by warding off these extrusions, capturing and stabilizing the contingency they create. As such, Badiou argues, the world 'is *not founded upon the social bond, which it ... express[es], but rather upon un-binding, which it prohibits*' (2007: 109, italics his). This contention mirrors Bauman's claim (see above) that all of human culture is built to constrain the endless and unknowable void of death, to limit and control its extrusions into the realm of the living. Indeed, for Badiou, the apparent solidity of the human world is no more than the result of its 'encounter with its own void' (2007: 93). In other words, although the void fundamentally threatens, indeed negates, existence, it is the very condition against which the world is staked and which makes any novelty possible.

By this account, humans forge their world by making something out of nothingness and negation. They may not be able to summon novelty or change from nothing, but they can bring it about by applying deliberate, directed agency to eruptions of the void. If change is to take place in the world created by humans, they must be 'patient watchmen of the void' (Badiou 2007: 111), closely attuned to the emergence of events and poised to intervene. When the void explodes through the presented and/or represented world like a plume of molten lava, it creates conditions called 'events'. Events are spatio-temporal points or sites of indeterminacy which might radiate into various (indeed, limitless) trajectories. Militants work by 'naming' events as such and positing them as the starting points of new ontological trajectories. They 'make something' out of radical contingency by helping to limit and close it off, and directing it towards one particular trajectory. Those for whom this new trajectory becomes the basis of become subjects-of-the-event; that is, their subjectivity and agency are shaped by the event and their 'fidelity' to it. Fidelity, in this context, refers to one's faithfulness to the belief in a particular event and its constitutive role in the world. Militants work to consolidate fidelity to the events they have named by using the forms of meaning-making mentioned above—art, science, love and politics—as 'truth procedures'. Truth procedures help to constitute a particular ontological trajectory as 'true' or 'real' and thus to embed it within the world.

So, by naming events, capturing their radical contingency, redirecting it and consolidating it through truth procedures, militants can intervene in their ontological conditions and bring about radical change. I shall now argue that intervenors do precisely this when they attempt to 'make something good come out of violence'. Large-scale violence dissolves human social structures, and thrusts manifestations of the void—death and destruction—into the realm of everyday life. Moreover, it creates conditions in which the future might unfold in numerous directions. When confronted by these situations, intervenors act as Badiouian 'militants'. First, they apprehend the emergence of the event, and rush to name it—usually as a 'war', 'disaster' or 'crisis', but perhaps also in more formal terms such as 'genocide' (see Chapter 6). Then, they interpose themselves into these conditions of contingency, in a range of ways: through the forms of meaning-making discussed in Chapter 5; the coercive acts explored in the previous chapter; or the more subtle, rituals discussed in the latter part of this chapter. By intervening in these moments of contingency, they attempt to sever trajectories of violence from their intended ends. Instead, they suture these trajectories to new outcomes: the creation of durable 'peace' or a new state, the restoration and transformation of everyday life. In so doing, they grasp moments of radical contingency and 'close' them around their own preferred ontological trajectories, simultaneously creating new conditions and sealing off the void—at least temporarily. Once this process of ontological intervention has been performed, the transformative processes discussed above use Badiouian truth procedures to set this new trajectory firmly in place. They manifest it in a number of ways: through the creation of new political regimes, the reconstruction of public spaces and homes, the constitution of new social relationships between conflicting groups, the creation of economic structures, and so on. As a result of this work, the deaths produced by violence are reframed as the ontological basis not for the ends of perpetrators (for instance, domination or the acquisition of resources), but rather for the creation and promotion of high life. This enables intervenors simultaneously to 'reclaim' disenchanted lives and to expand the reach of the ideal of 'high life'.

To see this strategy at work, we need look no further than the transformative ethos that has become central to contemporary intervention. It has come to be expected that intervention will not only put an end to violence, but also bring about a substantial transformation of the affected society 'for the better'. As Jabri remarks, it is now assumed that any discourse on peace assumes the possibility of transformation, of societal progression towards the institutionalization of modes of interaction that undermine the enabling conditions for violence.

(2007: 91)

In other words, intervention is expected not only to end violence but to transform the outcomes of violence, reversing (or at least erasing) its effects, and rooting out the conditions that enable it. Transforming the outcomes of violence is increasingly treated as a moral duty, as well as a pragmatic measure (see below). Consider Walzer's comments on the imperative placed on intervenors to 'rebuild' states in the wake of violence and military intervention undertaken to stop it. He states that:

Once we have acted in ways that have significant negative consequences for other people (even if there are also positive consequences) we cannot just walk away. Imagine a humanitarian intervention that ends with massacres stopped and the murderous regime overthrown; but the country is devastated, the economy in ruins, the people hungry and afraid; there is neither law nor order nor any effective authority. The forces that intervened did well, but they are not finished ... the work of the virtuous is never finished.

(Walzer 2004: 20–1)

Walzer beseeches his readers to 'imagine' a context in which intervention was simply a matter of fighting and 'walking away'. But is this image of intervention really so difficult to imagine, or even to recall? Up until the mid-1990s, intervention was understood largely in these terms: as a predominantly military practice intended to halt violence and create stability. But Walzer argues that the very legitimacy of post-war interventions, and their ability to bring closure to an episode of violence, rely '[on] something more than the restoration of the status quo ante—which gave rise, after all, to the crisis that prompted the intervention' (2004: 20). This is particularly the case, he suggests, in situations in which intervenors take action during an episode of violence, or act pre-emptively. Such cases 'radically shift the argument about endings, because now the war is from the beginning an effort to change the regime that is responsible for the inhumanity' (Walzer 2004: 19). In this context, military intervention is framed not only as a strategy for preventing conflict or limiting its effects, but also a means of pre-empting dehumanization and securing the category of humanity—by force.

What Walzer presents as a given—the abolition of hunger, fear, lawlessness, economic and other forms of ruin, and the transformation of a whole society—reflects a very distinctive, understanding of what intervention is and what it should accomplish. As John Darby argues, in the context of 'traditional' (that is, interstate) warfare, the 'post-war' commitments of parties were relatively minimal. Their priority was to establish regional security and ensure the withdrawal of combatants within their respective borders; 'anything beyond this [was] a bonus' (Darby 2010: 294–5). Of course, post-war conditions have regularly been used as opportunities for external forces to 'speed up history' by bringing in large-scale changes (Clark 2001: 54). Peace treaties, for instance, have been used throughout modern European history to reconfigure the borders, political systems and economic structures of states (see Ikenberry 2001; Howard 2000). These traditions of 'reconstruction' focused primarily on altering institutions and geopolitical configurations in order to create regional stability and guarantee the functioning of states. Contemporary discourses of reconstruction have taken this transformative impulse in a very different direction, to focus on the improvement of everyday human life and the social structures that sustains it.

The impetus to transform and enrich everyday life can be attributed at least in part to the emergence of a new conception of peace towards the end of the twentieth century. This notion of 'peace' emphasized social transformation, emancipation and the improvement of everyday life, contesting more traditional, state or military oriented conceptions (see Richmond 2007).

One of the most influential contributions to this trend was Johan Galtung's (1996) concept of 'positive peace', which differentiated between the mere cessation of violence (negative peace) and the creation of conditions of human flourishing. According to Galtung, even in situations in which overt, physical violence has run its course or been forcibly stopped, communities may suffer from 'structural violence'. This refers to social, economic, political or cultural forms of exclusion which prevent them from attaining a fully realized human life. The notion of positive peace suggests that any intervention seeking to create peace must do more than simply end an episode of violence. Specifically, it must transform the society in such a way that structural violence and the cultures that support it are removed. The closely related concept of 'root causes', which has become a basic principle of conflict management and transformation strategies, offers a similar perspective. Its proponents suggest that, in order to intervene effectively in a conflict, it is necessary to look beyond its obvious symptoms and goals. Specifically, one must pay attention to the often subtle social, cultural, political or even interpersonal structures that create and sustain friction between groups (Burton 1996; Miall 2007; Ramsbotham *et al.* 2005). For adherents of this approach, creating peace involves the gradual but comprehensive alteration of the symbols, attitudes, identities, norms, practices and institutions that have helped to foster conflict. Instead of measuring 'peace' in terms of the absence of physical violence, military victory or the reconstruction of a state, this understanding of peace also includes factors such as social harmony, economic prosperity and the reconciliation of conflicting groups. Throughout the last few decades, this transformative approach to peace has forged its way into the mainstream of policy-makers and practitioners concerned with the outcomes of intervention.

According to Hugh Miall, although security-driven and statist forms of peace-building are still common in practice, most scholars and practitioners now agree that peace 'should have some positive content' and produce desirable 'effects on the potential *realization* of human beings' (2007: 11, italics mine). Indeed, leading scholars on the subject suggest that a 'majority' of international actors and scholars 'se[e] transformation as the ultimate goal of the conflict resolution enterprise' (Miall *et al.* 1999: 60), or the 'primary aim of intervention' (Keating and Knight 2005: xxxiii).

The transformative impulse has also influenced how military intervention is understood and planned, particularly within the UN. The 'benevolent interventionism' (Liden 2009) now identified with the UN emerged through the production of a number of documents, statements, treaties and normative projects during the 1990s and early 2000s. In 1992, the publication of *Agenda for Peace* marked a significant change in the understanding of the UN's role in societies affected by violence. It introduced the idea of 'peace*building*' to the mainstream. 'Peace-building' is a positive concept which suggests that intervenors must employ strategies to create peace. It is defined in contrast to the notions of peacekeeping, which simply involves managing conflict, and preventive diplomacy, which is concerned solely with stopping it from emerging or limiting its effects. According to the framer of the concept, then-Secretary General Boutros Boutros-Ghali, intervention is intended to 'address the deepest causes of conflict: economic despair, social injustice and political oppression' (1992). In other words, from Boutros-Ghali's perspective, intervention should be oriented to transformative or emancipatory notion of peace discussed above. With the introduction of this idea, intervention became 'about' building peace, rather than simply about protecting national borders or upholding state sovereignty. In response to this conceptual shift, intervenors saw their job descriptions steadily expand to include a vast range of tasks: from the delivery of development aid to the disarmament of combatants and reform of security structures to the provision of technical advice to assist in the creation of governing structures (see Barnett *et al.* 2007). By the time Boutros-Ghali's successor, Kofi Annan, articulated his own version of 'peace', it contained three objectives: 'to consolidate internal and external security; strengthen political institutions and good governance; and promote economic and social rehabilitation and transformation' (cited in Bellamy 2010: 197). In this formulation, the goal of 'social transformation' is given equal weight to the original principle of 'ensuring security' and strengthening the capacities and sovereignty of states.

The influence of the transformative impulse is exemplified by the emphasis placed on 'rebuilding' in *Responsibility to Protect*. This document suggests that intervenors have a:

> Responsibility not just to prevent and react, but to follow through and rebuild. This means that if military intervention action is taken ... there should be a genuine commitment to helping to build a durable peace, and promoting good governance and sustainable development.
>
> (ICISS 2001: 39)

In short, *Responsibility to Protect* explicitly demands that rebuilding and social transformation for the better—exemplified in the ideas of 'good governance' and 'sustainable development'—are built into the process of military intervention from the outset.

Even military organizations such as NATO have reconfigured their strategies to emphasize peace-building and social reconstruction. Indeed, Alexandra Gheciu and Roland Paris (2011) argue that the continuing relevance of NATO in a post-Cold War world hinges on its ability to shed its traditional image and contribute to these goals. The work of NATO's Provincial Reconstruction teams in Afghanistan, in which military actors engage in 'community work' such as the construction of schools and hospitals, is a prime example of its efforts to do so. This transformative impulse is reflected in the most extreme sense in the militaristic doctrine of nation-building. Nation-building involves the use of military force to transform a state and society from the outside, the most illustrative examples being the US's post-2001 interventions in Afghanistan and Iraq. According to its framers, this doctrine is driven by 'the objective of transforming a society emerging from conflict into one at peace with itself and its Neighbours' (Dobbins *et al.* 2007: xvii). Francis Fukuyama describes nation-building as a project of 'creating or repairing all the cultural, social and historical ties that bind a people together as a nation' (2004). Within the rubric of nation-building, the transformation of societies for the 'better' (that is, the more 'democratic') is the *raison d'être* of intervention, not an auxiliary task or compensation for harms caused. It militarizes the transformative impulse, urging intervenors to *initiate* violence in order to bring about 'change for the better' in other societies.

As this brief analysis suggests, the desire not only to end violence but to transform whole societies in its wake cuts across a range of normative, practical, strategic and ideological approaches, as well as a number of key actors. I certainly do not wish to conflate these approaches, nor to gloss over the profound debates that are waged between their respective proponents (although this is not the place for these debates). The point is that, despite their differences, an astonishingly wide range of actors and organizations have converged around the image of transforming whole societies to improve the prospect of human flourishing.

What can explain this trend? Or, more to the point, what can persuade intervenors to invest the huge amounts of time, resources and political capital it requires? Standard explanations suggest pragmatic motivations related to states' desire to maintain international security and stability. From this perspective, a 'better life' functions as a 'carrot'—an incentive to prevent future violence, or to make peace seem more 'alluring' than war to potential combatants (see Keen 2008; Bellamy 2010). This is an accurate description of the overt, strategic goals of intervenors, and I do not wish to contest it on this level. However, I want to suggest that the motivations behind it run deeper. The various forms of transformative post-war strategy discussed above share a common basis in the Western secular aversion to bad death and the desire to assert the ideal of high life against it.[2] The process of 'making something good come out of violence' is a powerful *ontological* strategy through which intervenors seek literally to 'reclaim' deaths from violence in the way outlined above.

First, intervenors 'name' acts of violence as events by recognizing the contingency that they create. Then, upon intervening (whether through military or civilian means) they insert themselves into the trajectory of violence and become actors within it, attempting to seize hold of and redirect it. This is where the transformative strategies discussed above become relevant. They function as the truth procedures through which new ontological trajectories are realized and consolidated. The construction of conditions of 'positive peace', for instance, remove the traces of the previous social and cultural foundations, and offer new ones in their place. Likewise, peace-building and physical reconstruction projects offer tangible, material manifestations of the new ontological conditions of 'peace'. Through the gradual and small-scale processes of transformation, intervenors convert people living in societies affected by violence into subjects-of-the-event. In so doing, they *re*name the event so that it is not violence that lies as the basis of the newly constructed world, but rather intervention or its ends (such as 'peace'). This makes it possible for subjects-of-the-event to speak of living in conditions of peace, and to distinguish these from an era of violence; the two sets of conditions constitute different worlds separated by the act of intervention. In such cases, intervenors redirect the violent acts of others. In the context of nation-building, the main difference is that the violence in question originates from intervenors instead of from other actors, and requires no severing and suturing.

These ontological operations play an important role in the creation and extension of immortality strategies. First, they offer a very powerful and distinctive response to the problem of mass death: the ability to reverse its effects so that they ultimately produce and affirm human life, rather than negating it. By making violence ontologically productive of high life instead of (just) bad death, intervenors subvert the logical of killing while using its instrumental momentum to assert the primacy of human life. Transformative processes enfold deaths caused by violence into the very processes through which life is forged and affirmed. In so doing, they literally create life out of death in the way that Bauman describes. They convert deaths killed for an instrumental purpose into the ontological conditions for the creation of 'peace' or human flourishing. In so doing, they perform a distinctively Western secular form of redemption. The deaths in question are 'saved' from the grasp of meaningless or sacrificial violence and recuperated within structures that promote human flourishing. Those killed in episodes of large-scale violence can 'live on' in the new worlds that emerge from the work of intervenors, and in the flourishing that it promotes. In so doing, intervenors are able to re-enchant lives and deaths they deem to be disenchanted, while offering a Western secular form of life after death. This offers a powerful statement of the ability of human agency and institutions to overcome bad death and disenchantment—if not by preventing them, then by essentially hijacking their ontological trajectories and making them continuous with the production of high life.

Intervention and Western secular death rituals

In order to carry out the 'truth procedures' discussed above, intervenors rely on a number of distinctive death rituals. I use this term to refer to symbolic acts and practices intended to bring closure to the contingency created by death, to restore ontological stability in its wake, and to confirm the capability of intervenors to accomplish these tasks. In this sense, the social processes used in transformative interventions perform three important ontological tasks. First, they recognize the ontological ruptures created by violence—in the forms of physical harm, psychical suffering, the destruction of unique spaces, or the pain associated with the loss of irreplaceable loved ones (see Edkins 2011). Through transformative processes—whether literal 'rebuilding' projects or psycho-social healing—intervenors seek to close these holes in the category of humanity, and in the conditions of existence. Second, transformative processes mark the collective passing of lives. In this regard, they offer living memorials to the dead, and their products—a new state, a rebuilt village, an era of 'peace' or, crucially, the flourishing of those who survive—become monuments. As I have argued above, these emblems of high life are ontologically constituted in such a way that they appear to have 'come out of' the violence in question and the deaths it produced. As such, their existence is a testament to those who died, and to the human ability to live over and against death. Third, and paradoxically, transformative processes often attempt to remove the traces of death from human communities. The processes in question give expression to death, but they do so precisely by constraining it. Death might be 'allowed' into the realm of the living in the form of stone monuments, formal acts of public mourning, written or spoken eulogies. In these manifestations, death is brought under the control of human forms of meaning, and placed within the firm boundaries of social convention, propriety and order. Raw, uncontrolled embodiments of death—body parts thrown out of place by violence, bullet-ridden buildings, public spaces reduced to rubble—are removed as soon as possible. Indeed, from a certain perspective, the most effective monument to war is not the stately cenotaphs or public commemorations common in societies dominated by Western secularity, but rather the unadulterated evidence of violence. But in the context of intervention, and in line with Western secular attitudes towards death, the goal is not (only) to remember, but also to restore the dead to the realm of high life. So, the production of high life and the structures that sustain it are, simultaneously, a memorial to death and a means of effacing it.

Fourth, and crucially, death rituals allow for literal or symbolic segregation of dead bodies from the realm of the living. As I have argued in previous chapters, the dead body is one of the most potent manifestations of dehumanization and thus of disenchantment. Within a Western secular belief system, maintaining order between dead and living bodies is one of the most fundamental ways of upholding the category of humanity. The presence of dead bodies in the realm of high transgresses the border between the human and non-human, the enchanted and the disenchanted. Moreover, missing bodies upset the order enforced by this binary, and leave unbridgeable gaps in the category of humanity. They are fundamentally out of place and must be first returned, then segregated, in order for this order to be restored. This helps to explain the importance of repatriating the bodies of the dead (see Edkins 2011) even in processes of intervention which are overtly Western secular. The case of Cyprus offers an interesting example. The attempt to exhume, identify and 'return' the bodies of people killed in conflict between Greek Cypriot and Turkish Cypriot factions in the late twentieth century has unfolded in a multi-decade project pursued by the state and international organizations, not least the UN-sponsored Committee for Missing persons. As Paul Sant Cassia (2004) points out, these strategies of 'recovery' are bound up with the religious desire of family members to provide a proper burial for loved ones, but also with the political posturing of politicians eager to vilify the 'other side', and with the staking of land claims on the part of the bereaved. From this perspective, the process of recovering bodies is an amalgam of religious and secular motivations for the citizens in question. However, what is interesting for this argument is the central role of international organizations with an explicitly secular remit (in particular, the UN) in this project. Their approach to the project emphasizes the need to return bodies to 'their' families, as if they were the property of these relatives—or as if returning the bodies to relatives would restore the bodies to 'their' selves. This is reflected in the strong emphasis placed on the identification of corpses, which restores them to the status of individuals (see Chapter 5). The pervasive need to *identify* and *return* corpses is a clear reflection of the Western secular ideals of individuality, material integrity and self 'ownership' (see Chapter 1 in this volume; Edkins 2011). This allows intervenors to restore these bodies to the category of the human, and thus to reinstate the border between the living and dead on which it is staked. Of course, the very moment of 'recovery' is simply a prelude to the resegregation of these individuals from the land of the living. Only once they are retrieved, reinterred (or otherwise destroyed) and thus re-excluded can these bodies be reconciled—with Western secular beliefs, and perhaps also, simultaneously, with the religious beliefs of their families.

In these examples, the Western secular desire to create and maintain order between the living and dead converges with religious or transcendent beliefs about the appropriate way to treat the dead. However, intervenors do not stop at the goal of sealing off the disorder caused by violence. They also use death rituals in order to propel the process of re-enchantment by literally transforming death into manifestations of high life. It is to these transformative death rituals that I shall now turn.

In some cases, intervenors use very direct and literal strategies of re-enchantment to respond to the problem of bad death on a large scale.

Indeed, it is increasingly common for intervenors to appropriate elements of transcendent or enchanted belief systems for their own strategies of transformation. This is reflected in the rise of 'indigenous' approaches to peace-building and conflict transformation among major international organizations such as the UN and the World Bank (see MacGinty 2008). By tapping into the symbolic and constitutive power of transcendent beliefs, intervenors promote their own projects of re-enchantment. As I argued in Chapter 2, Western secularity is driven by a magpie tendency. At the individual level, it is manifested in the way that people selectively appropriate elements of various belief systems in order to attain authenticity. On a collective level, Western secular forms of meaning-making transform and internalize beliefs from other systems to feed the demand for re-enchantment. It is interesting to note that, in many of the cases I shall shortly discuss, members of transcendent belief systems have actively sought to integrate aspects of their beliefs into Western secular processes of meaning-making. It is difficult to tell whether this is a means of resisting the dominance or imposition of instrumental–rationality, a way of preserving 'traditional' culture, or a pragmatic attempt to influence the shape of the new society forged through intervention. Nonetheless, intervenors and 'local' actors both take part in the processes through which Western secularity appropriates transcendent beliefs for its project of re-enchantment. In such contexts, the boundary between the (Western) secular and the transcendent becomes changeable and blurred as elements of immanent and transcendent belief systems are merged and instrumentalized to one another.[3]

On one level, the appropriation of elements of transcendent belief systems by intervenors fulfils a straightforward purpose. This strategy is used to lend credence to, and increase acceptance of, the practices of intervenors among the communities in which they work. But I shall argue that the elements of belief instrumentalized by intervenors also play a deeper and much more literal role. As discussed above, Western secularity offers few resources for responding to death. By appropriating rituals or beliefs from other systems and infusing these into processes of transformation, intervenors amplify the power of their own death rituals, and the resonance of these rituals among the people they are intended to transform.

In some cases, appropriation happens simply through the redescription of transcendent death rituals as part of a process of peace-building, conflict transformation or a similar strategy. This framing does not necessarily undermine the constitutive value or efficacy of these rituals; indeed, in many cases, it relies on these properties. However, it subjugates the rituals in question to the Western secular project of peace-building, treating them as instruments for achieving its aims.

This mode of appropriation can be found in many anthropological accounts of violence and peace-building. Ironically, in most cases, the goal of these writers is to challenge dominant Western understandings of what 'peace' is and how it can be achieved, or to engender respect for alternative ways of life. Nonetheless, by framing the phenomena they observe as modes of

'peace-building' or similar strategies they reproduce the patterns of instrumentalization that are central to Western secularity. For instance, Lawrence
(2000) writes of the healing powers attributed to rituals at *Amman* ('goddess'/
'mother') temples in Sri Lanka, in which oracles interpret and acknowledge
the injuries caused by war. In so doing, they are believed to erase these injuries from the lives and bodies of victims, restore contact between the dead and
their families, and guard against further killing or violence. Lawrence
describes these rituals as an integral part of the process of creating 'peace',
folding the transcendent meaning of the rituals into the instrumental–rational
project of 'peace-building'. Similarly, Nordstrom's seminal study of civil war
in Mozambique describes a range of 'traditional' practices that were used in
the wake of its bloody civil war. In particular, she focuses on the magical
powers of *curandeiros*, or traditional healers. According to her respondents,
curandeiros were capable of rising from the dead, leading armies, using magic
to defeat enemy troops, and even restoring order between victims and perpetrators within communities. Nordstrom argues that the magical powers of
curandeiros were used to 'remove' war from victims and combatants, making
it possible for combatants to be accepted back into their communities after
the war. She translates their acts and the beliefs that they produce into terms
familiar to a Western secular mind: peace-building, reconciliation, the
restoration of selves and communities (see below). In a related example,
Volker Boege (2011) describes the way in which '*kastom*' (a pidgin term which
refers to traditional tribal custom) has become deeply implicated within
international peace-building in Bougainville. He argues that chiefs and elders
were heavily involved in 'achieving reconciliation' and using 'customary ways
of conflict resolution'. They did so through the symbolic exchange of gifts, and
through 'peace ceremonies', in which former adversaries feast together, eat,
drink, dance and engage in symbolic acts such as the breaking of spears. In
these cases, the practices in question are reframed and appropriated as alternative techniques for peace-building—ones which might offer more resonance
and durability than the externally determined forms of peace offered
by international intervenors. So, although they are intended to challenge
the dominance of Western, liberal–democratic, market-based notions of
'peace', these accounts ultimately instrumentalize these rituals to the goal of
peace-building.

   In other cases, elements of transcendent frameworks of belief are invoked
as internal sources of meaning and legitimation for the work of intervenors.
For instance, Lederach and Appleby claim that contemporary peacebuilding:

> Draws its core concepts from religious traditions—Judaism, Christianity,
> Islam—where reconciliation finds its richest and most ancient expression,
> but then seeks to synthesize these concepts with the best insights of the
> liberal tradition—human rights, democracy, and law—to form an ethic
> for modern politics.

(2010a: 92)

In this case, transcendent beliefs and rituals are located at the heart of strategies of transformation. They are drawn upon as a source of motivation and appealed to for legitimation. However, as Lederach and Appleby point out, the presence of transcendent beliefs does not render these practices wholly 'religious' (or, for that matter, wholly 'secular'). Instead, transcendent concepts offer metaphysical legitimation for immanent processes such as the institution of human rights, democracy and law.

The examples above refer to contexts in which transcendent beliefs are viewed either as external to, or an intrinsic part of, the strategies of intervenors. However, it is also common for rituals and beliefs of the kind described to be explicitly instrumentalized as part of a formal process of 'post-war' transformation or peace-building. Gerard Powers (2010) gives the example of the Acholi Religious Leaders' Peace Initiative in northern Uganda, initiated in 1997 by Anglican, Roman Catholic, Muslim and Orthodox religious leaders. This NGO has played a number of roles in responding to conflict in Northern Uganda, from consulting on the Juba peace process to assisting in the development of the Ugandan Amnesty Act. Powers suggests that the influence and global networks of these leaders helped them to achieve their aims. However, he insists that these actors had additional techniques at their disposal: 'ritual, prayer, and spiritual healing—that are not part of a secular NGO's peacebuilding portfolio' (Powers 2010: 324). In this case, rituals such as prayer and spiritual healing are directly and deliberately applied to Western secular projects such as the creation and alteration of laws. Crucially, prayer is not treated as if it were simply symbolic; rather, it is deemed to have the performative power to enable the changes in question.

Similar examples of the direct instrumentalization of transcendent rituals and beliefs can be found in processes of disarmament, demobilization and reintegration (DDR). Within these strategies, it is common for intervenors to integrate 'traditional cleansing ceremonies' based on tribal rituals (see Williamson 2006; Theidon 2007). Such ceremonies are intended ritually to remove the psychological, affective and moral stigma attached to combatants, symbolically restoring them to their communities. In this case, the constitutive power of these rituals is deemed integral to the Western secular goal of (re)integrating individuals within communities, and restoring social wholes. Similarly, Anne Brown and Alex Gusmao (2011) describe how non-secular cosmologies have become entwined with the process of international peace-building in Timor Leste. Communities in Timor Leste are based on clan networks, centred around *uma*, or houses, which include living human beings, but also the spirits of ancestors and elements of the natural world. Drawing on these sources of meaning, peace processes in the region have made use of *tar-abandus*—traditional agreements formed through a combination of negotiation among the living and the authority of biologically deceased ancestors. These agreements are simultaneously immanent and transcendent, secular and enchanted.

In all of these cases, transcendent rituals are treated as if they were constitutive of the changes in question. However, in order to use transcendent rituals and beliefs as tools of re-enchantment, intervenors need not literally believe in them. They must simply believe that these sources of enchantment hold meaning for the people whose lives they wish to re-enchant. However, these rituals and beliefs may also contribute to the Western secular ideals of human flourishing and authenticity. The beliefs and rituals discussed above have been adopted by intervenors precisely because they seem to support, or correspond to, the kinds of institutions and social relations that are associated with these ideals.

The trend towards appropriating transcendent or enchanted sources of meaning lends insight into the cosmological beliefs that underpin contemporary intervention. First, it highlights the belief of intervenors that large-scale violence must be responded to by means of symbolic and ritual acts. According to MacGinty:

> The principal advantage stemming from traditional and indigenous approaches to peacebuilding lies in its cultural intuitive nature. In theory, such approaches are able to connect with 'cultural memory banks' and conform to popularly held and accepted norms and expectations.
>
> (2008: 350)

Similarly, as Brown and Gusmao write, the integration of these beliefs and rituals with Western secular forms of meaning is not only a matter of ensuring that strategies of intervention are adopted by 'local' actors, but also:

> Of people struggling to deal with the always difficult and sometimes dire conditions facing them ... and endeavouring to shape their collective lives in ways that have meaning for *them*.
>
> (2011: 117, italics mine)

In other words, these elements of transcendent belief systems are valuable to intervenors not only because they are useful for generating support and acceptance of peace-building or conflict transformation strategies. They are also constitutive of the project of re-enchantment. The processes in question are intended to mark off epochs of violence, restore order and seal the holes created by violence and bad death. The rituals discussed above are very useful in this regard: they are expected to neutralize or even expunge the lasting effects of violence on human societies. They can also be used to restore order and to legitimate Western secular strategies aimed at achieving this. Furthermore, by engaging directly with transcendent death rituals, intervenors can enfold people who do not share their belief systems into the immortality strategies discussed above.

However, intervenors do not rely solely on transcendent belief systems in order to perform this task; Western secularity offers its own distinctive death rituals, even if they are not usually recognized as such. In the examples discussed above, the ritualistic aspect of intervenors' response to death might seem obvious (at least to a Western reader). However, Western secularity has its own distinctive death rituals that are rendered invisible by its false distinction between instrumental–rationality and the world of enchantment (of which rituals are usually considered a part, along with magic and beliefs in the supernatural). These practices are, too, based on the suspension of reason, the transfiguration of the self, and the metaphysical restructuring of people and societies. They are immanent rather than transcendent, but nonetheless perform the role of confirming the order of meaning, marking passages and constituting changes. Paying attention to them, in fact, helps one to avoid exoticizing the rituals discussed above in contrast to Western secular forms of meaning-making.

Several Western secular death rituals can be found in the transformative processes used in the context of 'post-war' interventions. By transforming bad death into high life, they perform a conversion that confirms the power of human agency to redeem itself. They also constitute powerful immortality strategies: they are used as 'truth procedures' to consolidate and realize the ontological projects discussed in the previous section. The production and flourishing of this kind of life offers a collective manifestation in which those lives 'lost' to violence can be reclaimed and 'live on'.

Among the most common and powerful death rituals used by intervenors are the processes associated with 'conflict transformation'. This strategy transposes the psychological concept of self-transformation to the collective level. It is based on the belief that, in order to exorcise conflict and move beyond the traumas caused by violence, whole societies must engage in processes of reflexive change. Although it is often veiled in the bureaucratic, pragmatic language of intervenors, a ritualistic image of transformation permeates this approach.

Specifically, society is framed symbolically as an individual who must undergo a massive and irreversible conversion in order to overcome the dark forces of violence. The processes through which this conversion takes place are simultaneously functional and symbolic. That is, they bring about the ritual of collective self-transformation and, by signalling to society that it has taken place, mark the end of one epoch and the beginning of the new one. In so doing, they solidify the ontological project of intervention discussed above.

Not surprisingly, this public ritual is modelled on the practices through which high life is produced (see Chapter 1). The collective goal of human flourishing, to which the ritual of transformation is oriented, is framed as the emergent product of myriad processes of individual self-realization. Indeed, although prompted by external actors, transformation is viewed as an immanent process in which the self-realization of millions of individuals combine to produce conditions of social change and enhanced quality of life (see Jabri 1996; Patomaki 2001; Miall 2007). As Hugh Miall argues:

the expression of individual realization collectively promotes the flourishing of the whole, and the flourishing of the whole enables the flourishing of individuals. Positive peace thus has the sense of 'wholeness' or 'flourishing-within-wholeness'.

(2007:12)

This approach places a strong emphasis on everyday life as the locus of ritual self-transformation. Elise Boulding claims that the most profound changes in 'post-conflict' societies emerge not from monumental acts, but rather from everyday practices such as caring, feeding, work and play (2000). This idea is reflected in the *Responsibility to Protect*, which states that:

> True and lasting reconciliation occurs with sustained daily efforts at repairing infrastructure, at rebuilding housing, at planting and harvesting, and cooperating in other productive activities.
>
> (ICISS 2001: 39)

In these processes, the banal activities that sustain everyday life are elevated into sources of redemption. Of course, this is part and parcel of Western secular beliefs, which raise everyday life to the status of an ideal. But in the context of 'post-conflict' strategies, these processes are sanctified more intensely: during the period of transformation, they become the basis of a ritual of collective re-enchantment, in which the restoration of everyday life signals its primacy and victory over death.

The quote above reflects another crucial death ritual used by intervenors: reconciliation. This is not, of course, an idea unique to Western secularity; in fact, the strategies discussed here can be quite explicitly traced to the Judeo-Christian concept of the reconciliation (see Lederach and Appleby 2010a). However, in the immanent tradition of Western secularity, they have been transformed to emphasize their human element rather than their potential for transcendence. In processes of conflict transformation, reconciliation is framed as a process of (re-)*humanization*. More specifically, it is understood as a process of 'mutual rehumanization' (Jeong 2005: 162) in which formerly warring parties join to carry out the everyday processes of societal transformation. Through formalized encounters with the other, 'perpetrators' and 'victims' are to be transfigured and (re)confirmed as members of the category of humanity. In other words, those people cast outside of the category of humanity by means of re-humanization are ritually reincluded.[4] These encounters are ritualized in the sense discussed above: they are planned and orchestrated; and they perform both a functional and a symbolic role in the ontological project of conflict transformation.

Rituals of reconciliation/(re-)humanization have a very specific structure. First, individuals must recognize others as 'fully human' beings and undertake acts that confirm this—whether working on a common project, apologizing or simply being present in the same room with a former enemy. According to

Louis Kriesberg (1998), this process involves the cultivation of empathetic relations that unfold over three stages. Initially, one must accurately perceive the other's feelings and goals. Then, one must attempt to experience these feelings and goals 'as if' they are one's own. Finally, one must distinguish one's own thoughts from those of the other in order to communicate the experience of empathy. The psychological concept of empathy has a very interesting ritual dimension: it asks one person symbolically to inhabit the mind (and perhaps also the body) of another, to 'become' the other person temporarily. In so doing, one is expected to undergo a profound personal transformation in which one feels intrinsically connected to the other. In other words, it calls for a symbolic transfiguration, in which one transcends the self in order to transform it.[5]

This ritual of transfiguration is intended to spark profound changes in the perceptions, attitudes and interactions of people affected by violence (see Lederach 2005). Proponents of conflict transformation argue that, through this process:

> Identities themselves become softened and transformed, as a broadening of self-understanding combines with a re-perception of others as fellow human beings.
>
> (Ramsbotham *et al.* 2005: 245)

Indeed, the ritual of transfiguration promotes the mutual re-enchantment of beings who, to each other at least, are considered to be dehumanized. In the process, it is expected that 'enemies [will] *become* persons with concerns that are recognized' (Kriesberg 1998: 297, italics mine). This process is reflexive: by engaging in the ritual of transfiguration, an individual can secure her own humanity by recognizing someone else's.

Another important ritual used by intervenors is psycho-social 'healing'. This imagery can be found in the work of John Paul Lederach and R. Scott Appleby (2010b). They describe the causes of violence and characterize its results as a 'failure of human flourishing' and advocate the transformation of social structures both as a prophylactic and a cure (Lederach and Appleby 2010b: 105). People harmed by violence, they contend, 'need radical healing— the kind of healing that restores the soul, the psyche, and the moral imagi- nation' (Lederach and Appleby 2010b: 28). So, for them, the most important question for practitioners of peace is 'how do we heal broken humanity?' (Lederach and Appleby 2010b: 28).

Although it makes use of medical language and imagery, this notion of healing is concerned not with the sustenance of biological life, but rather the 'meta-biological' aspects of life (see Chapter 3). In this sense, it has more in common with spiritual or magical concepts of healing used in many societies based on transcendent cosmologies (see above) than it does with Western medicine. Specifically, the strategies of healing used by practitioners of con- flict transformation respond to the harm caused by violence by seeking to restore or create conditions of human flourishing. According to Galtung (1996), the process of creating positive peace is one of 'diagnosis, prognosis and treatment' that take place at the level of social structures rather than individual bodies. From this perspective, any of the processes through which conflict transformation is carried out—processes of material rebuilding, 'reconciliation' efforts of the kind discussed above, memorializations, and socio-political reconstruction—can be construed as part of this 'treatment'.

Proponents of this 'healing' approach often liken the societal harms caused by violence to somatic harm—for instance, by referring to collective grief in terms of 'woundedness' or 'scarring', and to violence as a form of 'disease' or 'pathology'[6] (see Nordstrom 1997; Galtung 1996). Of course, literal injury and disease often attend war; but these references are not to human bodies, but to the symbolic collective body at the centre of transformative death rituals. Nonetheless, translating the harm of violence into bodily terms renders it tangible, bringing it within the realm of Western secular forms of meaning and response. As Bauman argues (see above), the Western secular response to death has focused largely on the development of biological, and medical strategies for forestalling it. Visualizing violent death as a form of disease renders the project of re-enchantment feasible. Instead of an inscrutable and unavoidable disaster, violence is reframed as a kind of chronic illness that can be worked on over time and perhaps even eliminated, through a combination of scientific advancement (the study of violence) and care (the use of conflict transformation strategies). At a deeper level, however, the medical metaphor underpins the ritual aspect of conflict transformation. Quite simply, it converts the war-damaged society into the body upon which rituals of re-enchantment can be performed.

Within these rituals of healing, intervenors (whether external or part of the society in question) play the role of healers. Their purpose is to catalyze the healing process and to prescribe courses of action that will expedite it. For Philpott:

> Peacebuilders are like doctors who understand that the body is composed of interconnected systems and then specialize in certain regions of connection with the conviction that these subsystems crucially sustain the entire anatomy. A feature of this medicine is its interest not only in laws, institutions, and policies but in emotions, attitudes, beliefs, legitimacy, and, broadly speaking, the wide range of relationships among citizens.
>
> (2010: 8)

The medical metaphor lends credence to the acts carried out by intervenors. Much of what they do, or claim to do, seems abstract and idealized: creating peace, generating stability, constituting new states. The purpose of ritual is literally to embody abstractions in concrete forms, confirming their constitutive or performative power. For instance, Scarry (see Chapter 3) argues that the destruction of bodies in war is a form of transubstantiation, in which the abstract ideals associated with war ('freedom', or 'power', for instance) are given concrete form. The notion of healing central to conflict transformation is simultaneously a continuation and a reversal of this process. It symbolically converts the harmed society into a ritual body in which violence is embedded, then construes the transformation of this society as an exorcism of this violence. By reversing the symbolic ritual of killing, intervenors seek not only to close off episodes of violence and remove their traces, but also to protect against future violence; indeed, conflict transformation is usually understood as a preventive strategy as much as a reactive one. In this sense, the brand of medicine wielded by intervenors is a talismanic one, and intervenors assume a role that might otherwise be occupied by psychopomps and shamans. Namely, they use rituals to ensure that the living and the dead are reconciled, that the radical contingency opened up by violence is restored to order, and that these processes are realized and confirmed in the production of flourishing human life.

These rituals play an important dramaturgical role in reversing the effects of violence and attempting to restore meaning to human lives and deaths. They involve very public and expressive assertions of the forms of agency associated with the Western secular ideal of high life—the reflexive activation of the capacity to transform oneself, and the ability to pursue and attain conditions of collective human flourishing. Most importantly, they frame these practices as strategies of re-enchantment—that is, of removing the effects of violence and restoring 'dehumanized' beings to the category of humanity. Just as they frame violence as a 'disease' embedded in the body, they present human flourishing as a concrete phenomenon, embodied in human social structures and the processes that sustain them. Secular 'healers' seek to guarantee the triumph of human life over death, and to restore the boundary between enchanted and disenchanted beings. Moreover, although they are focused on the living, these rituals offer powerful immortality strategies to those who have died in violence. They function as the 'truth procedures' through which the ontological interventions described in the previous section are realized. Moreover, in expressing the resilience and continuity of human life, they provide a framework in which lives 'lost' to violence can be recuperated and reflected. In this case, human flourishing is offered as a living memorial to those who died, and, simultaneously, a ritual negation of the events that killed them.

However, just as these processes can function as vehicles of re-enchantment, they also contribute to the forces of disenchantment and dehumanization, in a number of ways. First, and perhaps most fundamentally, the immortality strategies discussed above reproduce the phenomenon of effective dehumanization. Specifically, they frame people killed or harmed by violence as targets of re-enchantment—and, in some cases, (re-)humanization—confirming their status as disenchanted objects. It is important to note that the strategies discussed here (in particular, the immediate need to restore immanent, human meaning to lives and deaths affected by violence) are by no means 'natural' or 'universal' reactions to death. Instead, they reflect, and impose, a distinctively Western secular anxiety about the preservation of binaries of high life–bad death, human–inhuman and enchantment–disenchantment. In a related sense, the immortality strategies described above promote direct disenchantment by treating human lives and deaths as raw materials for the production of meaning. Just like the forms of counting, categorization and measurement discussed in Chapter 5, these strategies subject human lives and deaths to instrumental–rational processes, helping to *constitute* them as disenchanted objects. This is particularly pronounced in ontological strategies used to 'make something good come out of violence'. As part of these strategies, intervenors essentially hijack existing trajectories of violence, reorienting these towards new goals such as 'peace' and 'stability'. Ontologically, the distinction between these acts is fine; in the case of aggressive violence and intervention, human lives are instrumentalized as the fuel for transformation and the material conditions in which it is realized. Of course, in the case of intervention, the trajectories in question are set in motion by others, but the instrumentality of these strategies is undiminished.

Second, all of the strategies and processes discussed above promote very specific forms of meaning and responses to death. While they draw on a range of beliefs and rituals, both Western secular and transcendent, each of these phenomena are instrumentalized to Western secular immortality strategies— that is, to the production of high life. As I have argued above, the magpie tendencies of Western secular cosmology are magnified and projected through strategies of intervention. On the one hand, this approach recognizes diverse forms of belief and helps to preserve them amid rapid and often radical change. For this reason, the processes associated with Western secularity are not always as homogenizing as critics of secularizing processes (see Chapter 2) might suggest.

However, from another perspective, the selective appropriation of other belief systems, and their subjugation to Western secular forms of meaning, may have a profoundly disenchanting effect. This occurs for two reasons. For one thing, intervenors appropriate only *selected* elements of transcendent or enchanted systems of belief. They do not attempt to reproduce these systems of belief wholesale, cultivating the distinctive social, interpersonal, ritual and communal aspects of life in which these systems are embodied. To do this would involve quite literally reproducing societies as they were before the act of violence in question, which is at odds with the Western secular imperative to 'transform' societies in line with the ideal of high life. Instead, intervenors fragment these systems of belief, melding them into hybrids within which these fragments are protected, but the wholeness of which they form a part is lost. Moreover, as mentioned above, it is not common for intervenors to believe literally in the transcendent or enchanted beliefs they appropriate. Few intervenors convert to 'local' religions or become actual shamans (although of course it is possible that some do). For the most part, intervenors instru-mentalize transcendent forms of belief in the interests of promoting or expediting Western secular ideals of individuality and human flourishing. The upshot of this is that the appropriated beliefs may become devalued or even desacralized as they are subjugated to immanent beliefs. In this vein, MacGinty (2008) points out that the instrumentalization of 'traditional' rituals may deprive them of their contextual meaning by redefining them in terms of the instrumental goals and norms of intervenors. Similarly, Powers argues that:

> Religion cannot be simply a means to pursue peacebuilding. Instrumentalizing religion, even for the worthwhile objective of peacebuilding, will undermine religion as well as the effectiveness of religious peacebuilding.
>
> (2010: 329)

In other words, the risk of fragmenting and instrumentalizing transcendent belief systems to promote Western secular processes of re-enchantment is that they might lose the sacred character that inheres in their wholeness and interconnection as *systems* of belief. For societies experiencing serious rupture, this can only compound the sense of violence and ontological threat they experience.

For these reasons, the immortality strategies discussed above have ambivalent effects with regards to the project of re-enchantment. On the one hand, they offer powerful strategies for restoring meaning and order in the face of bad death. But on the other hand, they reproduce the same dialectic of disenchantment–re-enchantment discussed in previous chapters.

Conclusions

In order to protect the category of humanity, intervenors must find a way of closing the holes torn open by violence. Yet Western secularity offers few resources for dealing with death. Instead of confirming death as an integral part of life, or focusing on a transcendent afterlife, it calls for the rejection of death and the assertion of the primacy of high life. This chapter has explored the concept of immortality strategies, and the various processes and rituals through which they are used in intervention, particularly in efforts at 'postwar' transformation. By 'making something good come out of violence', and consolidating these efforts through symbolic, public rituals, intervenors seek to enfold the victims of violence into a Western secular framework of meaning. In so doing, they attempt to reverse the effects of bad death, to assert the primacy of high life, and to confirm the ability of human agents to redeem the category of humanity. The production and sustenance of high life functions, paradoxically, as both a memorial to the dead and a negation of bad death. However, as with the other strategies of intervention discussed in this book, these processes of re-enchantment also drive forward disenchantment. Is there any way to escape this dialectic?

Notes

1 This term is short for 'militant subjects-of-the-event'. A subject-of-the-event is someone who experiences an event as the beginning of a new ontological trajectory or set of conditions.

2 Of course, many conflict transformation theories are influenced by overtly religious thinking. However, I shall argue that they reflect a Western secular attitude towards death and the means of reconfiguring it. So, like many features of the contemporary world, they are hybrids of Western secularity and other belief systems (see Chapter 2).

3 Whether this process makes instrumental–rational processes more enchanted, or enchanted beliefs more instrumental–rational is difficult to ascertain; the strategy generates the potential for both results.

4 This is a mirror image of the rituals associated with retrieving and reinterring bodies discussed above, but in this case, the people in question are living.

5 In fact, Western secular beliefs place a strong emphasis on the idea of transfiguration. It is most clearly reflected in the central notion of authenticity, framed as a process of constant self-transformation.

6 Of course, the characterization of violence as a disease is ambiguous in its implications, since it frames violence not as the outcome of intentional, instrumental acts but rather as an immanent pathology. This, in turn, seems to dilute the responsibility of violent actors.

8 Conclusions—and beginnings

Western secularity is a powerful system of belief, which has furnished contemporary IR with some of its most compelling ideals and frustrating paradoxes. Its central concepts—of life and death, human and inhuman, enchantment and disenchantment, and even the concept of human intervention—both inspire and undermine the impulse to intervene in situations of mass violence. To understand the dilemmas and contradictions that contemporary intervenors face, it is necessary to pay attention to these cosmological foundations and their expressions in human action, institutions and social structures. *International Intervention in a Secular Age* has begun this task by contesting mainstream assumptions about the role of Western secularity and demonstrating its powerful influence on the norms, practices and ethics of intervention. It began by rejecting the standard story about secularity told in IR, which privileges the ideas of secularization and laicism. Instead, it argued that these are only two strands of the complex phenomenon of Western secularity, and drew attention to the alternative account presented in the 'trans-formation thesis'. It suggested that the rise of Western secularity came about through the shift to a totally immanent frame, in which human life and agency are the only sources of meaning. These transformations have produced distinctive beliefs, social formations and concepts of agency—including the idea that human beings can and must intervene in situations of violence. Building on this foundation, it then explored the distinctive concepts of life and death offered by Western secularity, and demonstrated how these have shaped international politics and the ethics of intervention. Images of high life and bad death fuel the desire to limit violence and ensure quality of life; yet they also make intervenors reluctant to sacrifice or relinquish their lives in the defence of others'. These concepts shed new light on the reasons for the strong public demand for intervention in situations of mass violence—and the resistance it may generate. Next, the book examined how these concepts of life and death are connected to the Western secular belief in disenchantment—that is, the belief that the non-human world is stripped of intrinsic meaning through instrumental–rational processes. Here, it highlighted a paradox: the creation and preservation of a distinctive, exclusively enchanted category of humanity requires the disenchantment of everything else (including humans cast out of the realm of high life). In other words, the very basis on which the category of humanity is staked is a constant source of its dissolution. This phenomenon can be seen at work in direct, effective and categorical forms of dehumanization. But Western secularity is equally driven by the desire to re-enchant, and these two forces form a powerful dialectic. The impulse to intervene reflects a desire to project meaning onto human beings who have been subjected to bad death or dehumanization, and to re-enfold them within Western secular forms of meaning-making. However, the instrumental–rational processes through which this strategy is carried out actually reproduce the dynamics of disenchantment. The book then traced this dialectic through its many twists and turns in the analysis, measurement and categorization of violence; the ethics of killing and letting die in contexts of military intervention; and the death rituals and immortality strategies that unfold in 'post-war' forms of intervention. Throughout all of these examples runs a common thread: Western secular cosmology and its paradoxical implications.

This book calls for a shift in the focus of discussions of intervention away from the realm of the strategic and ideological, and towards the realm of cosmology and ontology. At a moment when many scholars are calling for a 'post-secularist' orientation to international politics (see Chapter 2), this book has argued that we need, first, to take a closer look at what secularity means and enables in the context of intervention. To ignore the substantive features of Western secularity and their role in the international sphere is just as foolhardy as ignoring the influence of transcendent and 'religious' ideas—a mistake which 'post-secularists' caution against. This book embraces a specific kind of post-secularity in that it contests the practice of treating Western secularity as a neutral set of conditions, and seeks, in a sense to exoticize it by way of critique. It is also 'post-secularist' in that it contests the idea that secularism, or secularization—negative concepts which suggest the absence or corrosion of 'religion'—are the only ways of understanding secularity. Moreover, it embraces a vision of international politics shaped by various contesting, overlapping and transforming belief systems (of which Western secularity is one). However, it remains firmly secular in two regards. First, it moves away from the post-secularist focus on bringing 'religion' back into IR. It does not reject the importance of such a project, but rather suggests that the positive features of Western secularity should be treated with as much scrutiny as 'religious' beliefs. Second, it resists the temptation to believe that contemporary international politics is characterized by the eclipse of the secular. Certainly, it is almost impossible now to make an *empirical* secularist or laicist claim about the international sphere today (that is, to imply that religion plays no role in IR). But, as this book has argued, the features of Western secularity, understood through the trans-formation thesis, remain firmly embedded in the norms, logics and practices of IR. An understanding of Western secularity certainly does not explain everything that shapes intervention or international politics more generally, but it illuminates important elements thereof. Therefore, this book calls for a more subtle and attentive critique of secularity, in all of its contradictions.

To this end, I have tried to shift attention from the standard registers of knowledge employed by IR scholars and practitioners—juridical, ethical, strategic and scientific—to the much less fashionable lenses of cosmology and anthropology. An exploration of cosmology is crucial to any understanding of human action. It helps to determine how human beings see themselves, their place in the universe, and the possibilities and constraints of action. It also sets the parameters of ontology and meaning, without which the ethical and practical questions generally posed by IR scholars could not be posed. Cosmology in this sense of the word is generally ignored in IR scholarship—possibly because dominant, secularizing discourses associate cosmology with transcendent belief systems and presume that Western secularity lacks one. On the contrary, this book has demonstrated how deep, subtle cosmological assumptions shape how intervention is imagined and carried out. The anthropological sensibility of this book is a natural complement to this task. It approaches the assemblage of practices, structures, institutions, forms of agency, systems of meaning and other factors that make up the 'international' as a distinct form of human life. This makes it possible to observe how cosmology is expressed within it, and how people respond to their beliefs about it. Since the cosmological assumptions in question tend to be unspoken and unwritten, we can best observe them in the actions, institutions and discourses through which various actors respond to the challenges of life and death. An anthropological approach to the 'international' sphere offers a perspective that makes this kind of observation possible.

As this book has argued, adopting this approach allows scholars and practitioners of intervention (and of IR more generally) to view several perennial problems of intervention in a new light. For instance, it offers a fresh understanding of the sources of the contemporary idea of intervention, focusing on the transferral of responsibility for 'divine intervention' into human hands. It also provides insight into the fundamental sources of the aversion of states and international organizations to 'sacrifice' the lives of their troops, moving beyond pragmatic and ideological explanations. Furthermore, it plumbs more fully the disturbing consistency of the paradoxical logic through which human beings must be killed or allowed to die in order to protect 'humanity'. Crucially, this analysis also problematizes issues that have not yet been broached by scholars and practitioners of IR. Namely, it highlights the link between the Western secular notions of bad death, disenchantment and dehumanization that shape intervention. In so doing, it explores the deeply problematic impulse to 're-enchant' human life, which simultaneously responds to and compounds threats to human life.

Understanding the constitutive features of Western secularity is central to unlocking these problems, new and old alike. As such, discussions of its influence should be integral to discussions about the future of intervention and means of addressing its central problems. To this end, the remainder of this chapter will evaluate the role of Western secularity in contemporary intervention. The first part will highlight the substantial contribution this system of belief has made to human agency and ethics in the face of violence and death. Rather than advocating the abandonment of Western secular cosmology and ethics, it will argue that there is much to be preserved and retrieved from this framework. However, in order to retrieve Western secularity as one possible basis for international intervention and politics, its central paradox—the dialectic of disenchantment–re-enchantment—must be overcome. The chapter concludes by exploring two alternatives, each of which entails risks and ironies of their own. It concludes by calling for an international politics that rejects the concept of disenchantment and human exceptionalism. Only this ethical approach, I shall argue, can resolve the paradox at the heart of the Western secular impulse towards intervention.

In defence of Western secularity

The majority of this book has been devoted to the critique of Western secularity and its influence on contemporary intervention. Precisely because the concepts of life, death and humanity promoted by this system of belief are often taken for granted in IR, I wanted to focus on their paradoxes and ambiguous implications. However, I do not intend to excoriate Western secularity, which deserves as much respect and serious consideration as any other belief system. Nor am I advocating the rejection of this belief system, or the adoption of a transcendent basis for IR. As mentioned at the outset of this book, Western secularity is the belief system in which I have lived my life and from which perspective I write. The tone of this argument is one of immanent critique, rather than one of hostility. It does not suggest that Western secularity is the only possible basis for international politics. On the contrary, by refusing to take its influence for granted, this book has sought to relativize Western secularity, and to demonstrate that there are alternatives—both within and beyond this particular belief system. However, it does suggest that Western secularity offers several fundamental concepts and beliefs to IR—some of which are worth defending. As such, it is worth briefly reviewing the contributions that Western secularity has made to the various fields, practices and discourses explored throughout the book.

In Chapter 1, I explored 'transformation thesis', which suggests that many of the features of Western secularity emerged from the translation of transcendent ideals into human terms. This translation preserved some of the most powerful and evocative ethical principles of the Judeo-Christian tradition—for instance, the ethics of care, a commitment to the sanctity of human life. Yet through these transformations, human life was elevated above divine will or religious doctrine. What resulted were social and ethical structures wholly oriented to the value and meaning of human life, which did not require membership in any group other than that of humanity. This made possible the universal humanism that lies at the heart of contemporary discourses on human rights. Moreover, the Western secular emphasis on bodily integrity and the reduction of suffering have helped to provide momentum and public support for humanitarian action. Of course, people of many belief systems contribute to humanitarian causes (for 'religious' and 'non-religious') reasons. Nonetheless, the importance of Western secular beliefs should not be discounted as an explanatory factor in the rise of this movement. I also argued that Western secularity has made possible new conceptions of human agency—not least that of human intervention. This, I claimed, emerged from the transferral of divine responsibility and agency into human hands. By activating new images of agency, this world-view encourages human beings to respond directly to the 'evils' that face them, rather than waiting for divine action or judgement. In addition, the movement towards immanentization has privileged a 'human's eye' rather than a 'god's eye' view of life on earth and threats to it. This set a stage in which it makes sense to think of 'people-centred', rather than 'state-centred' understandings of security, law and sovereignty. In other words, international politics owes much of its 'humanization' (for better or for worse) to the transformations that produced Western secularity.

In addition, Chapters 2 and 8 argued that Western secularity is defined not by the absence of religion (a feature only of specific variants) but rather by the plurality of beliefs that it fosters. This element of Western secular belief can, as I shall argue shortly, be cultivated in order to generate care and attachment to various ways of human life (and perhaps even other forms of being). The 'magpie tendencies' of Western secular meaning-making simultaneously unsettle and preserve transcendent and enchanted sources of meaning. In this regard, Western secularity is not a nihilistic world-view, but one which infuses international politics with belief, optimism and richness of meaning. On the one hand, as I argued in Chapter 7, the encounter between Western secular and transcendent sources of meaning can fragment and desacralize the latter. But, it can also, sometimes simultaneously, sacralize instrumental–rational processes of meaning-making. Furthermore, the fragments produced are woven and recombined with other forms of belief, creating genuinely new sources of meaning. This is, in fact, a radically pluralizing process which extends well beyond the norms of toleration and accommodation promoted by many post-secularists. It expresses a belief that diverse rituals, practices and sources of meaning are necessary in order to sustain the category of humanity, embraces their fusion, and places meaning-making at the heart of human action. These features of Western secularity not only challenge the cliché that secularity and belief are mutually exclusive; they also put paid to the notion that the disenchantment of the universe can ever be completed within this system of meaning. On the contrary, the possibilities of Western secularity highlighted in this book offer a vision of an international sphere infused with myriad sources of inspiration, aspiration, hope and faith—all of which may be needed in order to guide ethical action in the face of massive threats.

In addition, the Western secular ideal of high life and the anti-ideal of bad death constitute significant innovations. Unlike the transcendent frameworks of meaning from which they are originally derived, they consistently abhor violence and destruction (with few exceptions—see Chapter 6). Moreover, they strongly discourage the use of violence by removing its meaning-making capacities. The profound abhorrence of death that they express is, if not strictly unique, a sharp departure from centuries of the glorification of death in the context of war (see Shapiro 1997) and thus an innovative contribution to IR. As this book has demonstrated, the Western secular abhorrence of death is paradoxical and at times contradicts with the actions taken in its name. Yet, it has made possible an entirely new way of understanding the conduct of wars: one driven by the desire to minimize (at least some) human deaths. This tenet has become so central to contemporary discourses on inter-vention that it is difficult to imagine them without it.

It is a trickier task to identify the positive contributions of Western secularity to the phenomena discussed in Chapter 6: the logics of killing and letting die which sustain the category of humanity. However, despite its often counter-productive consequences, the desire to protect the category of humanity and to guarantee the persistence of human life as such has made an innovative con-tribution to IR. Instead of states, monarchies, regimes or 'religious' ideals, human life—mortal and evanescent as it is—has come to be seen as a feature of the universe that is worth protecting in its own right. For better or for worse, this has transformed thinking and practice about the purpose of military action and the role of international actors.

Finally, in Chapter 7, I argued that Western secularity offers powerful strategies for responding to death and offering a form of earthly 'immortality' in the face of large-scale violence. That chapter suggests that non-transcendent systems of belief are capable of offering rituals that can restore meaning, provide hope, affirm the purpose of life and ensure the continuity life in the face of violence and death. Western secularity offers the possibility of redemp-tion even to those who are not embedded in a transcendent system of belief—or, indeed, those who have lost faith in one. Moreover, it ensures that even human beings who hold no transcendent beliefs are not entirely helpless in the face of death. On the contrary, they can engage in a range of acts, practices and rituals in order to retrieve meaning and assert the priority of human life.

From this perspective, Western secularity is a rich source of ethical, nor-mative and cosmological beliefs that have made possible many features of contemporary international politics. As stated above, I do not mean to sug-gest that Western secularity has produced these features in isolation; the account of Western secularity given here acknowledges its debts to various other forms of belief. However, the basic cosmological premises of Western secularity have made many of these phenomena seem possible, persuasive or normatively desirable. Moreover, I do not intend to suggest that any of the phenomena enabled by Western secular beliefs—from human rights to the idea of 'humanitarian intervention'—are prima facie desirable, in either theory or practice. Indeed, the majority of this book has suggested that the situation is much more complex than that. The point is that Western secularity offers a great deal to international thinking and practice, and that, without it, many of the ideals held dear by proponents of intervention (of one kind or another) would have little resonance. There is much to defend and retrieve from this belief system if its central paradoxes can either be accepted or overcome.

Addressing the central paradox of Western secularity

What are the prospects for overcoming the central paradox of Western secularity—its distinction between enchanted–disenchanted, and the dialectic it produces? In this section, I shall examine two alternatives. The first involves finding a place for violence, or (re)introducing an element of the transcendent into Western secular responses to violence. The second demands the rejection of the belief in disenchantment and the cultivation of an ethics based on care for being in all of its multiplicity. Neither approach can eliminate all of the problems addressed in this book, but each offers a way of overcoming the central problem: the fact that each attempt to re-enchant humanity drives forward disenchantment. Moreover, each alternative introduces new risks, pitfalls and paradoxes of its own. It is important to think through these alternatives not because they are only ones open to intervenors, but rather because they frame the problem in a new light and allow one to see beyond the dialectic of disenchantment–re-enchantment.

Negotiating with the transcendent: Taylor's maximal demand

Western secularity is, according to the 'transformation thesis', defined by its radical immanence. Human actions, institutions and capabilities form the frontiers of its cosmology, and the ideal to which all ethical action is oriented. The preservation of this immanent universe relies on the rejection and exclusion of the transcendent—in particular, the subjugation of human life to it. However, this severely constricts the sources of meaning that humans can draw upon in order to ensure the meaningfulness of their lives. In the absence of a transcendent realm, there is nothing to guarantee the value of human life, or to restore it when it is challenged. As I argued in Chapter 3, the total abhorrence of transcendent or 'sacrificial' forms of killing and dying presents a trade-off. On the one hand, it ensures that human life is enshrined as the highest ideal; but on the other hand, it strips death of its 'numinous' or meaning-making capacities. Death becomes, quite literally, a 'dead end' to human life, and a void that cannot be breached by human action. All human lives that fall victim to bad death are exiled from the category of humanity (unless they are retrieved through the strategies of re-enchantment discussed throughout this book). These individuals are, in fact, doubly banished: first, simply for being dead, and second, for being killed in a manner that threatens the ideal of high life. In this context, the category of humanity is always incapable of accommodating one half of the whole 'that constitutes [one] as human, that is, the sacredness of life *and* death' (Agamben 1999: 81, italics mine). Furthermore, those exposed to violence are deeply vulnerable to dehumanization—not only by their attackers, but also by those who would 'save' them. Indeed, I have argued that this abhorrence of bad death produces dehumanization and discourages the sacrifice of 'fully human' lives to save 'dehumanized ones' (see Chapters 4 and 7). In short, the total rejection of the meaning-making capacities of violence and death leave humanity extremely vulnerable to disenchantment.

Is there any way to broach this gap between the radical immanence of Western secularity and transcendent approaches to violence and death? Certainly, the (re)adoption of a transcendent framework would help to overcome the loss of meaning that attends death and violence, but it would entirely undermine the Western secular ideal of high life. Taylor (2007) argues, however, that there might be a middle way—that is, that it may be possible and necessary to restore some of the meaning-conferring capacities of violence. This amounts to extending (or perhaps fully embracing) the few exceptions to the category of bad death discussed in Chapter 6.

Taylor (2007) grapples with this task by seeking a balance between the elevation of everyday human life and the universal desire for transcendence that is so often expressed in violence. Within contemporary Western secular societies, he contends, the balance is skewed significantly in the direction of the former. According to Taylor, these societies constitute themselves by 'repressing and marginalizing violence' and degrading it to a 'pathology' (2007: 649) that can be removed with no cost and to the immense benefit of humanity. As Taylor puts it:

> Our new [exclusively human] stance allows us to imagine a world shorn of violence and suffering, at least as a conceivable long-term goal. The destructive forces which confront us are nothing but obstacles on the path to this goal.
>
> (2007: 651)

But Taylor urges us to note the historical specificity of this approach to violence, and its distinctiveness from other systems of belief. He argues that almost all known cultures—including the Judeo-Christian source of Western secularity—accepted it as normal, and even necessary, to find divine meaning in suffering and destruction (see also Asad 2003). Perhaps, he implies, this pattern suggests that there needs to be a role for violence within human societies. Only by giving meaning to violence, suffering and death were these cultures able to attain a secure sense of their place in the universe and of the durable meaning of their collective existence. According to Taylor, the inability to find meaning in violence and death is experienced as a profound loss within Western secular societies. This sense of loss, he avers, has produced a powerful internal struggle:

> Between aspirations to transcendence … and the cherishing of ordinary human desires; between the demand to understand and respect the meta-biological roots of human violence and the imperative moral demand to end it.
>
> (Taylor 2007: 676)

As a result of this struggle, he claims 'we are at war with ourselves, and responding differently to this inner conflict, we end up at war with each other' (Taylor 2007: 655). In other words, the attempt to suppress or eradicate violence produces contradictions and tensions which, ironically, render human life more vulnerable. For Taylor, the urgent imperative is to balance these seemingly conflictual demands in a way which can meet 'our highest spiritual or moral aspirations for human beings … which [nonetheless] doesn't crush, mutilate or deny what is essential to our humanity' (2007: 640). In other words, he argues that violence and death must be negotiated within the framework of Western secularity, not rejected out of hand.

To attain this goal, Taylor argues that Western secular societies must find a way of meeting what he calls the 'maximal demand': the trade-off between transcendence and the idealization of human life. Meeting this demand does not merely involve passive and reluctant acceptance of a certain amount of death as a 'necessary evil'. Instead, it calls for an explicit moral debate about the value of violence and its capacity to enhance human life. Moreover, the 'maximal demand' does not imply a simple 'reversion' to transcendent frameworks of meaning. Rather, it proposes that moral weight be given to both demands—or, at least, that both be recognized as legitimate and neces-sary to human life. To meet this demand, people living in Western secular world-views must either:

> Scale down [their] moral aspirations in order to allow [their] ordinary human life to flourish; or [they] have to agree to sacrifice some of this ordinary flourishing in order to achieve [their] higher goals.
>
> (Taylor 2007: 640)

How might the 'maximal demand' be met in the context of Western secular responses to large-scale violence? And how might it reshape these responses?

One option would be to emphasize the aesthetics of violence as a counter-challenge to processes of disenchantment. This would involve, as Taylor puts it, a 'reconciliation with violence and suffering through a beauty born of its necessity' (2007: 664). Violence has the power to bring about this reconciliation because 'it both beckons us as a means of self-affirmation, or giving numi-nous force to our lives; and also terrifies us' (Taylor 2007: 670). According to theorists of the 'sublime', this orientation is already a powerful force in international politics, and is reflected in collective responses to large-scale violence even in societies heavily influenced by Western secularity. According to Roland Bleiker, confrontations with violence (especially on a large-scale) produce a range of emotional responses:

> Fear of death and suffering, awe at the sheer magnitude of a traumatic event; anger and whoever or whatever caused the tragedy, relief for having survived it; hatred towards those deemed responsible, compassion for those who have died or are in pain.
>
> (2009: 67)

In other words, the experience of witnessing violence is charged with meaning, possibility and responsiveness. The terrible beauty of violence offers a heightened awareness of the nature of human being and its boundary conditions. Dwelling in this liminal space (even if only for a moment) opens individuals and collectives to multiple trajectories of action and response. In this way, violence opens up moments of contingency in the course of history, allowing people to enact major changes in human societies and even the international sphere. The experience of violence provokes the affective conditions in which such changes suddenly appear possible, enabling people to act as the Badiouian 'militants' discussed in Chapter 6. From this perspective, violence offers opportunities for making and altering meaning that would be smothered by uninterrupted process of everyday life. This is not a glorification of, or a call for violence, but rather a recognition of the plural, ambivalent possibilities opened up by its 'terrible beauty' and human responsiveness to it.

Francois Debrix (2007) makes a similar point. He avers that faraway images of violence are experienced by humans as:

> Necessary and sometimes pleasurable not so much because they evince an immediately evident beauty or artistic splendor, but because they require of the public to reach for ideas through and beyond the violent images in order to make sense of and find an eventual satisfaction with what is going on in the world out there.
>
> (Debrix 2007: 125)

In other words, the apprehension of large-scale violence intensifies processes of meaning-making, forcing humans to challenge their received beliefs and to (re)create meaning from a welter of chaos and destruction. What he describes is a profoundly creative impulse, which activates forms of agency that are highly prized in Western secular beliefs. Namely, this kind of creativity allows people to believe that they are located in comprehensible coordinates of time and space, within which they can play an active role in shaping history and ontology. In some cases, Debrix argues, this experience may also be profoundly humanizing, and can heighten the value attributed to human life. Observing violence from afar, Debrix suggests, enables human beings to see not only the destruction of human life but also to witness survival—including their own. This offers them a glimpse of '"humanity at its best" (... the human qualities that remain even in great suffering)' (Debrix 2007: 135). Watching others die violently underscores one's joy at having survived (see Bleiker 2009). However, it may also invoke a poignant sense of optimism about the capacity of humanity (as a category of being) to withstand violent death. This may be heightened further by affective responses to the efforts of intervenors to 'make something good come out of violence' through their own violent and non-violent action. Specifically, the forms of intervention discussed in Chapters 6 and 7 involve large-scale, spectacular acts of transformation which may themselves inspire the experience of the sublime.

So, both of these authors suggest that human affective responses to violence can offer unprecedented opportunities for meaning-making and catalysts for radical change or the self-constitution of collectives. While violence undercuts the ideal of high life, it also affirms many of the central beliefs and forms of agency that define Western secularity. As such, attention to the sublime elements of violence and death may offer a pathway for negotiating Taylor's 'maximal demand'.

However, intervenors, policy-makers and the global publics that call for intervention of various kinds tend to focus on the degradation of human beings in situations of violence, and the threat this raises to humanity 'as a whole'. In order to meet the 'maximal demand', it might be necessary to restore or publicly celebrate the images of heroism or valour not only in surviving violence, but also in succumbing to it with integrity, or as an act of altruism, or without fear and hatred. Another strategy might involve altering public orientations towards victims of violence to emphasize not (only) their suffering and the indignity of their deaths, but also their resilience and creativity in the face of violence. Numerous anthropologists of violence (see, for instance, Nordstrom 1997; Macek 2000; Richards 2005; Das 2007) have drawn attention to the remarkable capacity of humans to sustain and defend their ways of life in the face of violence. Asserting the meaning-conferring properties of violence in this way might invert the processes that produce bad death, using strategies intended to degrade human life as a means of bolstering its meaning. Agamben (1995) cautions strongly against interpreting the killing of *homo sacer* as a source of meaning for an important reason: this would reduce the shock and horror invoked by the violence, and, in this sense, let the killers off too easily. Agamben's stance offers a firm basis for resistance against sovereign power, but at the same time, it limits the opportunities for resisting and undermining this power by accepting its ability to dehumanize. Killing *homo sacer* may not intentionally or directly produce meaning, but it may do so *unintentionally and indirectly*. In other words, people may appropriate or (re)claim the meaning of this violence as a way of resisting it. As Agamben (1999) himself illustrates, the 'unspeakable' experience of surviving concentration camps has led to a proliferation of new concepts and forms of agency that have helped contemporary scholars to understand and fight against the phenomenon of dehumanization (for instance, the act of 'witnessing'). Thus, while it may be important to deny the *intention* of killers to produce meaning, deriving meaning from their actions is killing might be the most radical means of reversing its disenchanting effects.

In the context of intervention, this would involve adopting a new ethics based not (solely) on the desire to 'rescue victims', but also on the impulse to express solidarity with their suffering. It may even involve a positive desire to fight— and perhaps even to die—alongside them. Extended further, this approach may call for the (re)affirmation of an ethics of sacrifice into the ethics of intervention. Instead of framing the deaths of intervenors as entirely lost— that is, as wasteful and unnecessary—such an approach might emphasize the value of dying for 'humanity'. As Chapter 6 suggests, intervenors already apply this approach to various forms of killing and letting others die; to meet Taylor's 'maximal demand', they might have to extend it to themselves.

This move would create parity between intervenors and the people whom they wish to 'save' in more than one way. First, it would break down the dichotomy between 'fully human' and 'dehumanized lives', equalizing the value placed on these lives. It might involve reversing the trend towards using air strikes, UAVs and proxy tactics[1] as a replacement for ground troops. Moreover, it may entail further downgrading the priority of 'force protection' in peacekeeping missions. This idea is already expressed in the influential Brahimi Report (UN 2000), which suggests that force protection should never take priority over the humanitarian goals of a UN mission, and that person-nel taking part must accept this (see also Walzer 2004). However, reconciling an element of sacrifice with Western secular practices of intervention would require more than the reluctant acceptance of the risk of violent death. It would require the cultivation of a positive image of death, not as an excep-tion, but rather as an integral part of Western secular ethics and the ideal of high life. The deaths of intervenors would need to be linked explicitly the forms of individual and collective immortality discussed in Chapter 5, offering intervenors the chance to enhance the meaning of their lives through death. This, of course, is the same strategy that militaries have used for centuries to generate and maintain morale among their troops in conditions of war, and so it necessarily involves a reversion. The key difference, in this case, is that the ideals in question would be those of high life and 'humanity' rather than national pride, glory or territorial integrity.

The valorization of death required by Taylor's 'maximal demand' might sit uncomfortably with Western secular beliefs. However, as this brief discussion suggests, it already forms a strong undercurrent within practices of intervention arising from this system of belief. The experience of the sublime discussed above is widely experienced, but treated with a sense of shame or abjection (see Žižek 2009). Moreover, proponents of intervention are leery of affirming deaths (either of intervenors or those whom they wish to save) for fear of becoming apologists for violence. Attempting to meet the 'maximal demand' would involve overcoming these aversions and affirming the vestige of sacrifice that remains within Western secular ethics.

Even if these practical problems could be overcome, would it be desirable to attain the 'maximal demand'? The strategies outlined here are, of course, highly controversial and riddled with problems. Not only would they require a massive change (and, in some cases, a full reversal) of profound, entrenched beliefs, but they would also have significantly adverse consequences. In particular, they would significantly weaken the Western secular prohibition against violent death. Acknowledging the heroism of those who die or are harmed in the context of violence would, by definition, valorize this form of death and render it appealing. It may also break down distinctions between perpetrators and victims of violence, which is fuzzy at best in existing schemas of meaning. Specifically, it may be difficult to untangle acts of violence undertaken as a means of protecting oneself or others, and those executed as acts of revenge or aggression. This stance might also justify and even encourage military 'adventurism': the acts of states intent upon realizing their own visions of humanity and world order through military means (of which the doctrine of 'nation-building' is a prime example). Indeed, the promise of a 'good death' has been used for centuries to convince soldiers to relinquish their lives in the interests of sovereign power. One of the contributions of Western secular ethics has been to provide a basis for critiquing this practice by placing human life above the demands of power, and (re)introducing the ethics of sacrifice would likely reverse this trend. These objections fall largely into the category of 'slippery slope' arguments. They are plausible threats, but, at the same time, they represent extreme manifestations of the ideas presented above. For instance, restoring sacrifice to the heart of intervention need not mean that all military (or non-military) excursions should be glorified. On the contrary, the normative structures that are currently used to sanction states that break international law or diverge from agreed protocols need not be removed. Adopting this approach might simply involve changing public attitudes towards the lives and deaths of intervenors. Moreover, recognizing the meaningfulness of deaths lost to violence need not be interpreted as a comprehensive apology for violence of all kinds, or as evidence of impunity for violent actors. On the contrary, perpetrators of violence would still be subject to the same punishments and condemnations as they are now, but their victims could be afforded a different ethical status.

In either case, attempting to meet the 'maximal demand' would, as Taylor points out, require compromising some of the central tenets of Western secular ethics. The objections outlined above suggest the total reversal of these ethics, and a 'return' to a transcendent framework. However, the point of addressing the 'maximal demand' is to chart a course between the extremes of transcendence and radical immanence, not to oscillate between one and the other. This would involve constant attention and adjustment, and the work of maintaining balance between the two extremes could never be decisively completed. Intervenors—and human beings generally—would need to live with a certain degree of risk that the ideal of high life might be overturned. Moreover, they would need to place immense trust in the judgement of decision-makers. Potential intervenors would constantly need to weigh up the competing demands of privileging human life and accommodating transcendence. This would not mean capitulating to every form of violence or death, but rather attempting to 'eradicate the bad ones and encourage the good' (Taylor 2007: 646). This, of course, would be a highly subjective process of judgement, which would rely on an unfeasible degree of unity among the beliefs of intervening actors (something which Taylor's own account of secularity seems to preclude). Moreover, Taylor offers little guidance for precisely how these judgements should be carried out, and the 'good' forms of transcendent violence distinguished from the 'bad'. It seems that it might be necessary to continue to rely on the dichotomy between high life and bad death, or perhaps to create or adopt rigid, transcendent rules for making this distinction. For these reasons, the attempt to meet the 'maximal demand' seems to lead back to the same dichotomy that plagues existing Western secular approaches to violence and death.

The attempt to (re)affirm the sacrificial element of violence and death, therefore, creates a number of problems. It involves relinquishing many of the key tenets and ideals of Western secularity and diluting its power as a cosmology oriented towards human life. Furthermore, it opens up significant potential for the glorification and multiplication of violence, and offers little guidance for enacting the processes of judgement that might counter this problem. For these reasons, it seems to be a risky and potentially counterproductive way of addressing the central paradox of Western secularity. Is there any way to overcome the dialectic of disenchantment–re-enchantment without embracing the kind of 'radical transcendence' (see Connolly 2011) that Taylor describes?

Enchanting intervention: Bennett's rejection of disenchantment

Belief in dehumanization lies at the heart of Western secularity's central paradox. Indeed, as I have argued in this book, dehumanization is not an objective 'fact', but rather an intersubjective process. It does not inhere in specific actions or relationships; rather, it hinges on the beliefs of one or more parties that these acts are sufficient to denude a human life of its intrinsic meaning and that human action is capable of achieving this. Believing in disenchantment can have a depressive effect on human attachment to the world and care for its constituents. As Bennett argues:

> The depiction of nature and culture as orders no longer capable of inspiring deep attachment inflects the self as a creature of loss and thus discourages discernment of the marvelous vitality of bodies human and nonhuman, natural and artificial.
>
> (2001: 4)

In other words, the more humans look for disenchantment in a Western secular world-view, the more they will find it. This is a self-perpetuating cycle; once beings come to be seen as 'disenchanted', they become more vulnerable to the very processes that realize their status as disenchanted objects (killing, injuring or instrumentalization).

The modes of intervention discussed throughout this book seek to counteract this process by instrumentally *re*-enchanting human life, and by (selectively) integrating 'dehumanized' lives within Western secular systems of meaning. Yet this strategy produces troubling excesses: whole groups of people remain excluded from these processes of meaning-making, and are made subject to 'categorical dehumanization'. Even those who are enveloped within the project of re-enchantment are subjected to instrumental–rational strategies of meaning-making, which, ironically, reproduce them as disenchanted objects. As such, contemporary intervention appears to be hopelessly trapped within the dialectic of disenchantment–re-enchantment. Is there any way out of this cycle?

Bennett's work[2] offers a simple but radical option: humans should simply stop believing in disenchantment. More specifically, they should reject the dichotomy between 'enchanted' and 'disenchanted' forms of being on which the category of humanity is staked within Western secular cosmology.[3] Rejecting the possibility of disenchantment would undermine the logic that makes dehumanization possible. It would also remove the need for the clunky, mechanical dialectic of disenchantment–re-enchantment that have been explored in the latter half of this book. However, rejecting disenchantment would be a radical move, and not only because it would require a significant and large-scale shift in beliefs. It also raises a significant risk. Namely, denying the possibility of disenchantment and dehumanization would entail the claim that human beings remain enchanted—and therefore human—regardless of the harms, injuries or forms of death inflicted on them. It would deprive proponents of humanitarianism and human rights of two of their most important rallying cries: the fear of (mutual and total) dehumanization; and the intolerance of violence and suffering. This, in turn, would demand an ethics of intervention based not on the fear of mutual dehumanization, but rather on the sense of attachment, care and commitment that enchantment may inspire. How might this ethical orientation work?

To explore this option, it is necessary to dispense with zero-sum thinking about the relationship between humans and non-humans. Within the standard narrative of disenchantment, Bennett argues, human well-being and enchantment are placed in an inverse relation. Every advance in the scientific, social, productive, cultural and economic well-being of humanity seems to contribute to disenchantment, and to rely on the treatment of non-humans as mere objects for instrumental use. Moreover, this narrative of disenchantment frames *enchantment* instrumentally, as though it were a property that can be removed from and projected onto objects. Bennett rebuts this assumption, arguing that no being can be disenchanted provided that human beings remain willing to *be enchanted* with it. Enchantment, Bennett claims, is not an objective property that can be imbued and removed from particular beings by humans. Rather, it is a subjective state and a mode of experience characterized by affective sensations such as wonder and awe.[4] As Connolly (2011) argues, such states are produced through the infinitely complex and subtle interactions of the human brain and body with other material beings, sonic vibrations, colours and textures, patterns of motion, and so on. He argues that these states are not conscious or intentional; rather, they emerge at the level of the subconscious and express themselves in human affect. To be enchanted is to cultivate one's capacity to experience these sensations, and to respond to them ethically. This response is not limited to particular cases (for instance, the 'worst' acts of violence, or specific groups of human beings). Rather, Bennett suggests that humans may experience enchantment in response to just about anything—from technological marvels to garbage dumps (2010).[5]

According to Bennett, the capacity to be (and to remain) enchanted has powerful implications for ethical action. She suggests that it can engender a strong ethical commitment to preserving, protecting, celebrating or simply recognizing the special character of the world—much more so than deontological or fear-based motivators for action. This ethics of attachment is oriented towards protecting objects and beings for their own sake, not solely out of the desire to further human ambitions. Moreover, cultivating enchantment calls for efforts to immerse oneself in the wondrous elements of life even in the face of banality or horror. We can already see an element of this approach at work in the death rituals discussed in Chapter 7, in which intervenors draw on enchanted world-views to seal off the ruptures created by bad death. Western secular death rituals, too, can inspire enchantment in the face of destruction. The processes of transformation and healing are tinged with a sense of the miraculous, and military action can inspire a sense of wonder (it is not for nothing that the US military strategy of 'rapid dominance' is known colloquially as 'shock and awe'). This approach may also overlap with the notion of the sublime discussed above—the scale and magnitude of harms or responses to them may evoke a kind of fascination that corresponds to Bennett's descriptions of enchantment.

However, if enchantment is to become the basis for the ethics of intervention, it would need to be adopted in a much more radical way. Specifically, it would be necessary to remove the distinction between 'enchanted' and 'disenchanted' forms of life reproduced by the instrumental account of disenchantment. This, in turn, would demand that humans abandon the idea of human exceptionalism. Bennett (2010) argues that humans cling to exceptionalism in order to ensure that their needs are prioritized when disaster strikes. However, she claims, its historical 'track record' of achieving this aim is extremely poor, and it has led to circumstances (for instance, global warming) that may ultimately destroy human life. Instead of staking the protection of human life on its exceptional status, she offers '[an]other way to promote human health and happiness: to *raise the status of the materiality of which we are composed*' (Bennett 2010: 13). According to this argument:

> If matter itself is [recognized as being] lively, then not only is the difference between subjects and objects minimized, but the status of the shared materiality of all things is elevated. All bodies become more than mere objects.
>
> (Bennett 2010: 13)

Acknowledging that all beings—plants, non-human animals, objects, metals, machines—are more than 'mere' objects would remove the differential between enchanted and disenchanted beings. As I argued in Chapter 4, it is this differential that underwrites the logic of instrumental killing. Removing it would effectively render direct dehumanization deeply illogical, undermining effective dehumanization and making the whole project extremely difficult to realize. It would also protect human beings against categorical forms of dehumanization. According to Bennett, rejecting this dichotomy would:

> Set up a kind of safety net for those humans who are now, in a world where Kantian morality is the standard, routinely made to suffer because they do not conform to a particular (Euro-American, bourgeois, theocentric or other) model of personhood.
>
> (2010: 13)

In other words, if being ensconced in the category of humanity were no longer necessary to guarantee ethical status, it would no longer make sense to think of a being as a 'mere' object simply because it was cast outside of this category.

This shift in orientation would also involve rejecting the idea that death is always a source of disenchantment. As Bennett claims, there are many ways to respond to death in a Western secular context:

> One might seek to become resigned to a disenchanted world in which death is oblivion; one might look to a recuperated Romanticism in order to teach oneself how better to accept the meaninglessness of existence; or one might seek to overcome resentment over the fact of mortality by cultivating attachments to a world that allows numerous links to human, animal, material, technical and artificial bodies.
>
> (2001: 165)

In other words, enchantment, and the ethics of attachment that it promotes, might help to overcome the powerful sense of futility engendered by the Western secular notion of death as an absolute ending. The cultivation of attachment to life and being in all of its forms might work as a counter-balance against the meaninglessness of death.

Rejecting a belief in disenchantment and the dialectical dynamics it engenders would have important implications for many of the practices of intervention discussed throughout this book. Most importantly, perhaps, it would undermine the belief that the disenchantment of any individual or group of people poses a threat to 'humanity itself'—precisely because it would deny the possibility that 'humanity itself' could be disenchanted. Currently, the fear of disenchantment (or universal dehumanization) is one of the most powerful motivations for contemporary intervention. It is also a potent rallying call for proponents of human rights, humanitarianism and forms of intervention oriented towards protecting human life and its meaning. Indeed, one of the main ethical arguments made for upholding human rights in particular cases is that unless they are maintained universally, the very meaning of the term 'human' and the protections it offers would be moot. Similarly, as I argued in Chapter 6, the main rationale offered by intervenors for prioritizing responses to genocide is not that it threatens particular groups of people, but rather humanity 'as a whole'. The message reflected in both of these examples is clear: the only way to secure one's own humanity is to uphold the entire category. This leads to an ethics of intervention based on pessimism and nihilism, in which responsive action is driven by fear and revulsion rather than attachment and commitment.

Is an ethics of enchantment strong enough to replace the fear of mutual dehumanization as a motivating factor for ethical action? In the context of intervention, the stakes are terribly high. Fear, disgust, revulsion and resentment of death are powerful (if ultimately unstable—see Sontag 2003) motivations for action. Moreover, even these motivators fail to produce decisive responses to human suffering in all cases, as the problem of inconsistency in responses to mass violence attests to. Unless the sensation of enchantment is widespread and powerful enough to equal the motivation offered by these negative factors, then the abandonment of the current, negative approach might be even more disastrous.

Bennett's work suggests that we should take this wager. In fact, she argues that the capacity for ethical responsiveness prompted by enchantment is much stronger than the motivational capacity of fear and revulsion. Indeed, she claims, disenchantment is a strong suppressor of human action. It engenders a sense of futility, moroseness and impossibility, immersing human beings in the hopelessness of their condition, and driving them to actions that worsen this condition. In other words, when we see the universe as disenchanted, our resentment of this condition drives us to (ab)use it in ways that confirm its disenchantment, at least in our own eyes. In contrast, she claims, a well-developed sense of enchantment is crucial to overcoming resentment in the face of violence. She contends that a strong sense of enchantment is necessary in order to deal constructively with:

> The apocalyptic terror of the news and the despair or cynicism it breeds.
> Because the news media cultivate a crisis mentality, it is important to

heighten awareness of our profound—and empowering—attachment to life. For such attentiveness can help to transform shock at tragedy into a political will and to reform painful social structures.

(Bennett 2001: 160)

From this perspective, the current strategy of relying on negative motivations for ethical action is a risky gambit. It actually forecloses possibilities of action, and locks us into a cycle of fear and reaction that is difficult to break. Ultimately, this cannot function as an adequate basis for ethical action under extreme pressure. As Bennett puts it:

One must be enamoured with existence and occasionally even enchanted in the face of it in order to be capable of donating some of one's scarce mortal resources to the service of others.

(2001: 4)

Bennett's account of enchantment in the face of disenchantment seems to offer an antidote to the central paradox of Western secularity. Specifically, it resolves the dialectic of disenchantment–re-enchantment by removing belief in the possibility of disenchantment. This, in turn, makes the concept of dehumanization illogical, and therefore impotent as a motivator of instrumental violence. It also deals with the problem of meaninglessness in the face of bad death. Simply put, it suggests that the world can never become entirely meaningless if we remain willing to be enchanted with it, and that sources of enchantment exist even in the face of horror. But could this shift in approach work in the context of intervention discussed throughout this book?

A number of problems emerge in this regard. First, Bennett's argument that enchantment can inspire positive forms of ethical action is highly appealing, but she does not explain how it might work in practice. She is persuasive in her claim that the affective experience of attachment can produce care for, attention to, and attachment to other beings. But these experiences do not automatically produce action (let alone action appropriate to the context at hand). In some cases, affect is just that: a powerful experience that shapes a person's perceptions or world-view, but is not acted upon in any other way. If enchantment were to be the basis for ethical action, it would be necessary to offer much more specific guidance about how, and under what conditions, it translates into action. This is a complicated question, which relates to a range of dimensions—social, psychological, affective, and so on—and which is likely to vary considerably across individuals and social groups.

Second, the kind of responsiveness to the world that Bennett calls for is indeterminate. The language and imagery of disenchantment and dehumanization call for specified actions in objectively defined contexts. This is part of the reason why they are effective as calls to action: they identify a specific source of fear, and prescribe possible options for responding to it. Precisely because the experience of enchantment is intersubjective and highly individual, it is not possible or desirable to predetermine when it should take place, or what kinds of actions should result from it. Enchantment arises from concrete responses to unique situations; any attempt to predetermine it would deprive it of its essential character. However, the demands for coordination and urgent action created by situations of mass violence require that responses are predetermined to some extent, or at least based on precedents (particularly if military intervention is at issue). Without this element of pre-determination, responses to mass violence would be chaotic at best, and, at worst, would simply fail to emerge from myriad individual responses. While this approach may work very well in the context of the death rituals discussed in Chapter 7, it seems more limited as a guiding principle for responses to mass violence.

Third, the experience of enchantment might not produce the same effect for different people, which would raise problems for coordinated collective action. Enchantment, as Bennett describes it, is a largely affective experience. While highly powerful, affect is also unstable. As Susan Sontag (2003) and Luc Boltanski (1999) argue, human affective responses to violence and suffering do not always lead to constructive responses. They might also produce perverse effects—including a kind of pleasure derived from the sublimity of violence, or from the experience of abjection (see above). Moreover, affective response is uneven: while some people might have an overpowering affective response to an image of suffering, others might feel very little. The same could be said about the affective motivations behind the existing approach—namely, fear of dehumanization. Certainly, this fear is experienced differently by each individual on whom it has an impact. However, in existing discourses of dehumanization, one emotion (fear) has been parsed and channelled in a specific, instrumental way to motivate specific actions. The kind of responsiveness that Bennett's account calls for would demand that multiple, complex affective experiences motivate diverse responses. Indeed, the power of enchantment is precisely that it opens up multiple possibilities of experience and action. If this were channelled into a single, conditioned response (as fear has been in existing discourses) it would reproduce the same foreclosure of action as the current approach does, and there would be little point in substituting it.

Finally, adopting an ethics based on enchantment would not only require minor adjustments to existing approaches (for instance, the substitution of one concept of harm for another). Instead, it would demand that the entire basis of intervention be changed. As the emergence of Western secularity attests to, massive changes in belief are possible, but they take place over long periods of time and through emergent, transformative processes (not usually the intentional efforts of specific actors). So, it would be difficult to affect the inversion of beliefs that this approach calls for and remain responsive to emergencies unfolding in the present. Furthermore, the dichotomous logic of the existing approach to dehumanization exerts a paralyzing effect. Specifically, it suggests that any lapse in efforts to uphold the category of humanity could be disastrous. As such, the idea of suspending the processes of re-enchantment in order to allow for this kind of transformation would most likely be ruled out for fear of its consequences. For these reasons, the risk associated with abandoning the language and concept of disenchantment is high, and would require leaps of faith that might be beyond the scope of most Western secular minds.

This brief discussion suggests that a total rejection of the narrative of dis-enchantment would be difficult to realize. Nonetheless, of the two alternatives discussed here, it holds the most promise for rethinking the Western secular basis of intervention. Instead of calling upon humans to embrace violence or to relinquish the immanent framework offered by Western secularity, it encourages us to multiply the possibilities of ethical action within this sphere. Furthermore, rather than capitulating to transcendent beliefs or compromis-ing the ethical values of Western secularity it seeks forms of transcendence that affirm human (and other forms of) being in this world. Although a total rejection of the narrative of disenchantment is problematic in the context of intervention, Bennett's account suggests that the experience of enchantment may be infused into action—perhaps even action of an instrumental kind. For instance, it may reshape the way in which various kinds of intervenors frame the victims of violence, or their own motivations for acting (or failing to act) in response to this violence. Even if it is not adopted wholesale as the foundation of the ethics of intervention, it can, on a micro-level, help to gradually counteract—and perhaps eventually overcome—the dialectics of disenchantment–re-enchantment. An important challenge for the future, then, is to find ways of enfolding an ethics of enchantment into existing prac-tices, and of translating affective responses like enchantment and attachment into concrete, protective action.

Conclusions

International intervention is not just about 'saving' human lives: it is also an attempt to secure humanity's place in the universe. This book has explored the cosmological beliefs that underpin contemporary practices of intervention—most importantly, Western secular beliefs about life, death and the primacy of humanity. These beliefs shape a wide range of practices: the idea that human beings should intervene when human lives are at stake; the apprehension of violence and harm; practices of intervention and peace-building; and logics of killing and letting die. Ironically, however, the Western secular desire to ensure the meaningfulness of human life at all costs contributes to processes of dehumanization, undercutting the basic goals of intervention. As a result, intervenors are trapped in a seemingly endless dialectic of disenchantment and re-enchantment. An urgent challenge, therefore, is to explore the possi-bilities of escaping this paradox. Doing so will be necessary if we are to address the most problematic aspects of intervention: the apparent unwill-ingness to 'sacrifice' some lives to 'save' others; inaction in the face of large-scale violence; the instrumentalization of human lives and deaths; and the processes of dehumanization which intervenors may (unintentionally) enact.

The main message of this book is that Western secularity cannot be ignored in discussions of international intervention. Nor can it be oversimplified, reduced to the 'absence of religion', or rejected as irrelevant in the face of a perceived 'resurgence of religion'. For better or for worse, it is deeply embedded in the structures, processes and forms of agency through which intervention is carried out. It is necessary to recognize the powerful influence that it exerts in this sphere, and to respond to the problems it raises. What form, then, should this response take?

One option may be simply to accept the ambivalence of Western secularity and its outcomes. In other words, one might argue that the benefits of the Western secular emphasis on everyday human life outweigh the costs of dehumanization (although of course such an argument would most likely emerge from individuals who enjoy the most protection from dehumanization). Another option would be to give up on Western secularity and to adopt (or readopt) a transcendent basis for international action. However, despite the many problems that arise in a Western secular approach to intervention, this book has not argued that it should be rejected or abandoned wholesale, or that it is impossible to address its paradoxes. I agree with Taylor (2007) that Western secularity is not a lost cause, and that it is a source of rich and potent values. As this chapter has argued, it has also greatly strengthened and expanded the scope of humanitarianism, the value placed on earthly life, and the possibilities of human action. There is much to defend within this framework, and ample opportunities for reframing it.

This final chapter has explored two different options for retrieving Western secularity as a basis for ethical action: Taylor's 'maximal demand' and Bennett's rejection of the standard narrative of disenchantment. Each promises to offer a way out of the central impasse faced by intervenors, but each brings its own disturbing implications and risks. Meeting the 'maximal demand' may involve glorifying violence or compromising the value of earthly existence that is so central to Western secular beliefs. Rejecting the narrative of disenchantment, and the entire cosmological structure that it supports, might undermine the basis of concerted, collective action in the face of large-scale violence. I have concluded that the latter approach offers the most promising option for retrieving Western secularity as a basis for the ethics of intervention. However, if it is to work, much more thinking needs to be done about how the diverse, affective impulses associated with enchantment can be translated into the kind of rapid, determinate, collective action demanded by situations of mass violence.

Nonetheless, these hypothetical alternatives suggest that there is considerable scope for rethinking the basic assumptions that underpin Western secularity— and international intervention. None of this is possible, however, unless we take into account the positive features of Western secularity and their concrete effects on intervention. By highlighting these points, this book has sought to open up discussions about how Western secular beliefs, ontology and ethics might be reconfigured in order to address their undesirable effects. In order for these discussions to take place, it is necessary to turn the searchlight of IR thinking to the most fundamental questions that confront human beings: questions about the nature of humanity, death and the meaning of life.

Notes

1 For instance, the arming and support of 'rebel' groups by foreign governments, which has recently been used in both Libya (2011) and Syria (2013).
2 Bennett's work calls for a range of radical political reforms including the redefinition of publics and the rethinking of the nature of moral responsibility, which are beyond the scope of this discussion. For the purposes of this discussion, I shall limit my analysis to her argument about the power of enchantment to motivate ethical action.
3 An indispensable element of Bennett's framework is that she argues that our ethical responses should extend beyond human beings. This approach is often rejected by proponents of human well-being, for fear that it might posit the equality of humans and non-humans, making it impossible to prioritize action in emergency situations. However, it is important to note that the inclusion of non-human beings within this ethics of intervention need not necessarily mean that all beings should be given equal protection. It simply suggests that non-humans, and the complex assemblages they help to constitute, should be given some consideration. However, this debate is beyond the scope of the current argument.
4 As noted above, it remains anthropocentric in that it appears only to apply to humans or to other beings capable of experiencing these forms of affect.
5 Similarly, Thomas Birch (1993) makes a persuasive argument that humans may experience a 'deontic' moment (that is, a compulsion to attend to another being) for *anything*—whether another person, living being, or even a rock.

Bibliography

African Union (2012) 'The Continental Early Warning System', *Peace and Security: African Union Commission*. Online. Available www.peaceau.org/en/pages/cmd-au-ce ws-continental-early-warning-system (accessed 26 February 2012).

Agamben, G. (1995) *Homo Sacer: Sovereign Power and Bare Life*, Stanford, CA: Stanford University Press.

——(1999) *Remnants of Auschwitz: The Witness and the Archive*, New York: Zone Books.

——(2004) *The Open: Man and Animal*, Stanford, CA: Stanford University Press.

Amnesty International (2011) 'About the Conflict', *Amnesty International Annual Report*. Online. Available www.amnesty.org.uk/content.asp?CategoryID=610 (accessed 23 December 2011).

Arendt, H. (1963) *Eichmann in Jerusalem: A Report on the Banality of Evil*, New York: Penguin.

——(1976) *The Origins of Totalitarianism*, New York: Harvest.

——(1998) *The Human Condition*, Chicago, IL: University of Chicago Press.

Asad, T. (2003) *Formations of the Secular*, Stanford, CA: Stanford University Press.

——(2007) *On Suicide Bombing*, New York: Columbia University Press.

——(2011) 'Freedom of Speech and Religious Limitations', in Calhoun, Craig, Mark Juergensmeyer and Jonathan van Antwerpen, *Rethinking Secularism*, Oxford: Oxford University Press, pp. 282–97.

Autessere, S. (2010) *The Trouble with the Congo*, Cambridge: Cambridge University Press.

Ayoob, M. (2004) 'Third World Perspectives on Humanitarian Intervention and International Administration', *Global Governance*, 10(1): 99–118.

Badiou, A. (2007) *Being and Event*, trans. O. Feltham, London: Continuum.

Balibar, E. (2004) 'Dissonances within Laicite', *Constellations*, 11(3): 353–67.

Ban, K.M. (2011) 'Ban outlines need for long-term transitional arrangements in Libya', *UN News*. Online. Available www.un.org/apps/news/story.asp?NewsID=37933 &Cr=Libya?#.Ue13TPtwbmQ (accessed 22 July 2013).

Barbato, M. and Kratochwil, F. (2009) 'Towards a Post-Secular Political Order', *European Political Science Review*, 1(3): 317–40.

Barnett, J. (2001) *The Meaning of Environmental Security: Ecological Politics and Policy in the New Security Era*, London and New York: Zed.

Barnett, M. (2010) *The International Humanitarian Order*, New York: Routledge.

Barnett, M. and Stein, J.G. (2012) 'Introduction', in M. Barnett and J.G. Stein (eds) *Sacred Aid: Faith and Humanitarianism*, Oxford: Oxford University Press.

Barnett, M., Kim, H., O'Donnell, M. and Sitea, L. (2007) 'Peace-building: What Is in a Name?', *Global Governance*, 13: 35–58.

Bastian, B., Laham, S.M., Wilson, S., Haslam, N. and Koval, P. (2009), 'Blaming, Praising and Protecting Our Humanity: The Implications of Everyday Dehumanization for Judgments of Moral Status', *British Journal of Social Psychology*, 50: 469–83.

Bauman, Z. (1992) *Mortality, Immortality and Other Life Strategies*, Cambridge: Polity Press.

——(2006) *Liquid Fear*, Cambridge: Polity Press.

BBC (2002), 'Moral combat: NATO at war', *Panorama*. Online. Available http://news.bbc.co.uk/hi/english/static/events/panorama/transcripts/transcript_12_03_00.txt (accessed 9 January 2012).

——(2011a) 'Counting the cost of NATO's mission in Libya', *BBC News*. Online. Available www.bbc.co.uk/news/world-africa-15528984 (accessed 12 June 2012).

——(2011b) 'Fight to save the world: Sergio', *Storyville* (broadcast 1 June 2011).

Bellamy, A.J. (2010) 'The Institutionalisation of Peacebuilding: What Role for the UN Peacebuilding Commission?', in O. P. Richmond (ed.) *Palgrave Advances in Peacebuilding: Critical Developments and Approaches*, Basingstoke: Palgrave Macmillan.

Benjamin, W. (1986) 'Critique of Violence', in P. Demetz (ed.) *Reflections: Essays, Aphorisms, Autobiographical Writings*, New York: Schocken Books.

Bennett, J. (2001) *The Enchantment of Modern Life: Attachments, Crossings and Ethics*, Princeton, NJ: Princeton University Press.

——(2010) *Vibrant Matter: A Political Ecology of Things*, Durham, NC: Duke University Press.

Bhargava, R. (ed.) (1998) *Secularism and Its Critics*, Delhi: Oxford University Press.

Bilgin, P. (2008) 'The Securityness of Secularism? The Case of Turkey', *Security Dialogue*, 39: 593–614.

Bilgrami, A. (2004) 'Secularism and relativism', *Boundary 2*, 31(2): 173–96.

——(2010) 'What Is Enchantment', in M. Warner, J. van Antwerpen and C. Calhoun (eds) *Varieties of Secularism in a Secular Age*, Cambridge, MA: Belknap Press of Harvard University.

Birch, T. H. (1993) 'Moral Considerability and Universal Consideration', *Environmental Ethics*, 15(1): 313–15.

Bleiker, R. (2009) *Aesthetics and World Politics*, Basingstoke: Palgrave Macmillan.

——(2010) *Vibrant Matter: A Political Ecology of Things*, Durham, NC: Duke University Press.

Boege, V. (2011) 'Hybrid Forms of Peace and Order on a South Sea Island: Experiences from Bougainville (Papua New Guinea)', in O. P. Richmond and A. Mitchell (eds) *Hybrid Forms of Peace: From Everyday Agency to Post-Liberalism*, Basingstoke: Palgrave Macmillan.

Boltanksi, L. (1999) *Distant Suffering: Morality, Media and Politics*, Cambridge: Cambridge University Press.

Boulding, E. (2000) *Cultures of Peace: The Hidden Side of History*, Syracuse, NY: Syracuse University Press.

Boutros-Ghali, B. (1992) *Agenda for Peace*, New York: United Nations.

Braidotti, R. (2010) 'The Politics of "Life Itself" and New Ways of Dying', in D. Coole and S. Frost (eds) *New Materialisms: Ontology, Agency and Politics*, Durham, NC: Duke University Press.

Brigg, M. and Bleiker, R. (2010) 'Autoethnographic International Relations: Exploring the Self as a Source of Knowledge', *Review of International Studies*, 36(3): 779–98.

Brown, M. A. and Gusmao, A. (2011) 'Looking for the Owner of the House: Who Is Making Peace in Rural East Timor?', in O.P. Richmond and A. Mitchell (eds) *Hybrid Forms of Peace: From the Everyday to Post-liberalism*, Basingstoke: Palgrave Macmillan.

Brown, W. (2008) *Regulating Aversion: Tolerance in the Age of Identity and Empire*, Princeton, NJ: Princeton University Press.

Burton, J.W. (1996) *Conflict Transformation: Its Language and Processes*, Lanham, MD, and London: Scarecrow Press.

Butler, J. (2004) *Precarious Life: The Powers of Mourning and Violence*, London and New York: Verso.

——(2009) *Frames of War*, London: Verso.

Buzan, B., Waever, O. and de Wilde, J. (1999) *Security: A New Framework for Analysis*, Boulder, CO: Lynne Rienner Press.

Calhoun, C., Juergensmeyer, M. and Van Antwerpen, J. (2011) 'Introduction', in C. Calhoun, M. Juergensmeyer and J. Van Antwerpen (eds) *Rethinking Secularism*, Oxford: Oxford University Press.

Casanova, J. (2010) 'A Secular Age: Dawn or Twilight?', in M. Warner, J. Van Antwerpen and C. Calhoun (eds) *Varieties of Secularism in a Secular Age*, Cambridge, MA: Belknap Press of Harvard University.

Chan, S. (2000) 'Writing Sacral IR: An Excavation Including Kung, Eliade and Illiterate Buddhism', *Millennium Journal of International Studies*, 29(3): 565–89.

Chandler, D. (2003) 'Rhetoric without Responsibility: The Attraction of "Ethical" Foreign Policy', *British Journal of Politics and International Relations*, 5(3): 295–316.

——(2004) 'The Responsibility to Protect? Imposing the Liberal Peace', *International Peacekeeping*, 11(1): 59–81.

Chesterman, S. (2001) *Just War or Just Intervention?* Oxford: Oxford University Press.

Chong, A. and Troy, J. (2011) 'A Universal Sacred Mission and the Universal Secular Organization: The Holy See and the United Nations', *Politics, Religion and Ideology*, 12(3): 335–54.

Christie, R. (2010) 'Critical Voices in Human Security: To Endure, to Engage, or to Critique?', *Security Dialogue*, 41(1): 169–90.

Clark, I. (2001) *The Post-Cold War Order: The Spoils of Peace*, Oxford: Oxford University Press.

Commission on Human Security (CHS) (2003) *Human Security Now*, New York: Commission on Human Security.

Connolly, W. (1999) *Why I Am Not a Secularist*, Minneapolis, MN: University of Minnesota Press.

——(2011) *A World of Becoming*, Durham, NC: Duke University Press.

Coward, M. (2006) 'Against Anthropocentrism: The Destruction of the Built Environment as a Distinct Form of Political Violence', *Review of International Studies*, 32: 419–37.

Crawford, N. (2002) Argument and Change in World Politics, Cambridge: Cambridge University Press.

CSP (2009) 'Global Conflict Trends', *Measuring Systemic Peace*. Online. Available www.systemicpeace.org/conflict.htm (accessed 22 December 2011).

Dalby, S. (2002) *Environmental Security*, Minneapolis, MN: University of Minnesota Press.

Dallmayr, F. (1999) 'Rethinking secularism (with Raimon Panikkar)', *Review of Politics*, 61: 715–35.

Darby, J. (2010) 'Reconciliation (Reflections from Northern Ireland and South Africa)', in O. P. Richmond (ed.) *Palgrave Advances in Peacebuilding: Critical Developments and Approaches*, Basingstoke: Palgrave Macmillan.

Darby, P. (ed.) (2006) *Postcolonizing the International: Working to Change the Way We Are*, Honolulu, HI: University of Hawaii Press.

Dardagan, H. (2011) 'Libya: he toll NATO didn't count', *Guardian*, 29 August 2011.

Das, V. (2007) *Life and Words: Violence and the Descent into the Ordinary*, Berkeley, CA: University of California Press.

Debrix, F. (1999) *Re-envisioning Peace-keeping: The UN and the Mobilization of Ideology*, Minneapolis, MN: University of Minnesota Press.

——(2007) *Tabloid Terror: War, Culture and Geopolitics*, London: Routledge.

Debrix, F. and Weber, C. (eds) (2003) *Rituals of Mediation: International Politics and Social Meaning*, Minneapolis, MN: University of Minnesota Press.

Dillon, M. and Reid, J. (2009) *The Liberal Way of War: Killing to Make Life Live*, London: Routledge.

Dobbins, J., Jones, S.G., Crane, K. and DeGrasse, B.C. (2007) *The Beginner's Guide to Nation-Building*, Santa Monica, CA: RAND Corporation.

Edkins, J. (2003) *Trauma and the Memory of Politics*, Cambridge: Cambridge University Press.

——(2011) *Missing: Persons and Politics*, Ithaca, NY: Cornell University Press.

Erskine, T. (2004) 'Blood on the UN's Hands? Assigning Duties and Apportioning Blame to an Intergovernmental Organization', *Global Society*, 18(1): 21–42.

Esmeir, S. (2006) 'On Making Dehumanization Possible', *PMLA*, 121(5): 1544–51.

Evans, G. (2008) 'The Responsibility to Protect: An Idea Whose Time Has Come … And Gone?', *International Relations*, 22(3): 283–98.

Foucault, M. (2003) *Society Must Be Defended: Lectures at the College de France, 1975–1976*, London: Picador.

Fox, D.J. (1998) *An Ethnography of Four Non-governmental Development Organizations*, New York: Edwin Mellen Press.

Freeman, M. (2004) 'The Problem of Secularism in Human Rights Theory', *Human Rights Quarterly*, 26(2): 375–400.

Fukuyama, F. (2004), 'Nation-building 101', *Atlantic Monthly*, January/February, 2004. Online. Available www.theatlantic.com/past/docs/issues/2004/01/fukuyama.htm (accessed 22 July 2013).

Galtung, J. (1996) *Peace by Peaceful Means*, London: Sage.

Gane, N. (2002) *Max Weber and Postmodern Theory*, Basingstoke: Palgrave Macmillan.

Genocide Watch (2011) 'Current Countries at Risk of Genocide, Politicide, or Mass Atrocities'. Online. Available www.genocidewatch.org/alerts/countriesatrisk2011.html (accessed 23 December 2011).

Gheciu, A. and Paris, R. (2011) 'NATO and the Challenge of Sustainable Peacebuilding', *Global Governance*, 17(1): 75–79.

Goetze, C. (2013) 'What peacebuilders read', *paper presented at the International Studies Association Convention on the Politics of International Diffusion: Regional and Global Dimensions*, San Francisco, April.

Goldstone, J.A. (2008) *Using Quantitative and Qualitative Models to Forecast Instability*, Washington, DC: US Institute of Peace.

GPI (2011) *2011 Methodology, Results and Findings: Global Peace Index*, Sydney: Institute for Economics and Peace.

Grayson, K. (2008) 'Human Security as Power/Knowledge: The Biopolitics of a Definitional Debate', *Cambridge Review of International Affairs*, 21(3): 383–401.

Habermas, J. (2006) 'Religion in the Public Sphere', *European Journal of Philosophy*, 14(1): 1–25.

Hagan, J. and Ryder-Richmond, W. (2008) 'The Collective Dynamics of Racial Dehumanization and Genocidal Victimization in Darfur', *American Sociological Review*, 73: 875–902.

Haslam, N. (2006) 'Dehumanization: An Integrative Review', *Personality and Social Psychology Review*, 10(3): 252–64.

Held, D. (2010) *Cosmopolitanism: Ideals and Realities*. Cambridge: Polity Press.

HIICR (2009) 'HIIK Conflict Barometer 2009'. Online. Available http://hiik.de/en/index.html (accessed 23 December 2011).

Howard, M. (2000) *The Invention of Peace*, London: Profile.

HSRG (2010) 'Human Security Report 2009–10'. Online. Available www.hsrgroup.org/human-security-reports/human-security-report.aspx (accessed 23 December 2011).

Hurd, E.S. (2008) *The Problem of Secularism in International Relations*, Princeton, NJ: Princeton University Press.

ICISS (2001) *The Responsibility to Protect*, Ottawa: IDRC.

ICRP (2011) 'The Crisis in Libya'. Online. Available www.responsibilitytoprotect.org/index.php/crises/crisis-in-libya (accessed 24 July 2012).

Ignatieff, M. (2001) *Virtual War: Kosovo and Beyond*, London: Picador.

Ikenberry, G.J. (2001) *After Victory: Institutions, Strategic Restraint and the Rebuilding of Order after Major Wars*, Princeton, NJ: Princeton University Press.

Institute for Economics and Peace (2010) *2010 Methodology, Results and Findings*. Online. Available http://economicsandpeace.org/wp-content/uploads/2011/09/2010-GPI-Results-Report.pdf (accessed 22 July 2013).

International Institute for Strategic Studies (IISS) 2011. 'Armed Conflict Database' Available www.iiss.org/publications/armed-conflict-database/ (accessed 23 December 2011).

Jabri, V. (1996) *Discourses on Violence: Conflict Analysis Reconsidered*, Manchester and New York: Manchester University Press.

——(2007) *War and the Transformation of Global Politics*, Basingstoke: Palgrave Macmillan.

Jakobsen, J.R. and Pellegrini, A. (2008) 'Times Like These', in J.R. Jakobsen and A. Pellegrini (eds) *Secularisms*, Durham, NC: Duke University Press.

Jenkins, R. (2000) 'Disenchantment, Enchantment and Re-enchantment: Max Weber at the Millennium', *Max Weber Studies*, 1(1): 11–32.

Jeong, H. (2005) Peacebuilding in Postconflict Societies, Boulder, CO: Lynne Reiner Press.

Juergensmeyer, M. (2011) 'Rethinking the Secular and Religious Aspects of Violence', in C. Calhoun, M. Juergensmeyer and J. Van Antwerpen (eds) *Rethinking Secularism*, Oxford: Oxford University Press.

Kaldor, M. (2006) *Old and New Wars*, Cambridge: Polity Press.

Kaldor, M., Martin, M. and Selchow, S. (2007) 'Human Security: A New Strategic Narrative for Europe', *International Affairs*, 2: 273–88.

Keane, J. (1996) *Reflections on Violence*, London: Verso.

——(2000) 'Secularism?', *Political Quarterly*, 71(1): 5–19.

Keating, T.F. and Knight, A.W. (2005) 'Introduction', in T.F. Keating and A.W. Knight (eds) *Building Sustainable Peace*, Tokyo: United Nations University Press.

Keddie, N.R. (2003) 'Secularism and Its Discontents', *Daedalus*, 132(3): 14–30.

Keen, D. (2008) *Complex Emergencies*, Cambridge: Polity Press.

Kelman, H.C. (1973) 'Violence without Moral Restraint: Reflections on the Dehumanization of Victims and Victimizers', *Journal of Social Issues*, 29(4): 25–61.

Kennedy, D. (2004) *The Dark Side of Virtue: Humanitarianism Reassessed*, Princeton, NJ: Princeton University Press.

Khong, Y.F. (1992) *Analogies at War: Korea, Munich, Dien Bien Phu and the Vietnam Decisions of 1965*, Princeton, NJ: Princeton University Press.

Khong, Y.F. and McFarlane, N.S. (2006) *Human Security and the UN: A Critical History*, Bloomington, IN: University of Indiana Press.

Kleinman, A. and Kleinman, J. (1996) 'The Appeal of Experience: The Dismay of Images: Cultural Appropriations of Suffering in Our Times', *Daedalus*, 125(1): 1–23.

Kriesberg, L. (1998) *Constructive Conflicts*, Lanham, MD: Rowman and Littlefield.

Kristeva, J. (1982) *Powers of Horror*, New York: Columbia University Press.

Large, J. and Sisk, T. (2006) *Democracy, Conflict and Human Security: Pursuing Peace in the 21st Century*, Stockholm: IDEA.

Latour, B. (1993) *We Have Never Been Modern*, Cambridge, MA: Harvard University Press.

Laustsen, C.B. and Waever, O. (2000) 'In Defense of Religion: Sacred Referent Objects for Securitization', *Millennium Journal of International Studies*, 29(3): 705–39.

Lawrence, P. (2000) 'Violence, Suffering, Amman: The Work of Oracles in Sri Lanka's Eastern War Zone', in V. Das, A. Kleinman, M. Ramphele and P. Reynolds (eds) *Violence and Subjectivity*, Berkeley and Los Angeles, CA: University of California Press.

Lederach, J.P. (2003) *The Little Book of Conflict Transformation*, Intercourse, PA: Good Books.

——(2005) *Moral Imagination: The Art and Soul of Peace-Building*, Oxford: Oxford University Press.

——(2010a) 'Reconciliation: an Ethic for Peacebuilding', in D. Philpott and G. F. Powers (eds) *Strategies of Peace*, Oxford: Oxford University Press.

Lederach, J.P. and Appleby, R.S. (2010b) 'Strategic Peacebuilding – An Overview', in D. Philpott and G. F. Powers (eds) *Strategies of Peace*, Oxford: Oxford University Press.

Lehmann, H. (2008) 'Max Weber and the Dialectics of Disenchantment and Reenchantment in Modern History', *Max Weber Programme Working Papers*, 35: 73–80.

Liden, K. (2009) 'Building Peace Between Global and Local Politics: The Cosmopolitical Ethics of Liberal Peacebuilding', *International Peacekeeping*, 15(5): 616–34.

Luban, D. (2012) 'What would Augustine do?', *Boston Review*. Online. Available http://bostonreview.net/david-luban-the-president-drones-augustine-just-war-theory (accessed 6 June 2012).

Lynch, C. (2011) 'Religious Humanitarianism and the Global Politics of Secularism', in C. Calhoun, M. Juergensmeyer and J. Van Antwerpen (eds) *Rethinking Secularism*, Oxford: Oxford University Press.

Macek, I. (2000) *War Within: Everyday Life in Sarajevo Under Siege*, Uppsala: Acta Universitatis Upsaliensis.

MacFarlane, N.S. and Khong, Y.F. (2006) *Human Security and the UN: A Critical History*, Bloomington, IN: University of Indiana Press.

MacFarlane, N.S., Thielking, C.J. and Weiss, T.G. (2004) 'The Responsibility to Protect: Is Anyone Interested in Humanitarian Intervention?', *Third World Quarterly*, 25(5): 977–92.

MacGinty, R. (2008) 'Indigenous Peace-making versus the Liberal Peace', *Cooperation and Conflict*, 43(2): 139–63.

Malachuk, D.S. (2010) 'Human Rights and a Post-Secular Religion of Humanity', *Journal of Human Rights*, 8(2): 127–42.

Mann, M. (2005) *The Dark Side of Democracy*, Cambridge: Cambridge University Press.

Mavelli, L. (2012) 'Security and Secularization in International Relations', *European Journal of International Relations*, 18(1): 177–98.

Mbembe, A. (2003) 'Necropolitics', trans. L. Meintjes, *Public Culture*, 15(1): 11–40.

Miall, H. (2007) *Emergent Conflict and Peaceful Change*, Basingstoke: Palgrave Macmillan.

Miall, H., Ramsbotham, O. and Woodhouse, T. (1999) *Contemporary Conflict Resolution*, Oxford: Blackwell.

Morgenthau, H. (1967) 'To Intervene or Not to Intervene', *Foreign Affairs*, 45: 425–36.

Nandy, A. (1998) 'The Politics of Secularism and the Recovery of Religious Tolerance', in R. Bhargava (ed.) *Secularism and its Critics*, Delhi: Oxford University Press.

Newman, E. (2011) 'A Human Security Peace-building Agenda', *Third World Quarterly*, 31(10): 1737–56.

Nordstrom, C. (1997) *A Different Kind of War Story*, Philadelphia, PA: University of Pennsylvania Press.

——(2004) *Shadows of War: Violence, Power and International Profiteering in the Twenty-First Century*, Berkeley, CA, and London: University of California Press.

Norris, P. and Inglehart, R. (2004) *Sacred and Secular: Religion and Politics Worldwide*, Cambridge: Cambridge University Press.

O'Brien, S.P. (2010) 'Crisis EarlyWarning and Decision Support: Contemporary Approaches and Thoughts on Future Research', *International Studies Review*, 12: 87–104.

Paris, R. (2001) *At War's End: Building Peace after Civil Conflict*, Cambridge: Cambridge University Press.

Patomaki, H. (2001) 'The Challenge of Critical Theories: Peace Research at the Start of the New Century', *Journal of Peace Research*, 38(6): 723–37.

Philpott, D. (2002) 'The Challenge of September 11 to Secularism in International Relations', *World Politics*, 55(1): 65–95.

——(2010). 'Introduction', in D. Philpott and G. F. Powers (eds) *Strategies of Peace*, Oxford: Oxford University Press.

Pink, S. (1998) 'The White "Helpers": Anthropologists, Development Workers and Local Imaginations', *Anthropology Today*, 14(6): 9–14.

Pouligny, B. (2006) *Peace Operations Seen from Below: UN Missions and Local People*, London: Hurst.

Powers, G.F. (2010) 'Religion and Peacebuilding', in D. Philpott and G. F. Powers (eds) *Strategies of Peace*, Oxford: Oxford University Press.

Pupavac, V. (2005) 'Human Security and the Rise of Global Therapeutic Governance', *Conflict, Security and Development*, 5(2): 161–81.

Ramsbotham, O., Woodhouse, T. and Miall, H. (2005) *Contemporary Conflict Resolution*, 2nd edn, Cambridge: Polity Press.

Richards, P. (ed.) (2005) *No Peace, No War: An Anthropology of Contemporary Armed Conflicts*, Athens, OH: Ohio University Press.

Richmond, O.P. (2007) *The Transformation of Peace*, Basingstoke: Palgrave Macmillan.

Rieff, D. (2002) *A Bed for the Night: Humanitarianism in Crisis*, London: Vintage.

Roberts, D. (2013) 'US reconsiders its opposition to arming Syrian rebels', *Guardian*. Online. Available www.guardian.co.uk/world/2013/may/03/us-reconsiders-arming-syrian-rebels (accessed 3 May 2013).

Saferworld (2011) 'Where We Work: Central Asia'. Online. Available www.saferworld. org.uk/where/central-asia (accessed 4 February 2012).

Sant Cassia, P. (2004) *Bodies of Evidence: Burial, Memory and the Recovery of Missing Persons in Cyprus*, Oxford: Berghahn.

Scarry, E. (1985) *The Body in Pain: The Making and Unmaking of the World*, New York and Oxford: Oxford University Press.

Sen, A. (2008) *Human Security Now*, New York: UN Commission on Security.

Shapiro, M.J. (1997) *Violent Cartographies: Mapping Cultures of War*, Minneapolis, MN: University of Minnesota Press.

Sheikh, M.K. (2012) 'How Does Religion Matter? Pathways to Religion in International Relations', *Review of International Studies*, 38(2): 365–92.

Singer, P.W. (2009) *Wired For War: The Robotics Revolution and Conflict in the 21st Century*, New York: Penguin.

SIPRI (2002) *An Internet-Based Early Warning Indicators System for Preventive Policy*, Stockholm: SIPRI.

——(2011) 'Facts on International Relations and Security Trends'. Online. Available www.sipri.org/databases (accessed 23 December 2011).

Slaughter, A. (2005) 'Security, Solidarity and Sovereignty: The Grand Themes of UN Reform', *American Journal of International Law*, 99(3): 619–31.

Sontag, S. (2003) *Regarding the Pain of Others*, London: Penguin.

Sparrow, R. (2007) 'Killer Robots', *Journal of Applied Philosophy*, 24(1): 62–77.

Stanton, G.H. (1999) *The Eight Stages of Genocide*, Washington, DC: Genocide Watch.

Stollznow, K. (2008) 'Dehumanisation in Language and Thought', *Journal of Language and Politics*, 7(2): 177–200.

Tadjbaksh, S. and Chenoy, A.M. (2007) *Human Security: Concepts and Implications*, London: Routledge.

Taylor, C. (1985) *Philosophy and the Human Sciences – Philosophical Papers (vol. 2)*, Cambridge: Cambridge University Press.

——(1989) *Sources of the Self*, Cambridge: Cambridge University Press.

——(1991) *The Ethics of Authenticity*, Toronto: Canadian Broadcasting Corporation.

——(1998) 'Modes of Secularism', in R. Bhargava (ed.) *Secularism and Its Critics*, Delhi: Oxford University Press.

——(2004) *Modern Social Imaginaries*, Durham, NC, and London: Duke University Press.

——(2007) *A Secular Age*, Cambridge, MA: Belknap Press of Harvard University.

——(2010) 'Afterword: Apologia pro libro suo' in "Can secularism be other-wise?", in M. Warner, J. van Antwerpen and C. Calhoun (eds) *Varieties of Secularism in a Secular Age*, Cambridge, MA: Belknap Press of Harvard University.

——(2011a) *Dilemmas and Connections*, Cambridge, MA: Belknap Press of Harvard University.

——(2011b) 'Western Secularity', in C. Calhoun, M. Juergensmeyer and J. Van Antwerpen (eds) *Rethinking Secularism*, Oxford: Oxford University Press.

Thakur, R. (2002) 'Outlook: Intervention, Sovereignty and the Responsibility to Protect: Experiences from ICIS', *Security Dialogue*, 33(3): 323–43.

Theidon, K. (2007) 'Transitional Subjects: The Disarmament, Demobilization and Reintegration of Former Combatants in Colombia', *International Journal of Transitional Justice*, 1, 66–90.

Themner, L. (2013) *Armed Conflict Dataset Codebook*, Oslo: UCDP/PRIO.

Thomas, S. (2005) *The Global Resurgence of Religion and the Transformation of International Relations: The Struggle for the Soul of the Twenty-First Century*, Basingstoke: Palgrave Macmillan.

Tirman, J. (2011) *The Deaths of Others: The Fate of Civilians in America's Wars*, Oxford: Oxford University Press.

Tokača, M. (2010) *Personal interview with the author in Sarajevo*, 12 March.

UN (2000) *Report on the Panel of United Nations Peace Operations*, New York: UN.

UN Development Programme (UNDP) (1994) *UN Development Report*, New York: United Nations.

Vatican (1995) *Address of His Holiness John Paul II at the Fiftieth General Assembly of the United Nations Organization*, New York, on 5 October 1995. Online. Available www.vatican.va/holy_father/john_paul_ii/speeches/1995/october/documents/hf_jp-ii_spe_05101995_address-to-uno_en.html (accessed 29 April 2013).

Walzer, M. (1977) *Just and Unjust Wars: A Moral Argument with Historical Illustrations*, New York: Basic Books.

——(2004) *Arguing About War*, New Haven, CT: Yale University Press.

Warner, M., Van Antwerpen, J. and Calhoun, C. (2010) 'Introduction', in M. Warner, J. Van Antwerpen and C. Calhoun (eds) *Varieties of Secularism in a Secular Age*, Cambridge, MA: Belknap Press of Harvard University.

Weber, M. (1922) 'Science as a Vocation', in H.H. Gerth and C.W. Mills (trans. and eds) *From Max Weber: Essays in Sociology*, New York: Oxford University Press.

Weiss, T.G. (2004) 'The sunset of humanitarian intervention? The Responsibility to Protect in a Unipolar Area', *Security Dialogue*, 35(2): 135–53.

Weizman, E. (2011) *The Least of All Possible Evils: Humanitarian Violence from Arendt to Gaza*, London: Verso.

Welsh, J. (2003) 'Introduction', in J. Welsh (ed.) *Humanitarian Intervention and International Relations*, Oxford: Oxford University Press.

Wendt, A. (1999) *Social Theory of International Relations*, Cambridge: Cambridge University Press.

Wheeler, N. (2000) *Saving Strangers: Humanitarian Intervention in International Society*, Oxford: Oxford University Press.

Wikipedia, 'Casualties of the 2011 Libyan Civil War'. Online. Available http://en.wikip edia.org/wiki/Casualties_of_the_2011_Libyan_civil_war#Deaths_caused_by_Coalition_forces (accessed 9 January 2011).

Williamson, J. (2006) 'The Disarmament, Demobilization and Reintegration of Child Soldiers: Social and Psychological Transformation in Sierra Leone', *Intervention*, 4(3): 185–205.

Wood, R.M. and Gibney, M. (2010) 'The Political Terror Scale: A Re-introduction and Comparison to CIRI', *Human Rights Quarterly*, 32(2): 367–400.

Žižek, S. (2002) *Welcome to the Desert of the Real!*, London: Verso.

——(2009) *In Defense of Lost Causes*, London: Verso.

Index